Welcome to a world where the shadows come to life and the thrill of the unknown awaits your artistic touch. 'Nocturnal Nightmares: Adult Horror Coloring' invites you to embrace the enigmatic, to dance with the darkness, and to explore the eerie in a way that's uniquely creative.

Within these pages, you'll find a curated collection of illustrations that blur the line between horror and artistry. From creatures that go bump in the night to haunted scenes that send shivers down your spine, each intricate design is a canvas for your imagination to roam.

As you color, remember that you're not just adding hues; you're crafting your own interpretation of the uncanny. The power to transform the chilling into the beautiful rests within your hands, and each stroke is an invitation to confront and conquer the shadows.

Whether you're a seasoned colorist or new to the world of adult coloring, 'Nocturnal Nightmares' offers you a chance to engage with fear and fascination in a way that's both therapeutic and exhilarating. Let your colors tell stories of both dread and courage as you breathe life into these haunting scenes.

So, if you're ready to challenge the darkness with your creativity, if you're eager to reimagine fear as a work of art, then turn the page, pick up your coloring tools, and step into a world where nightmares and creativity intertwine. Let the journey into the nightmarish begin.

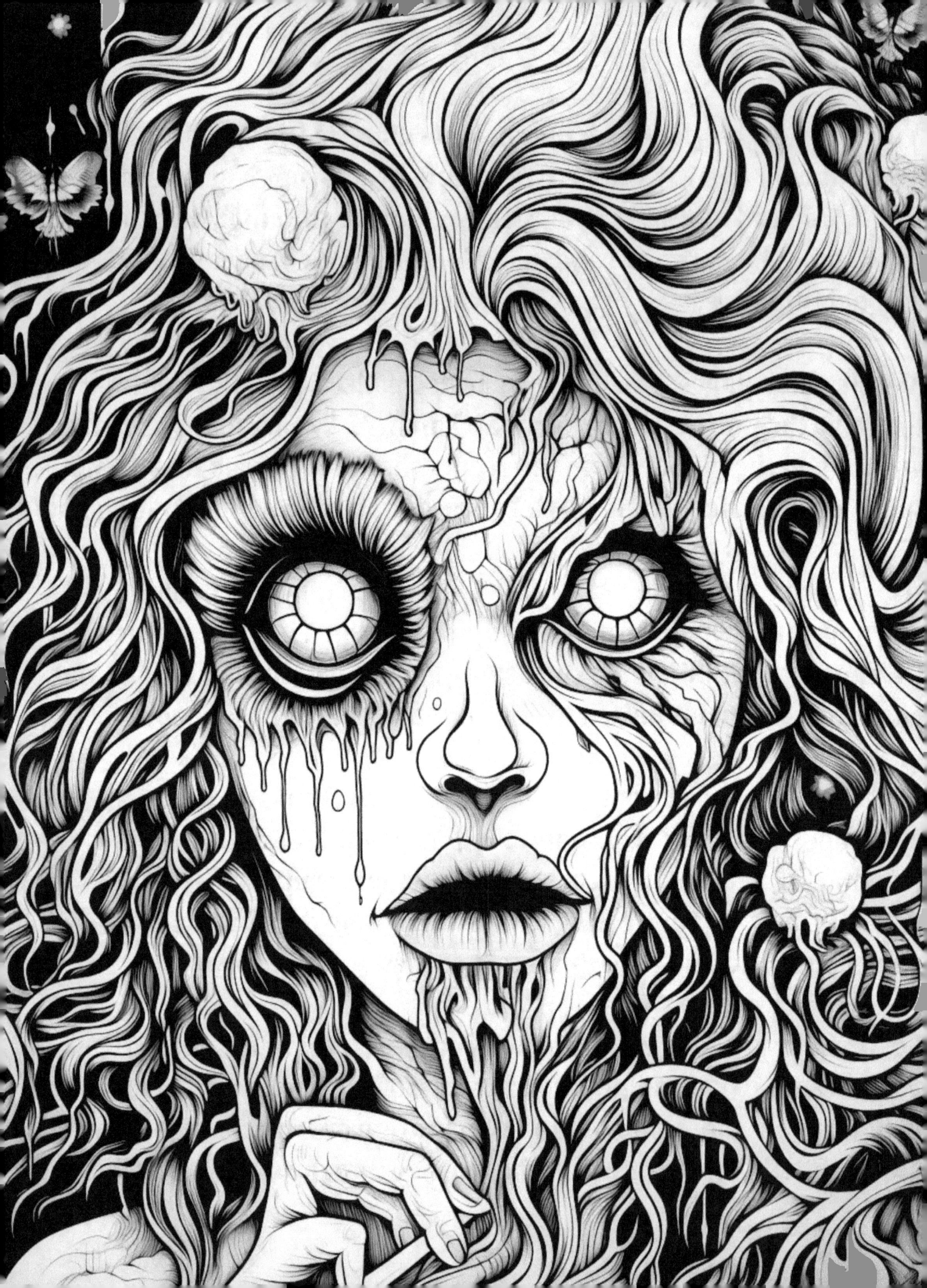

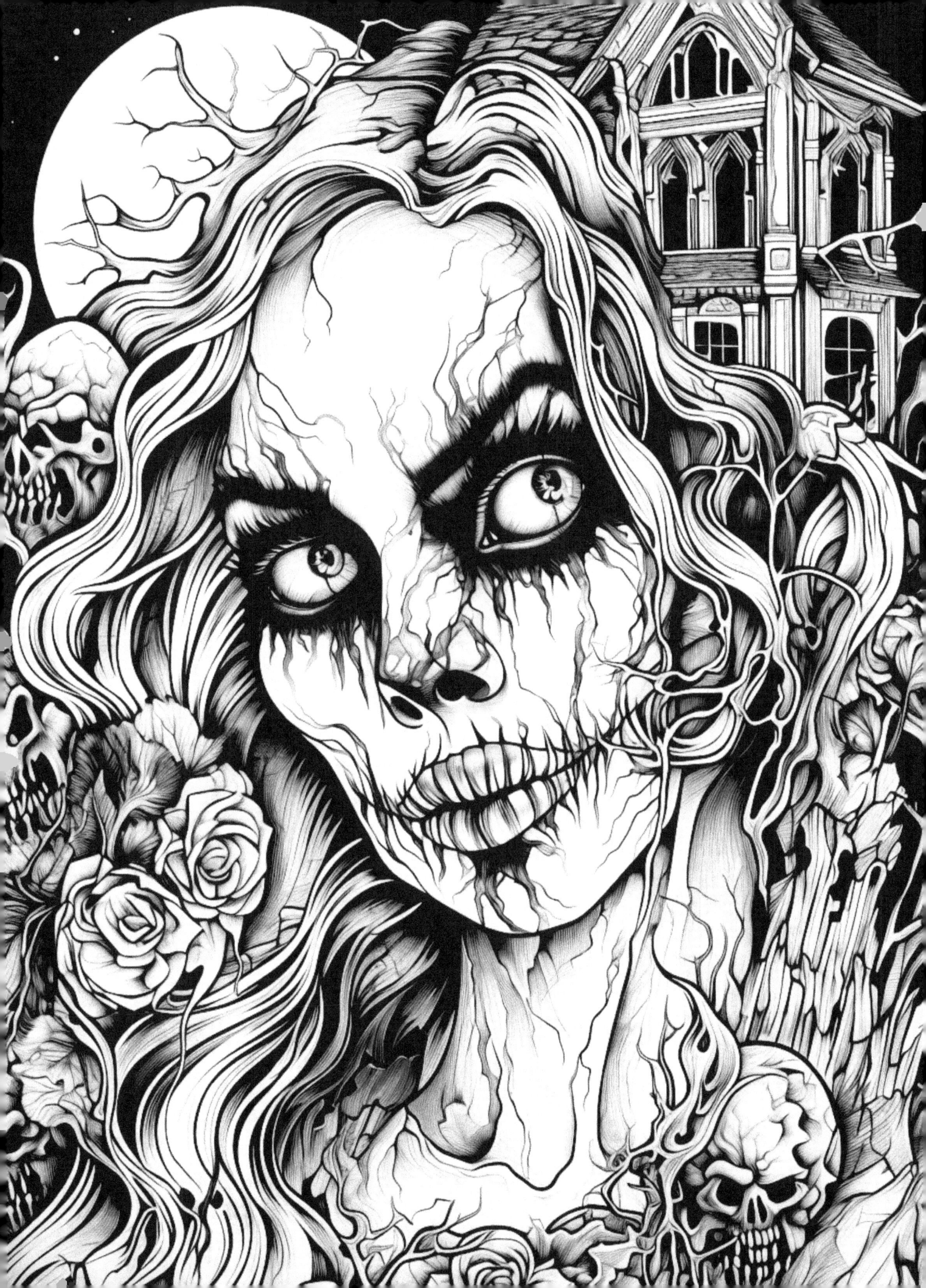

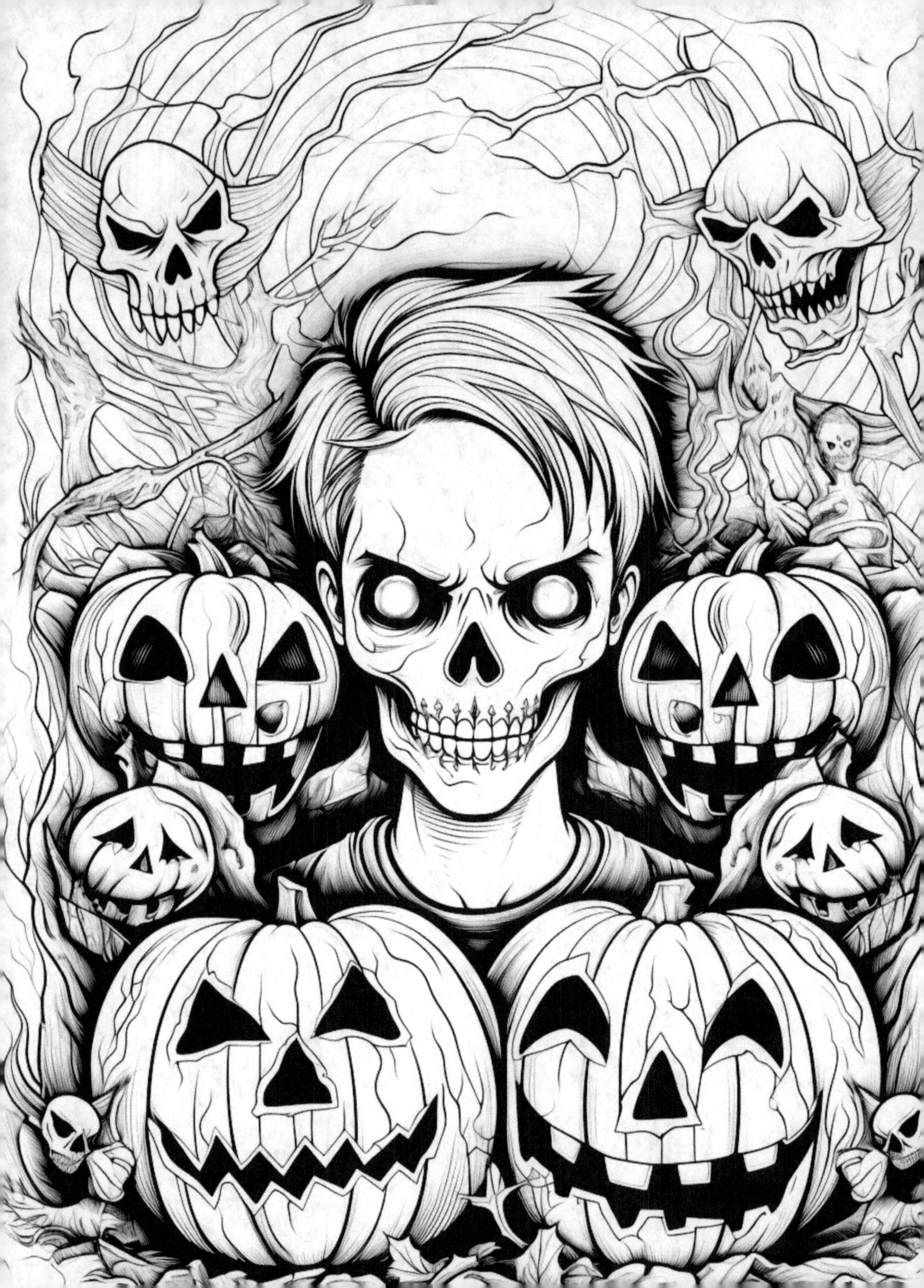

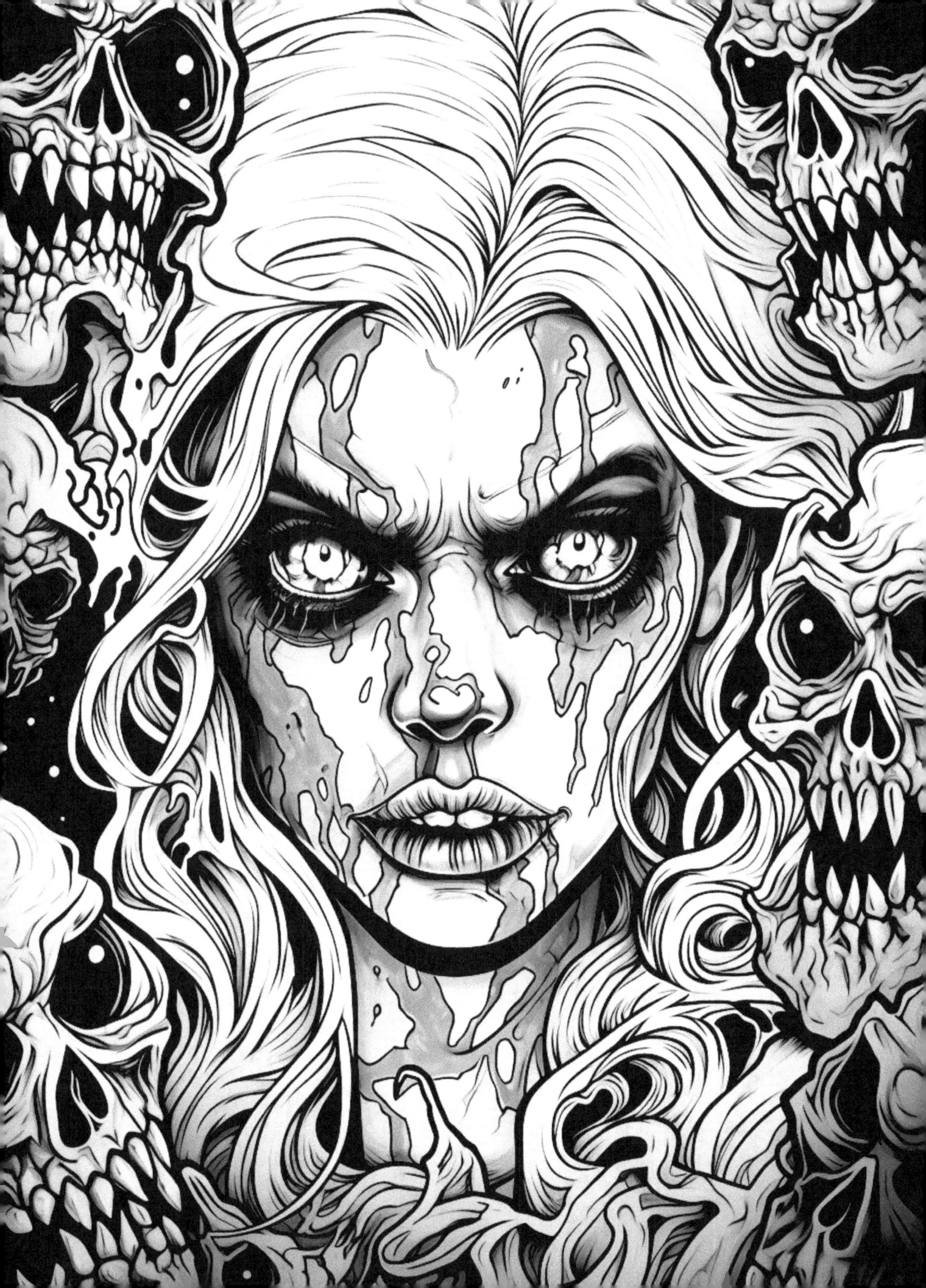

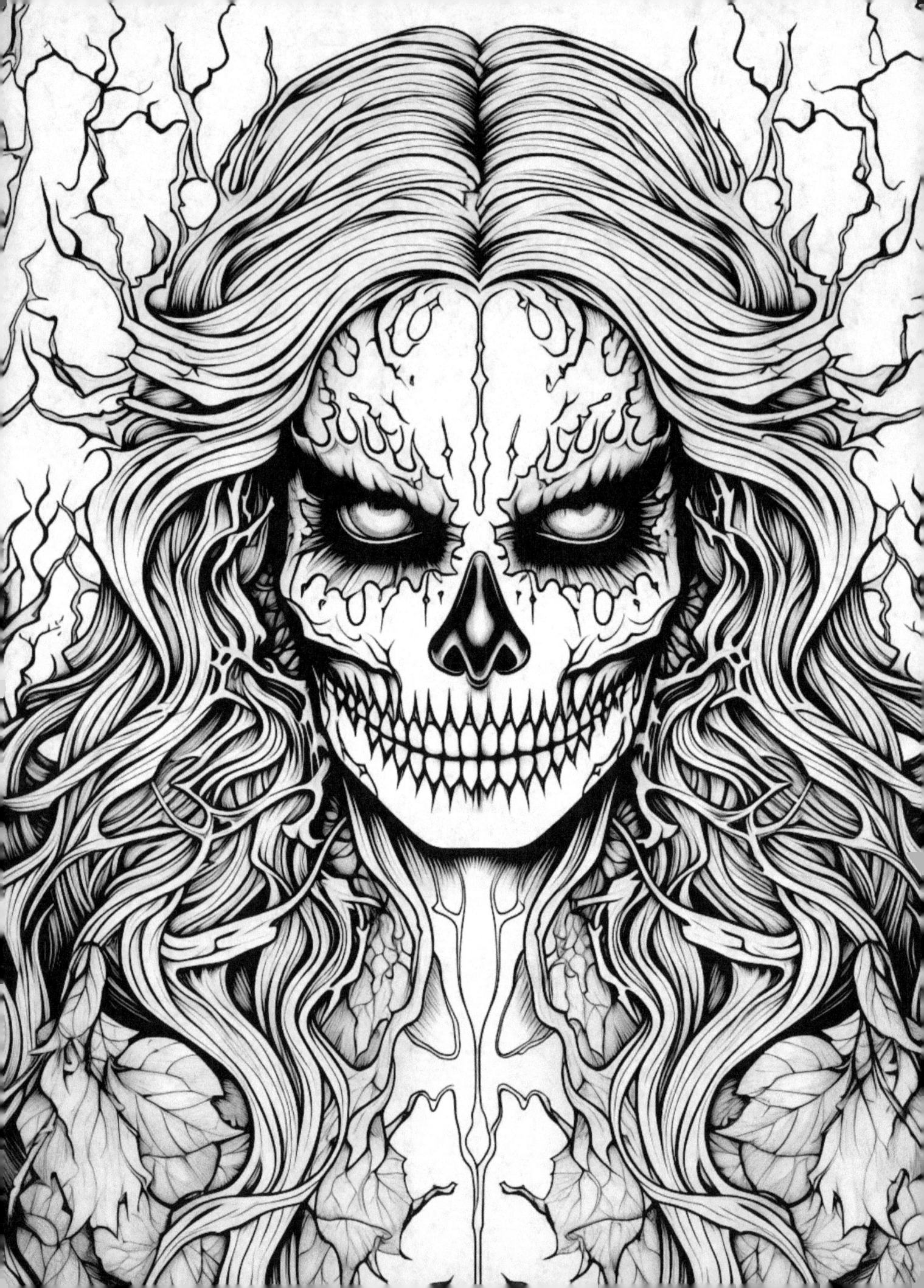

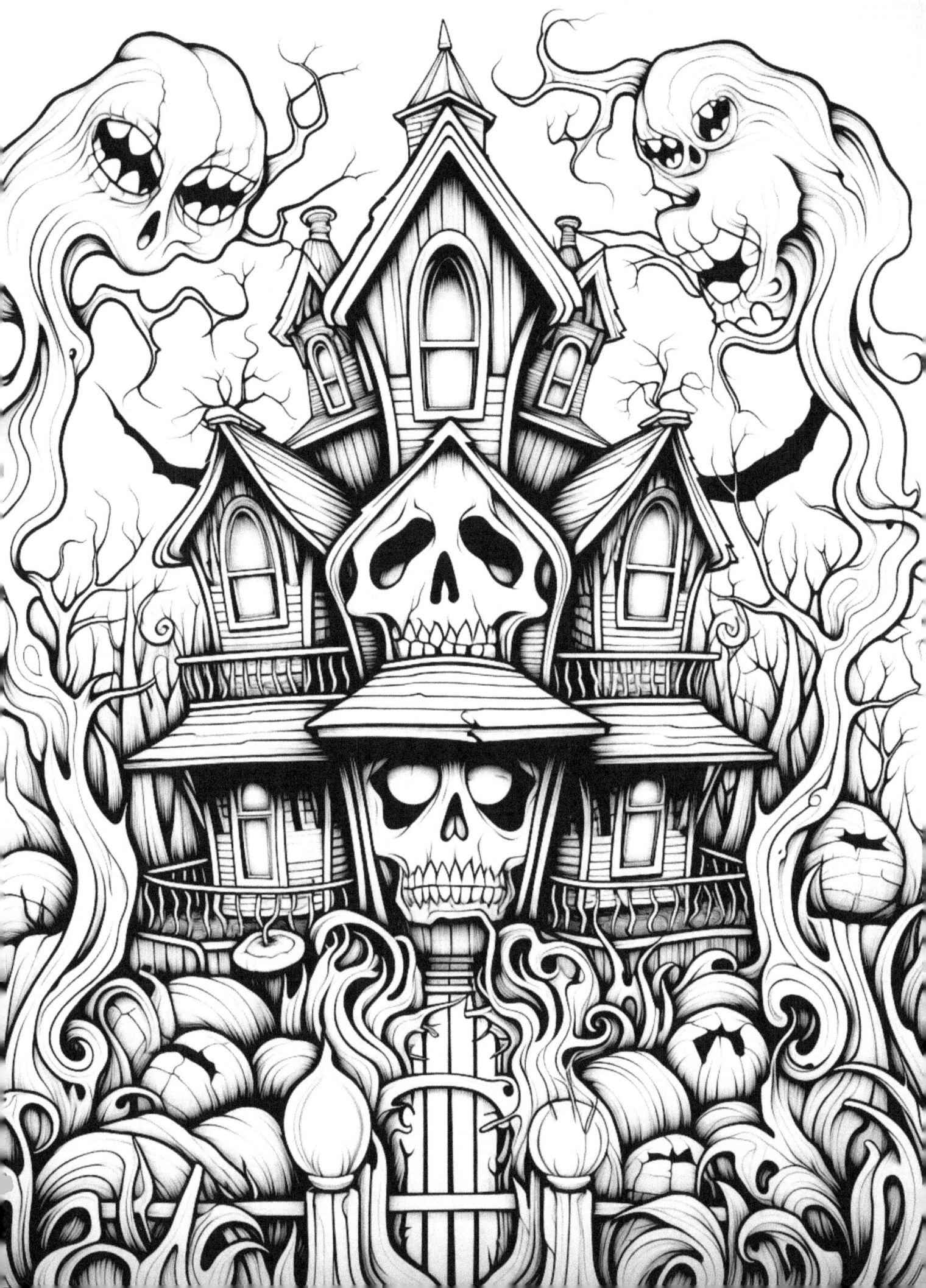

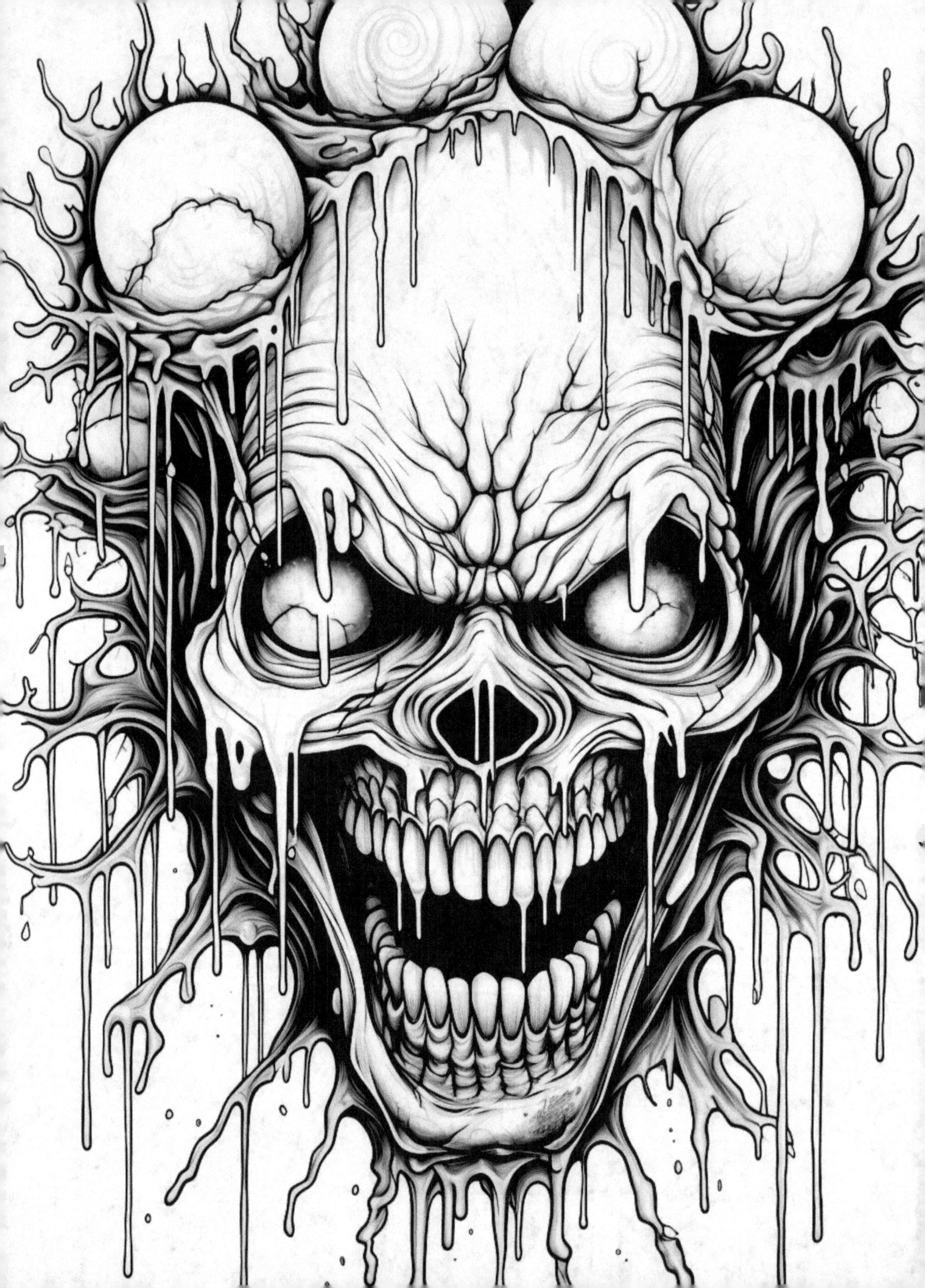

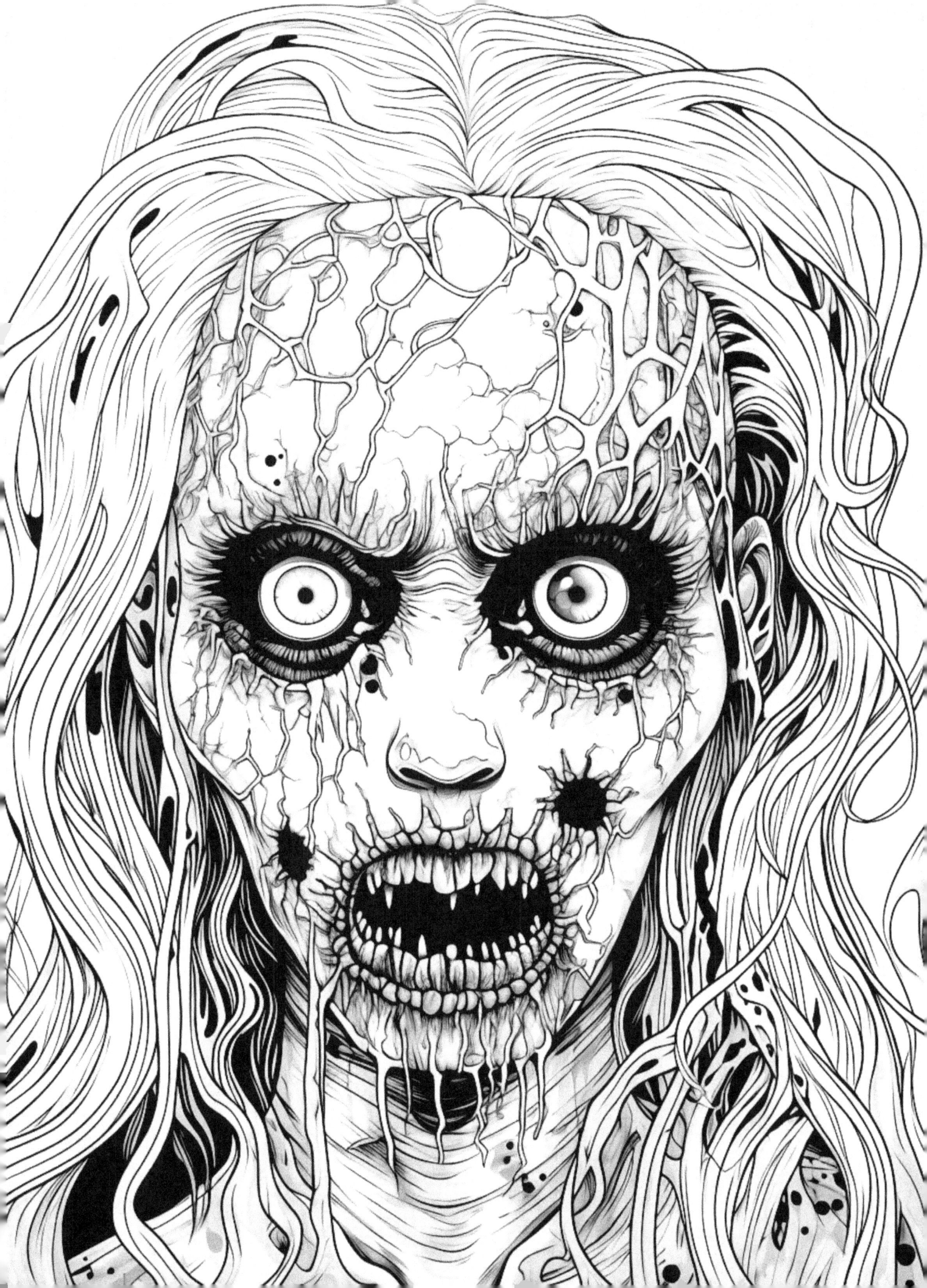

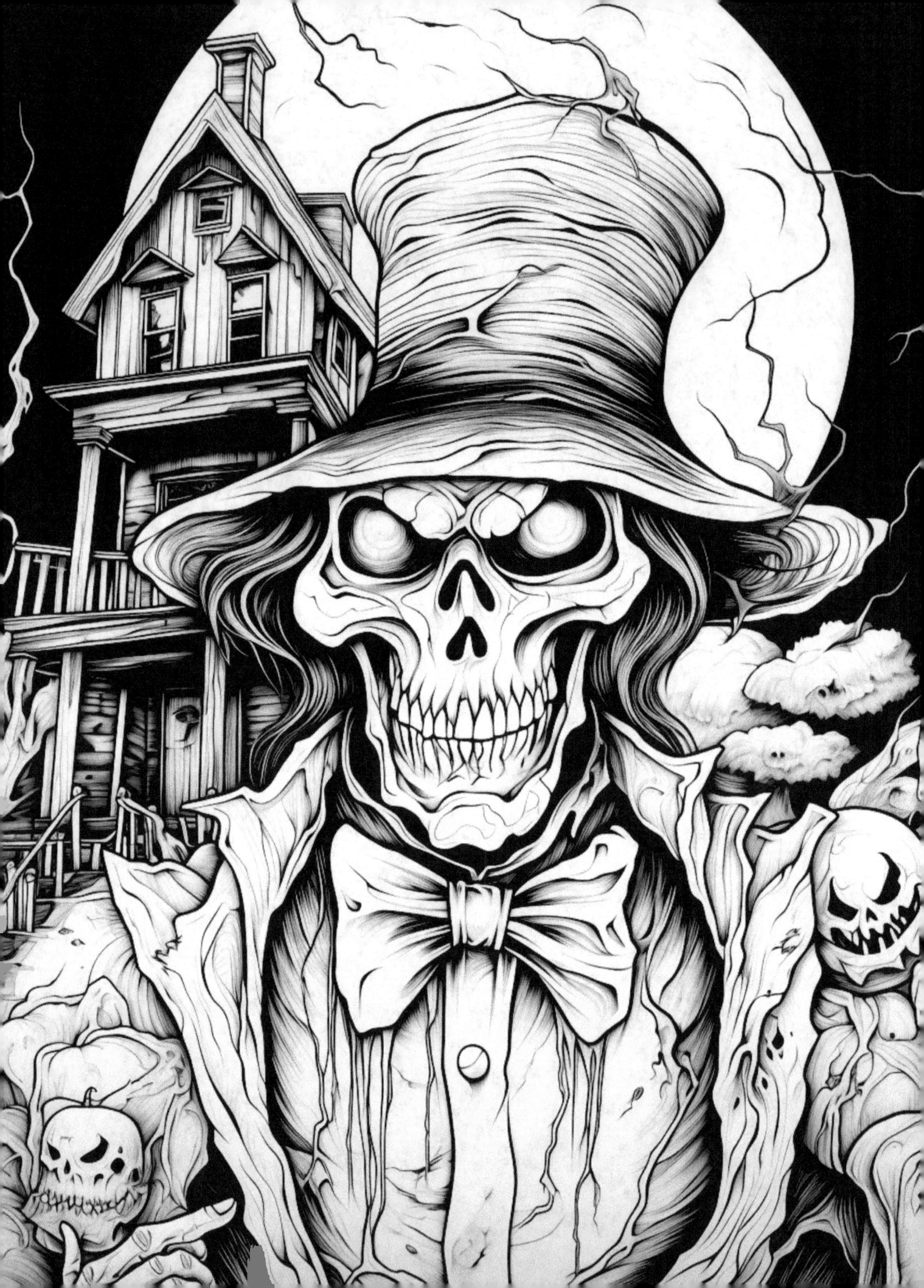

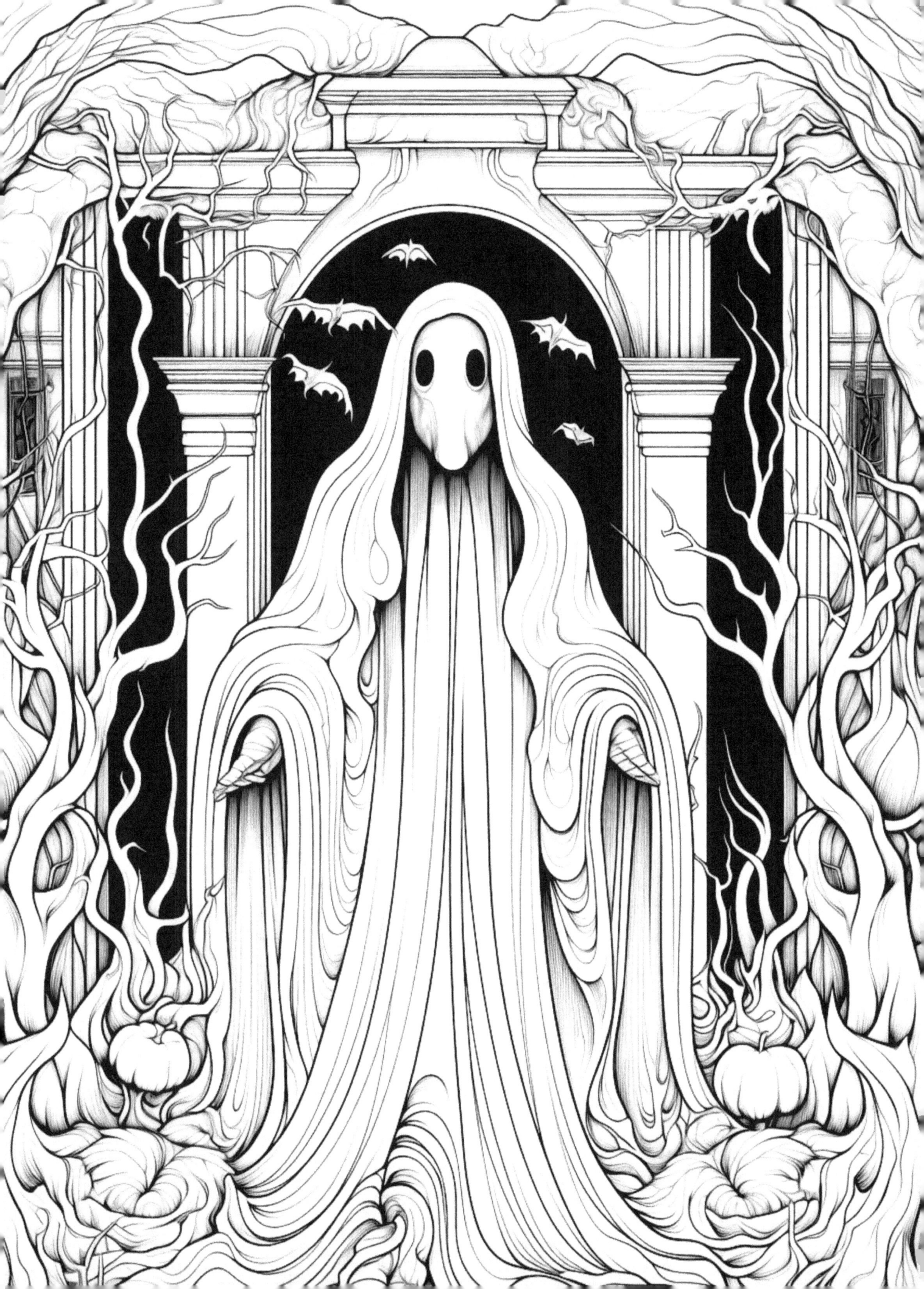

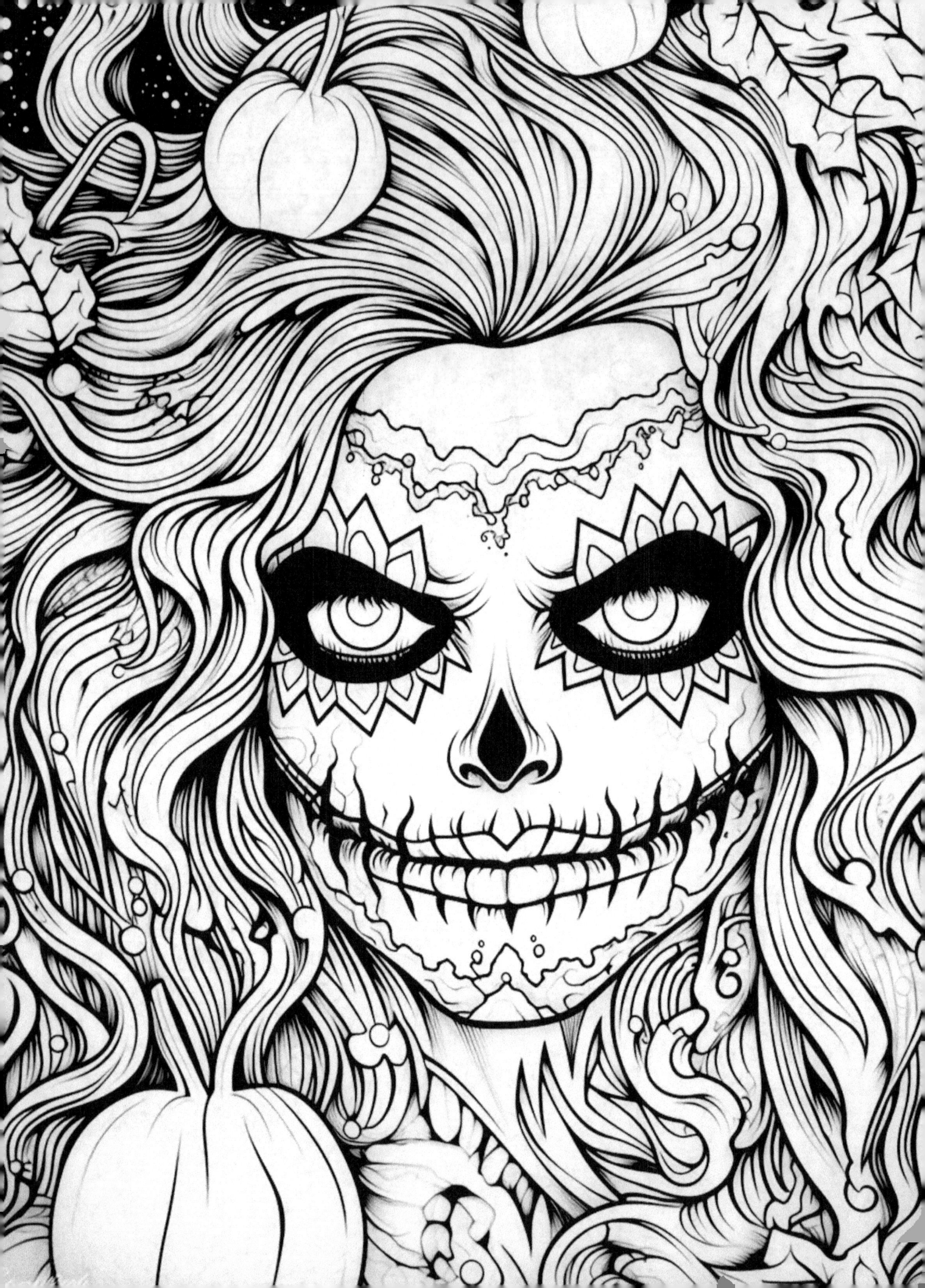

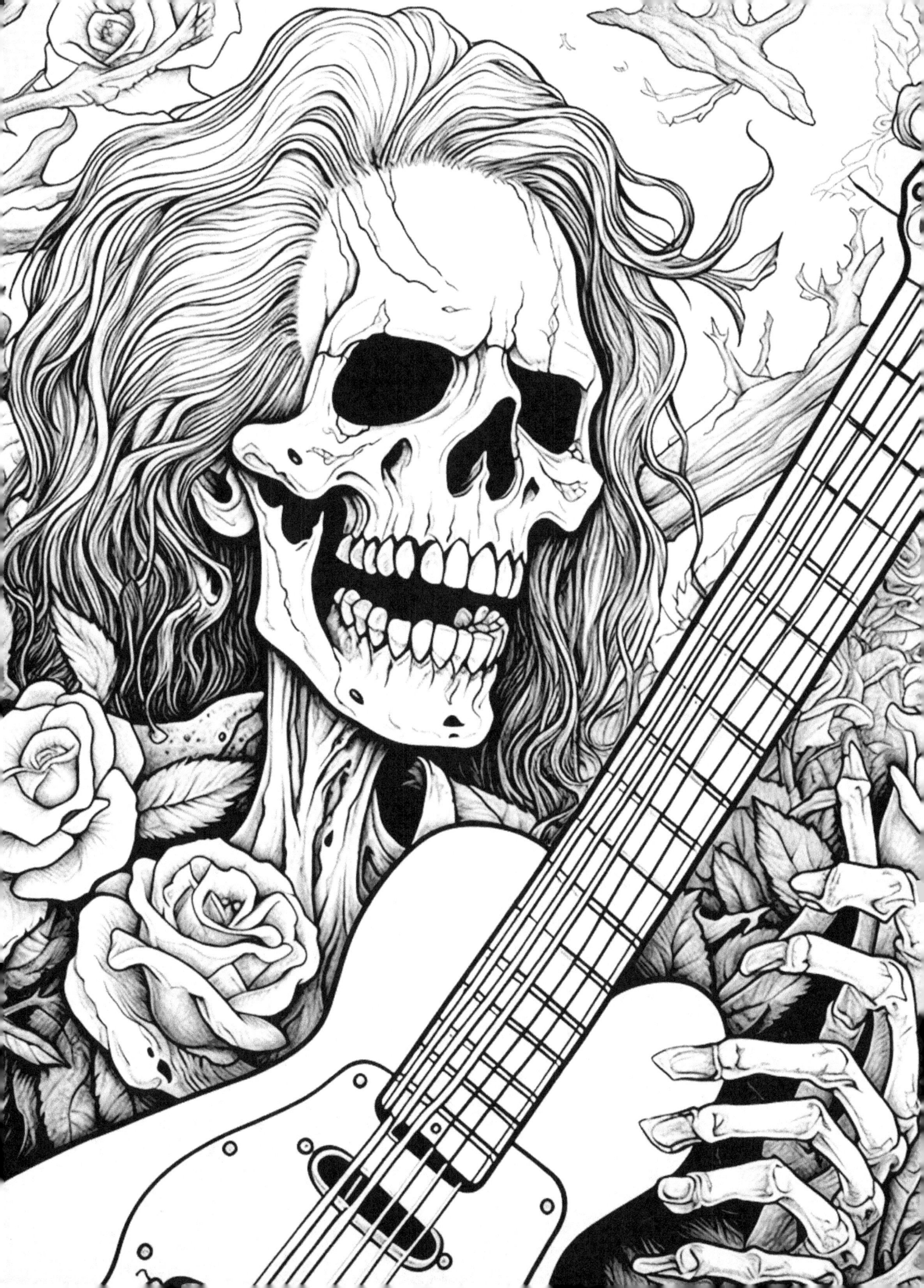

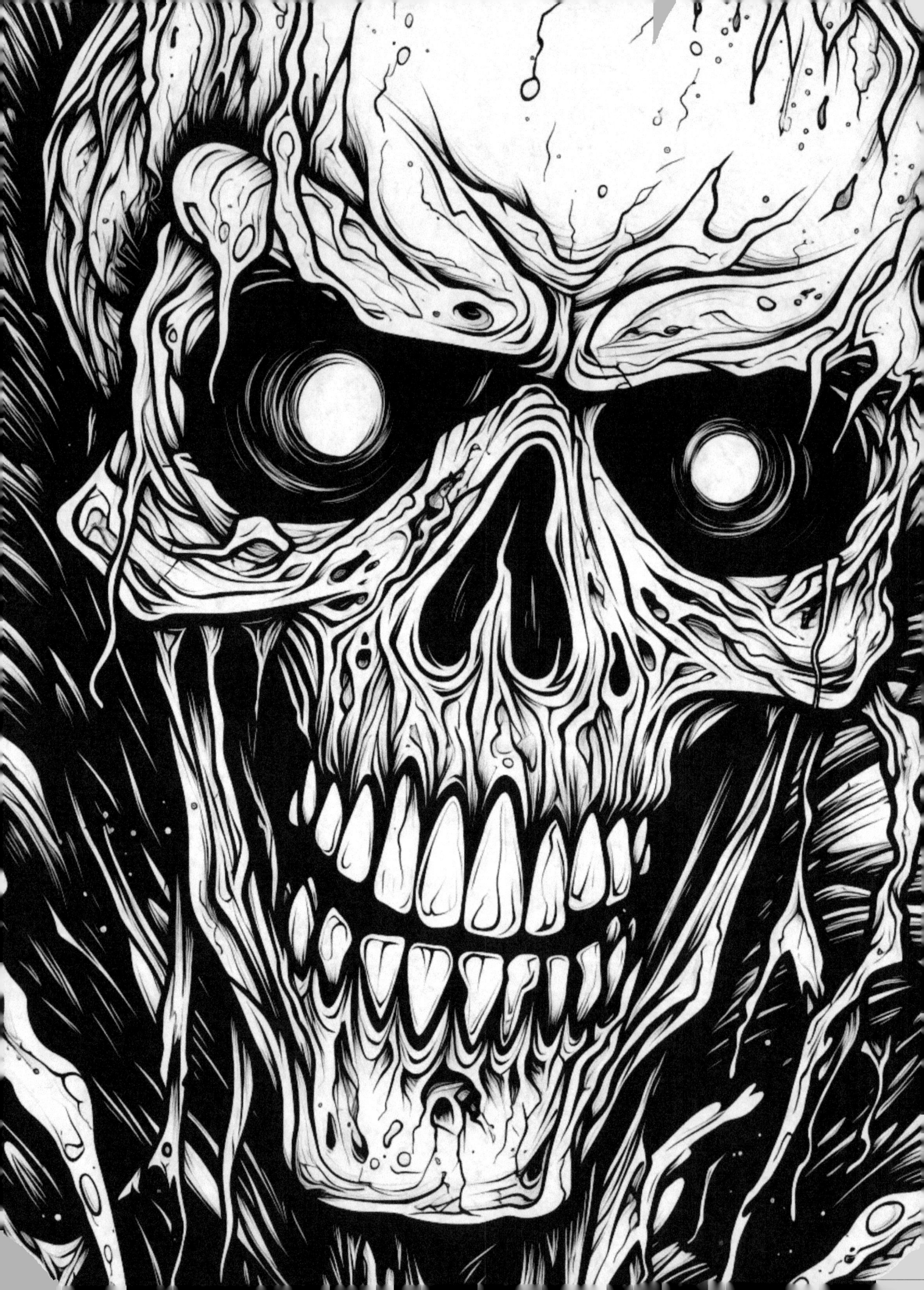

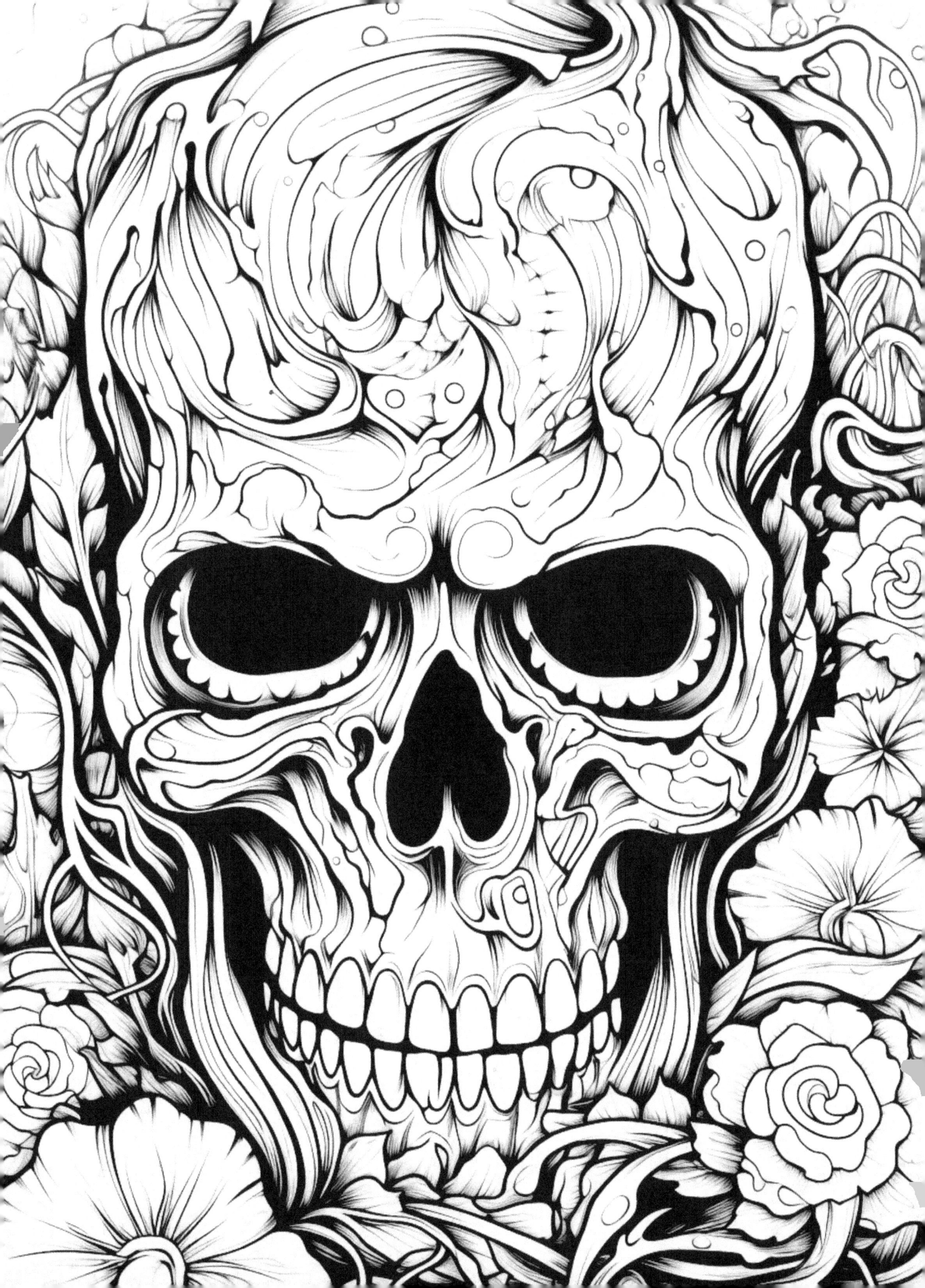

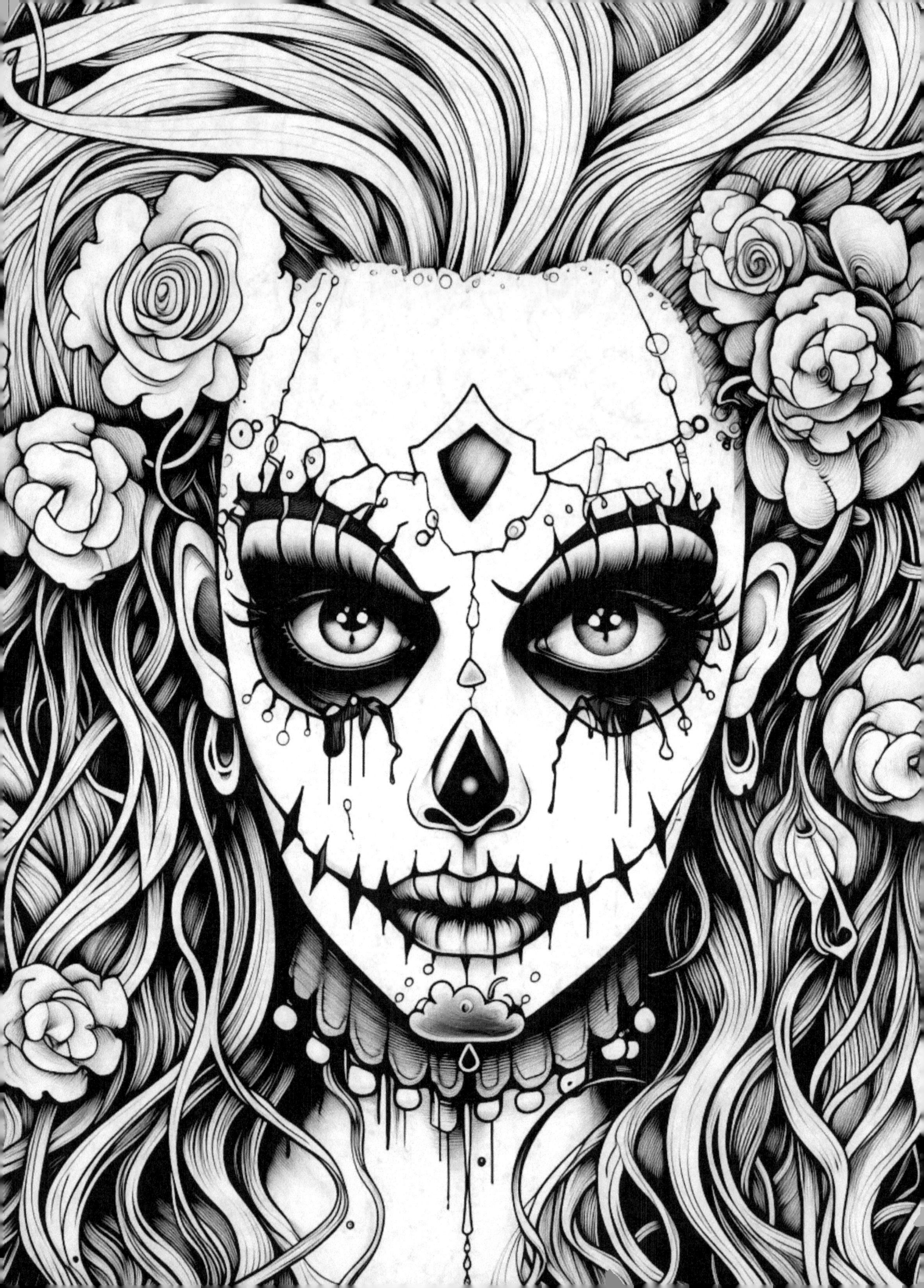

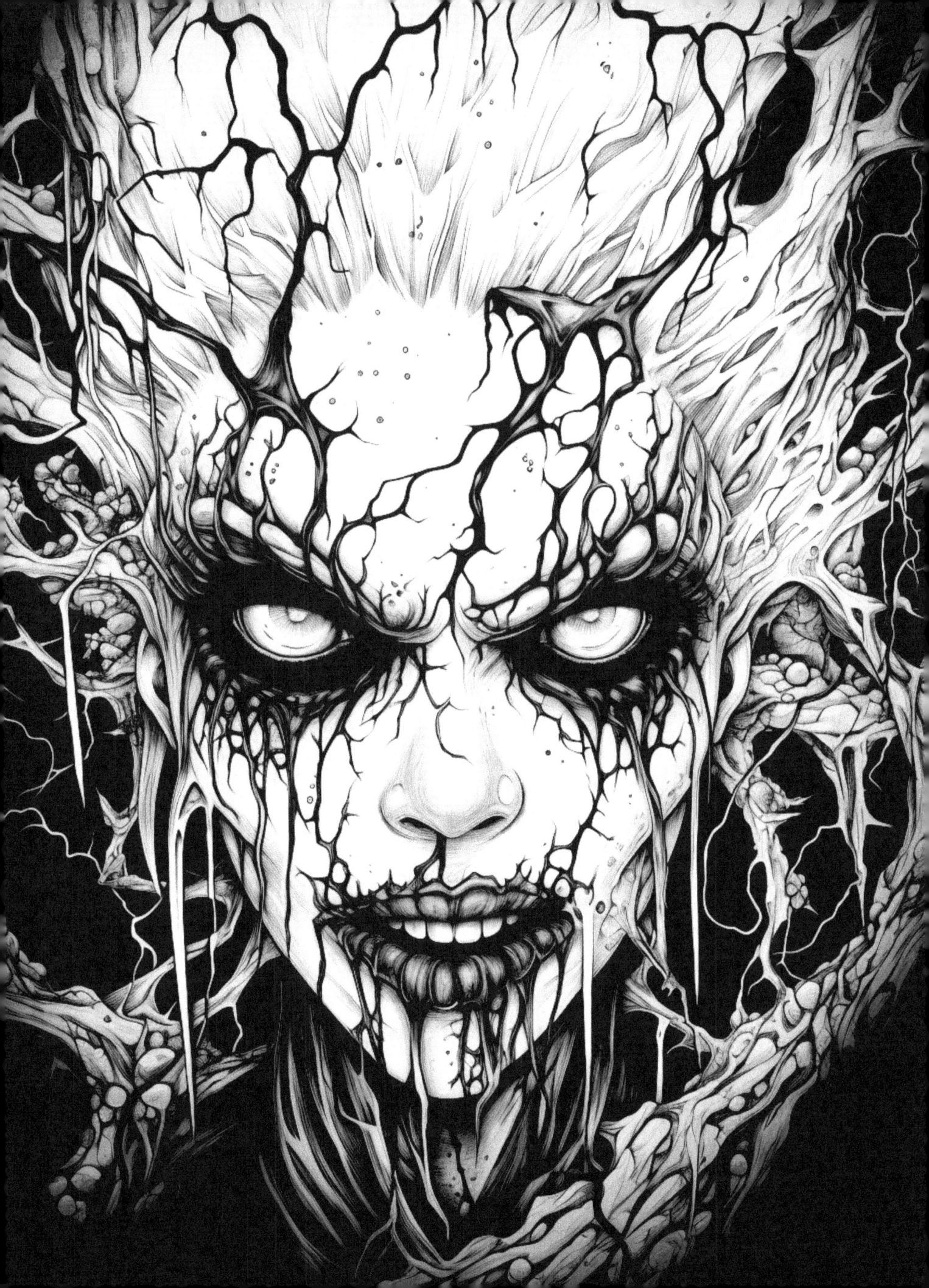

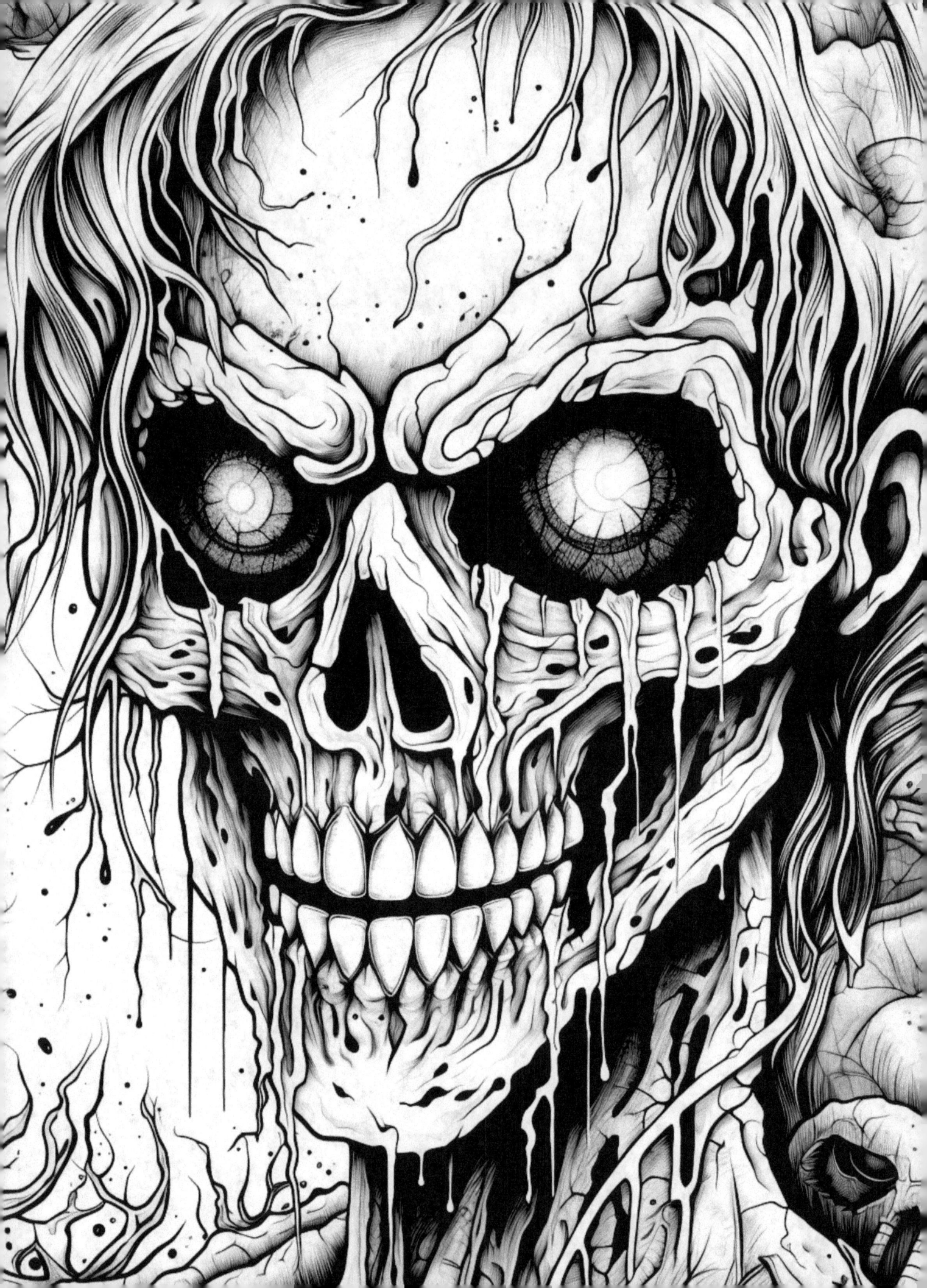

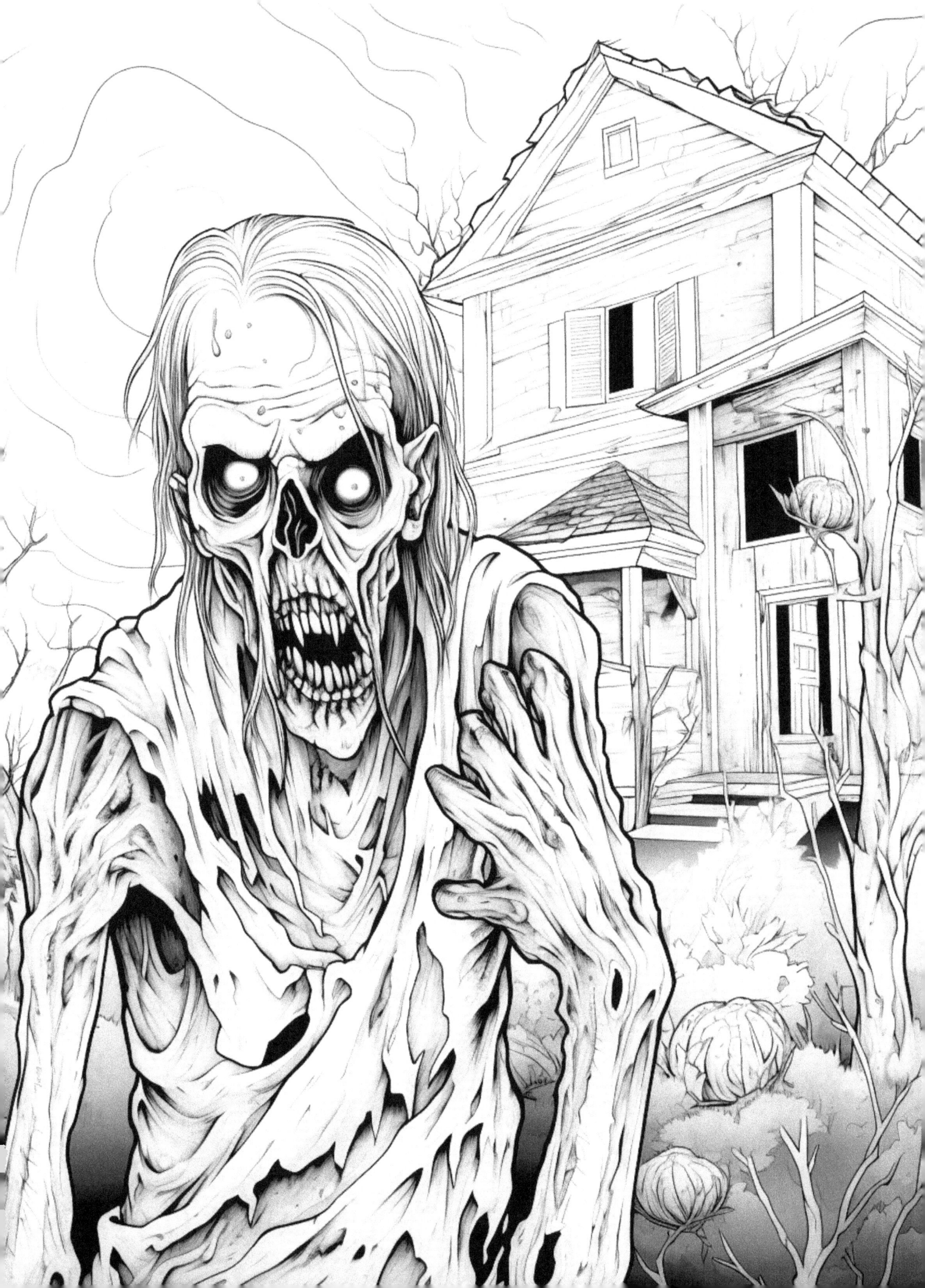

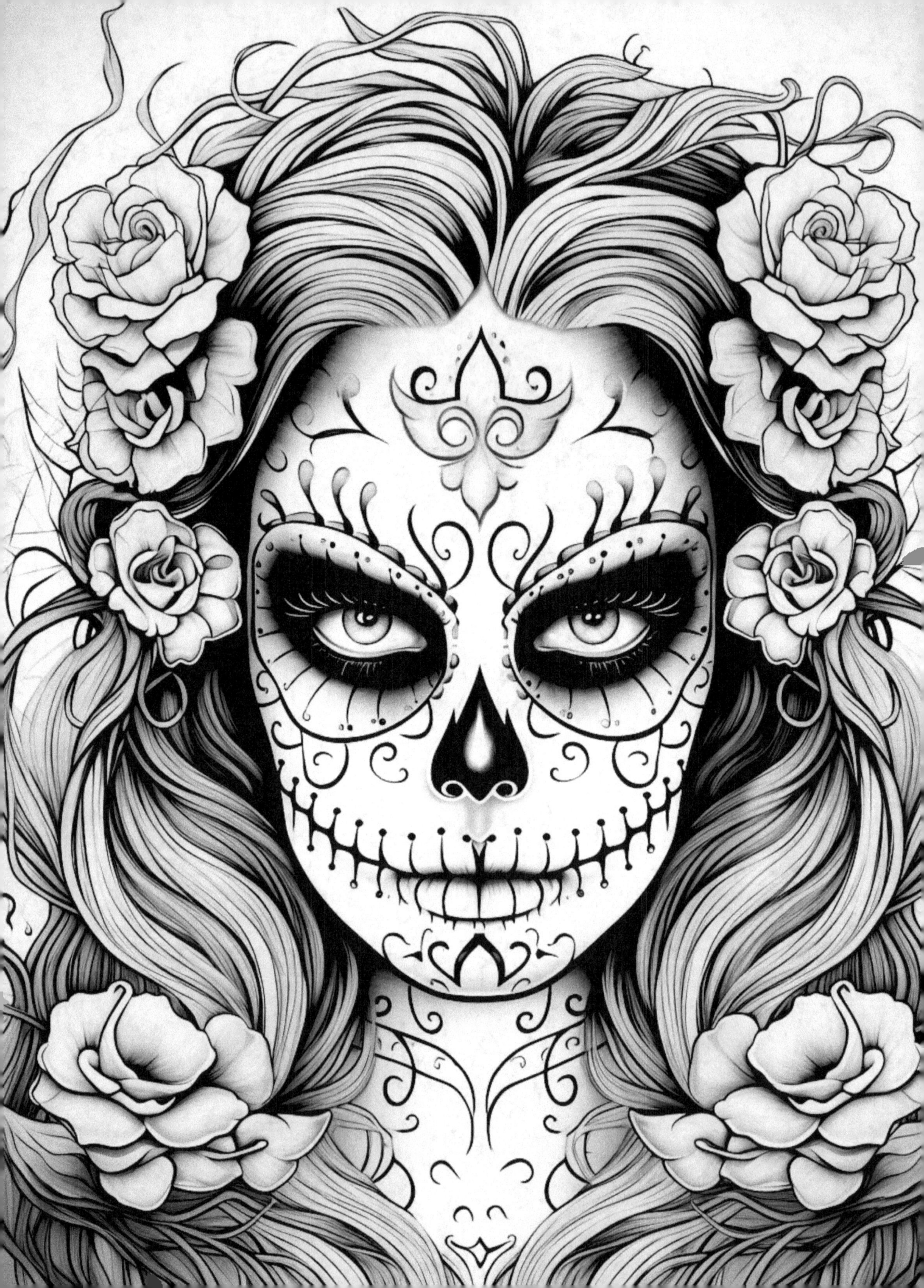

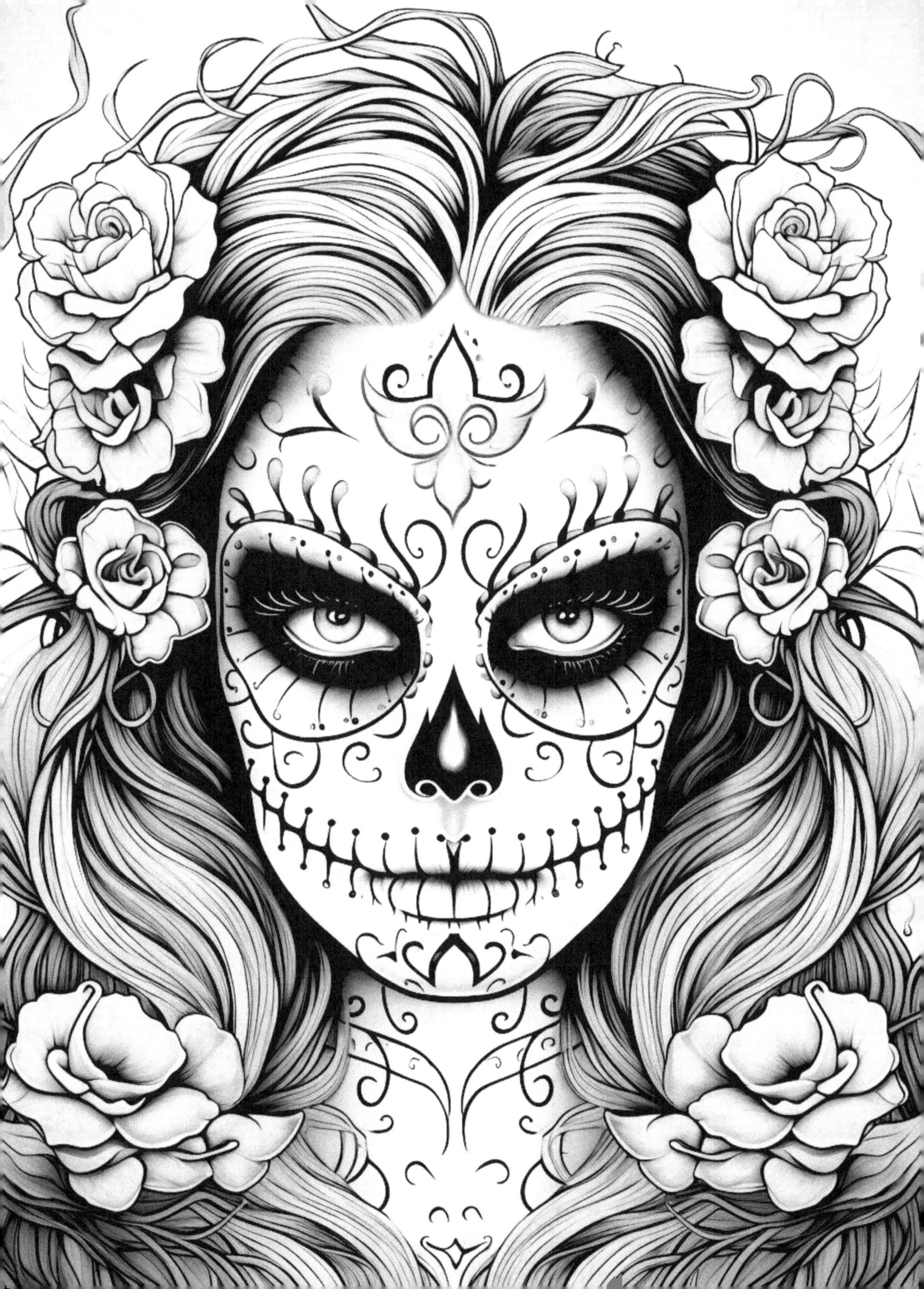

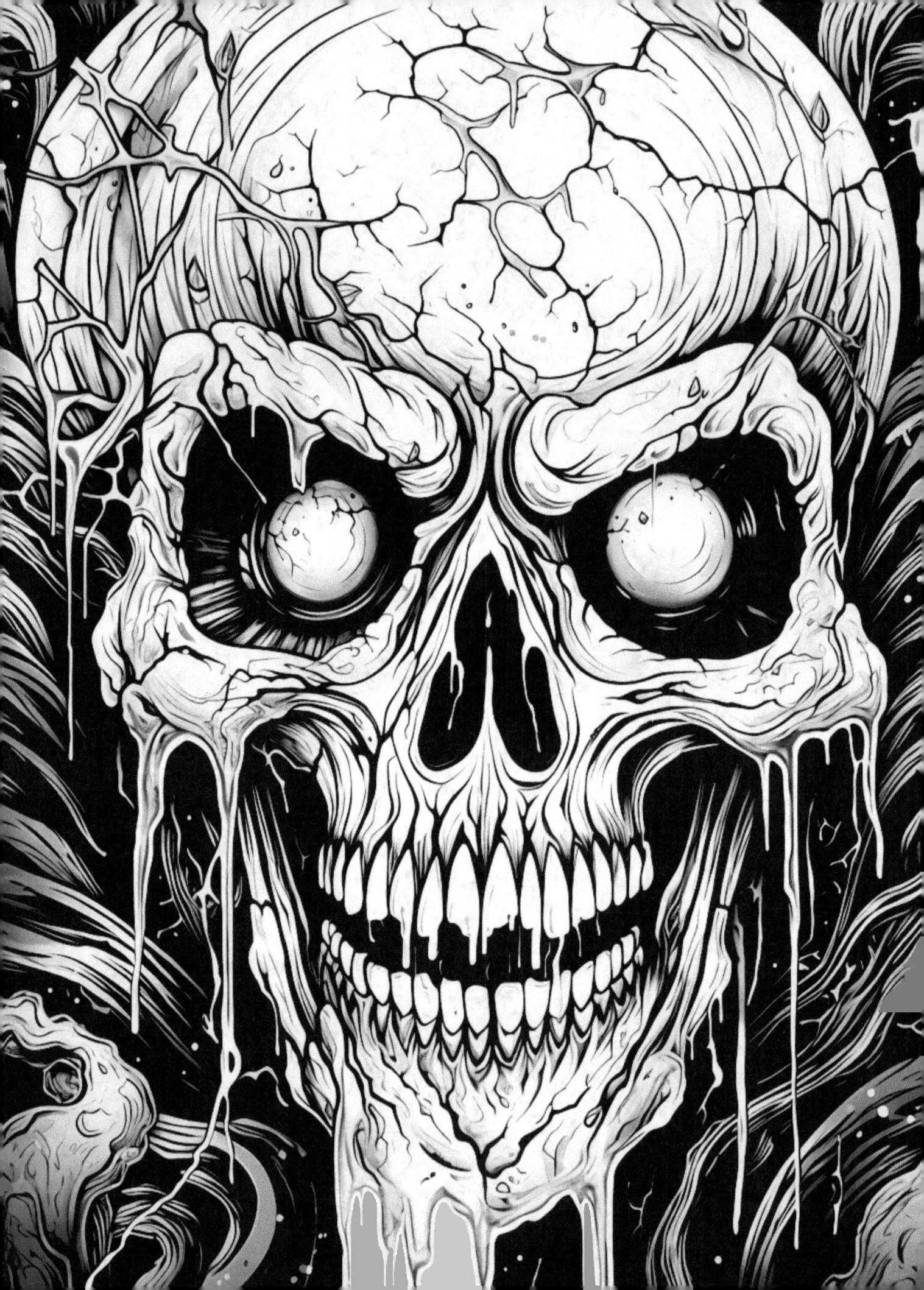

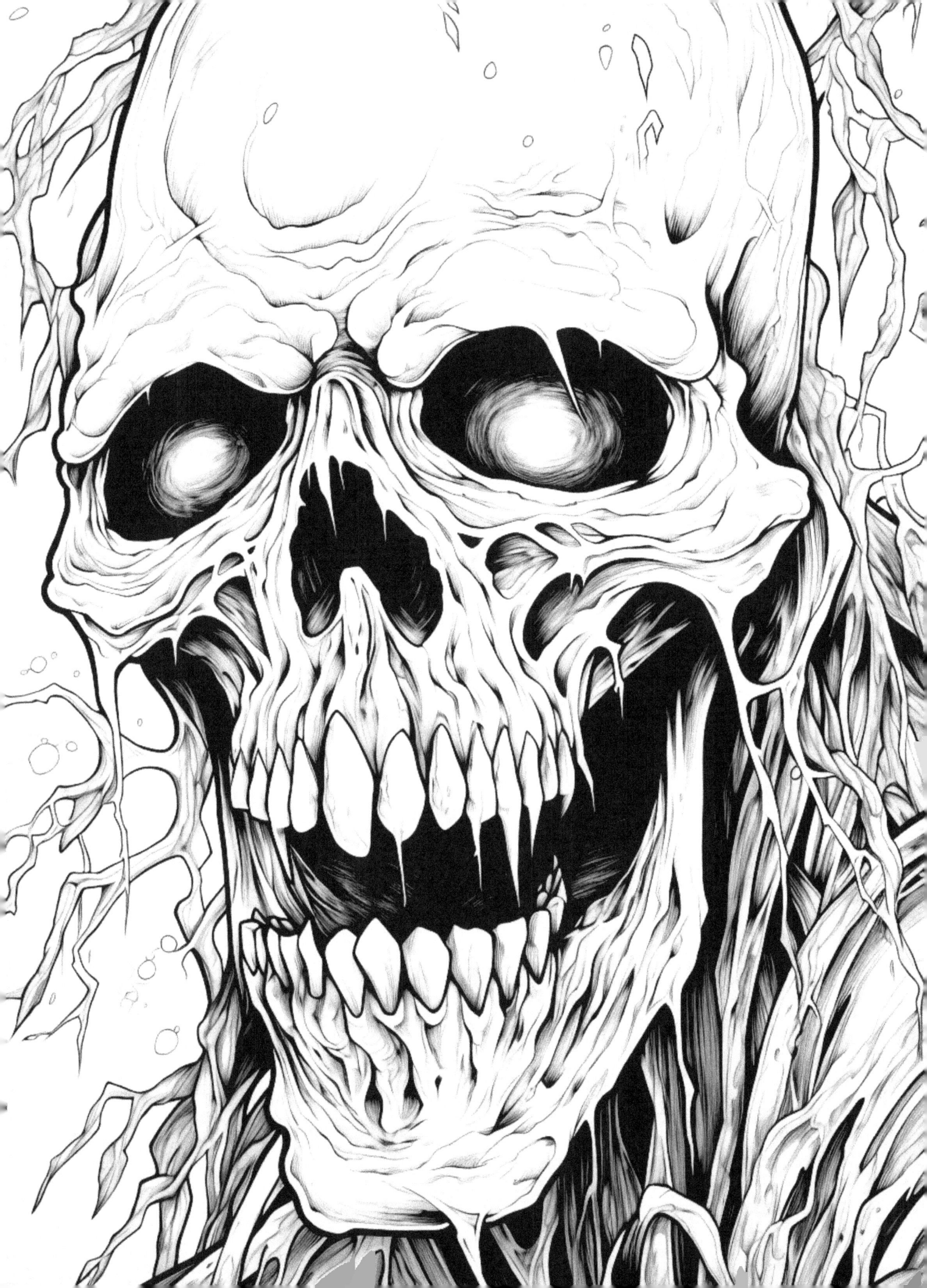

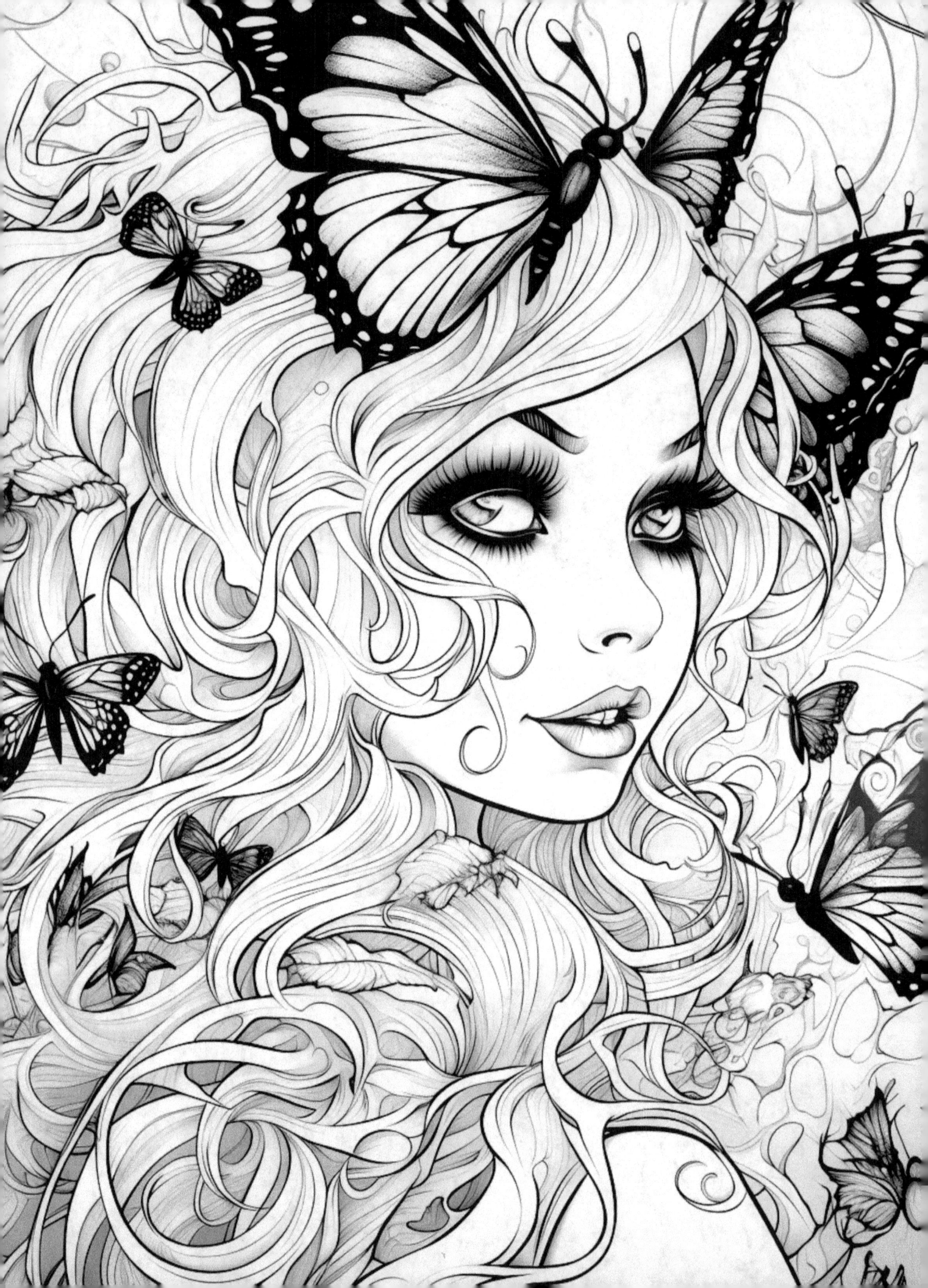

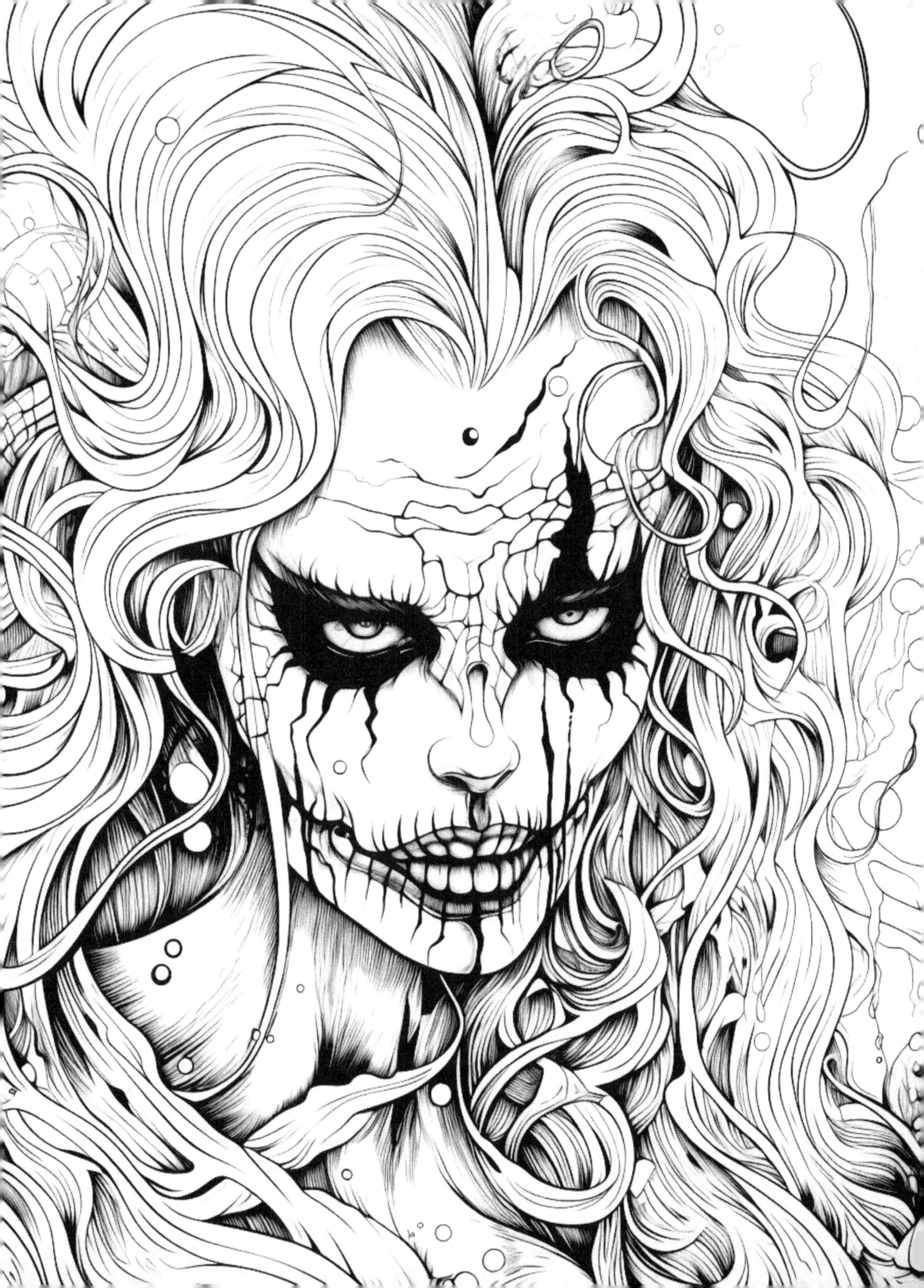

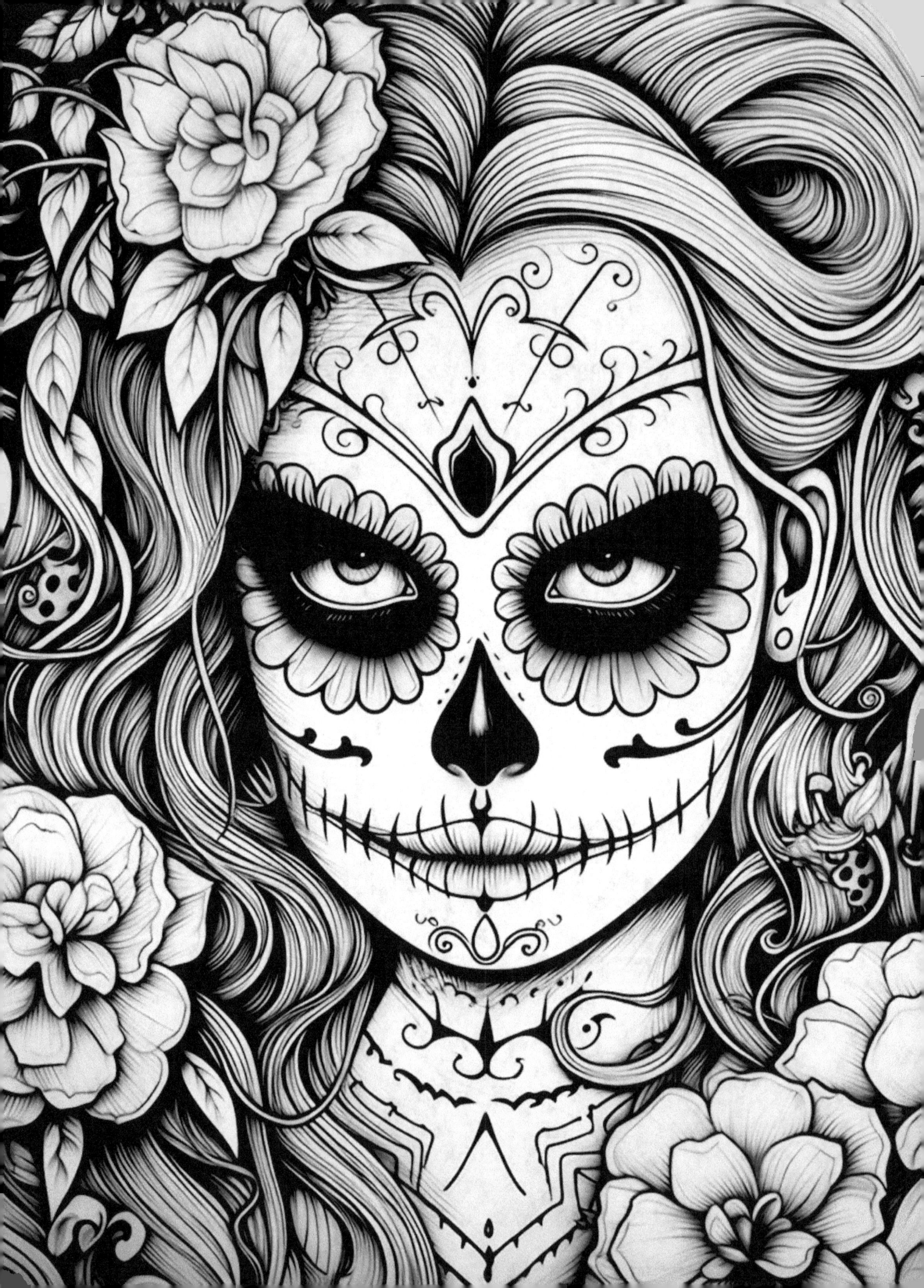

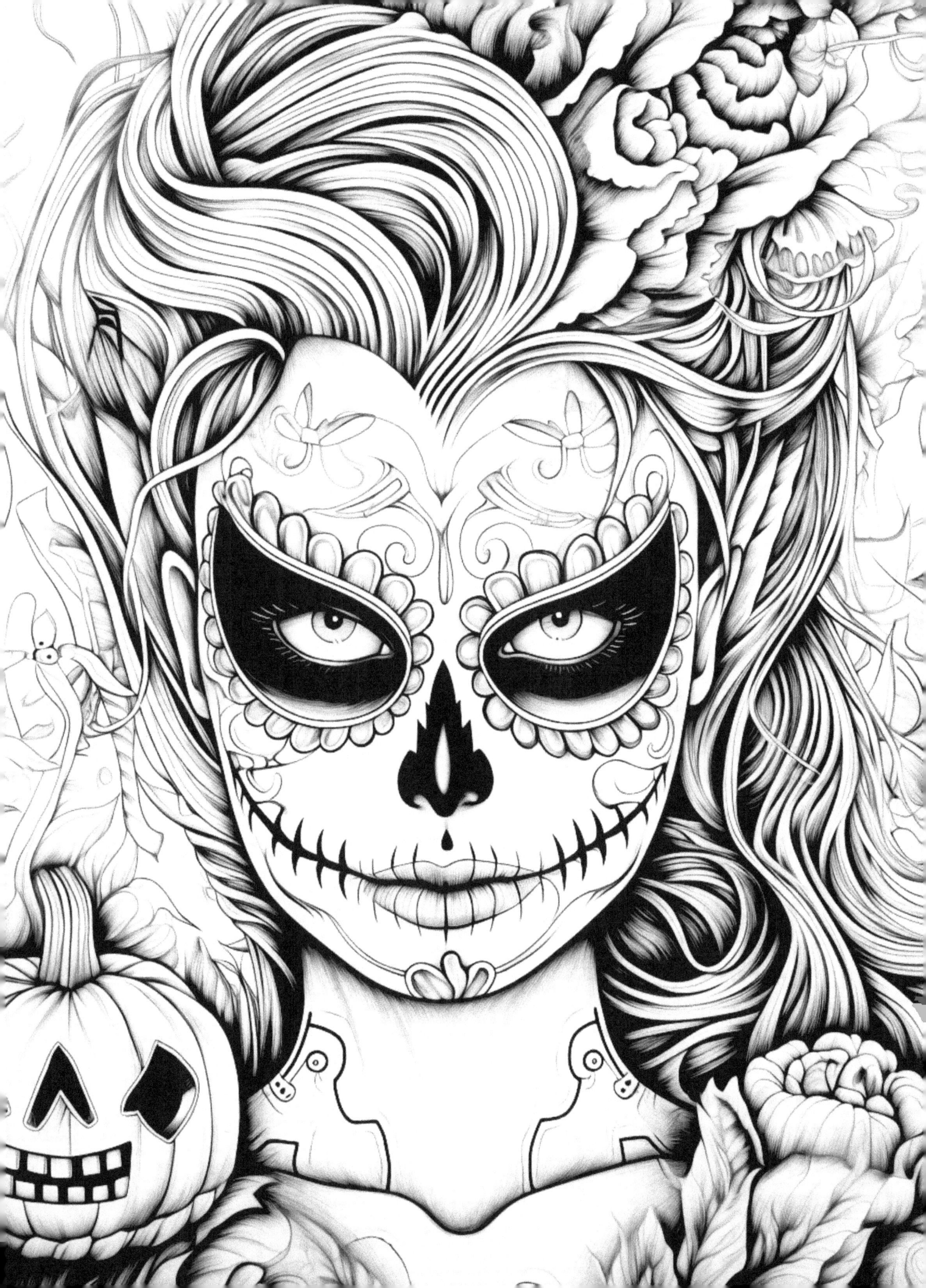

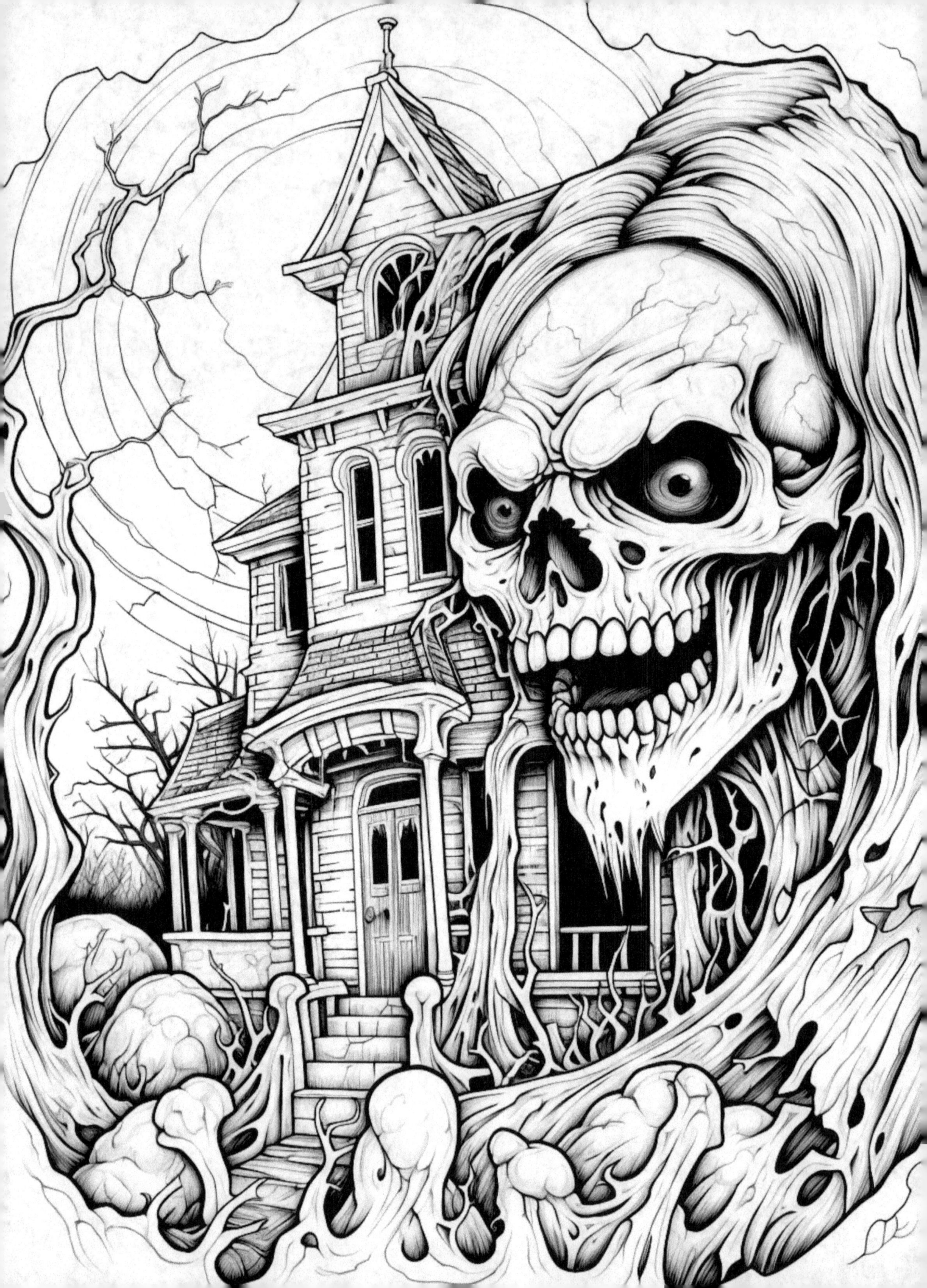

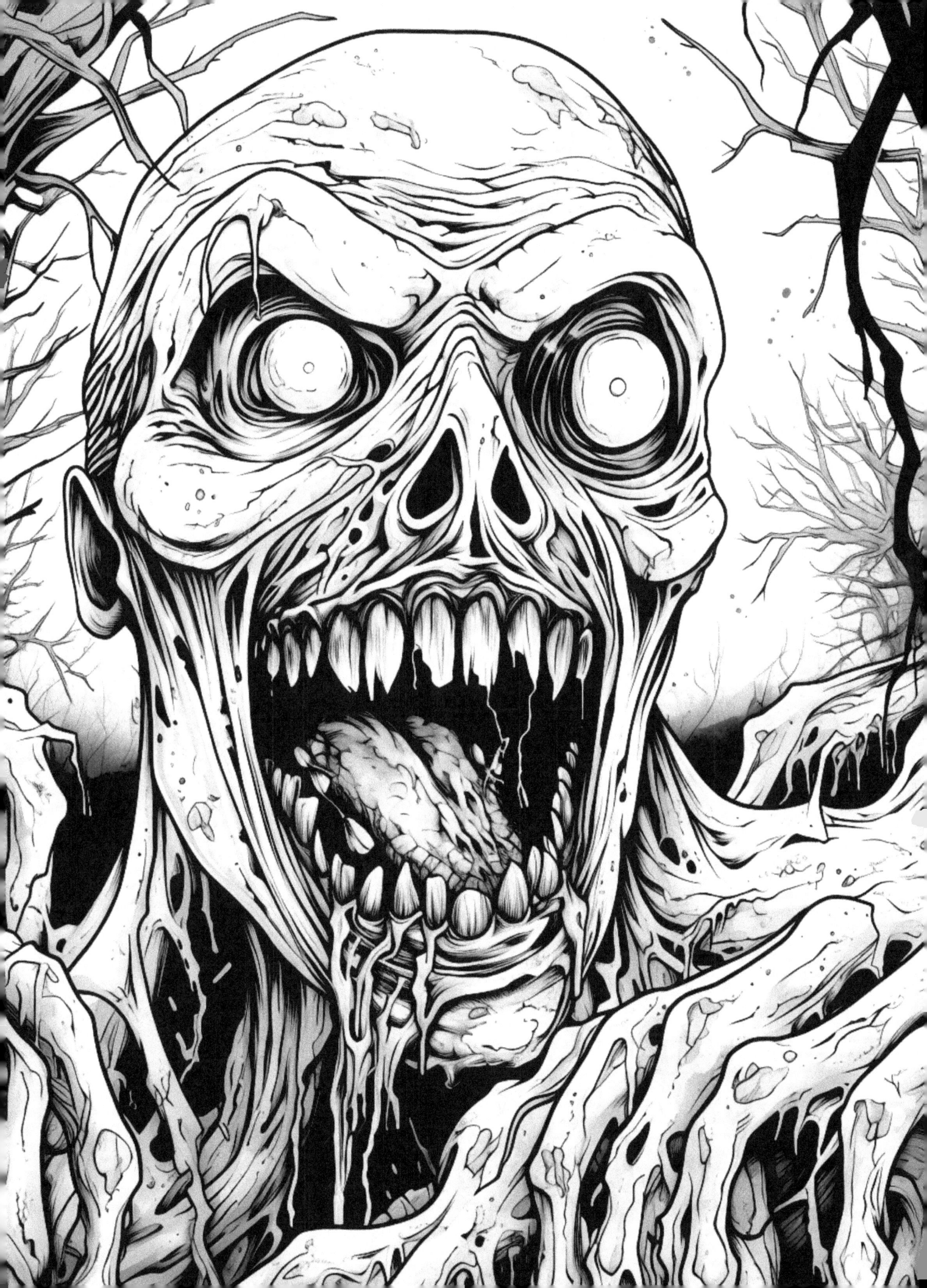

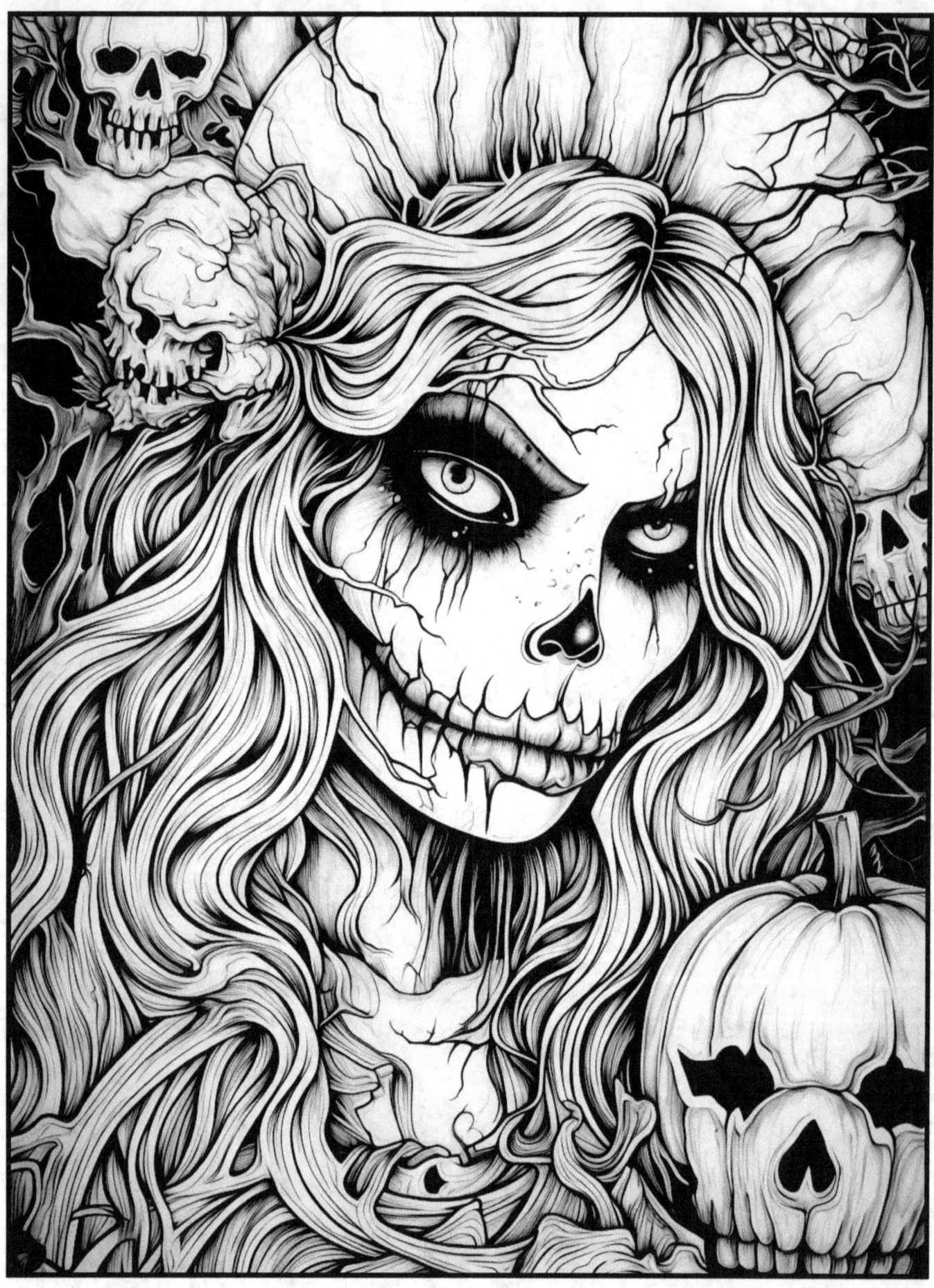

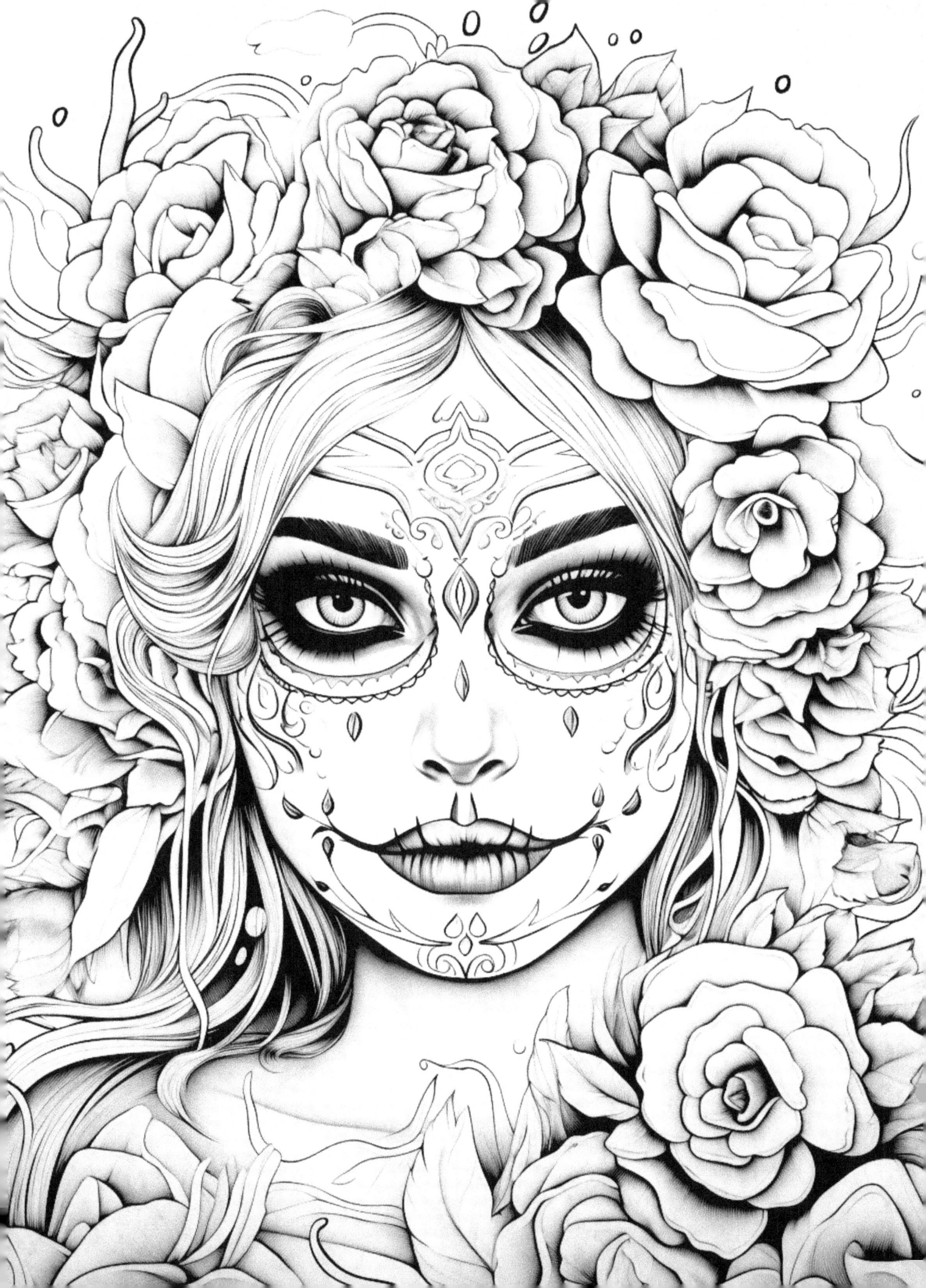

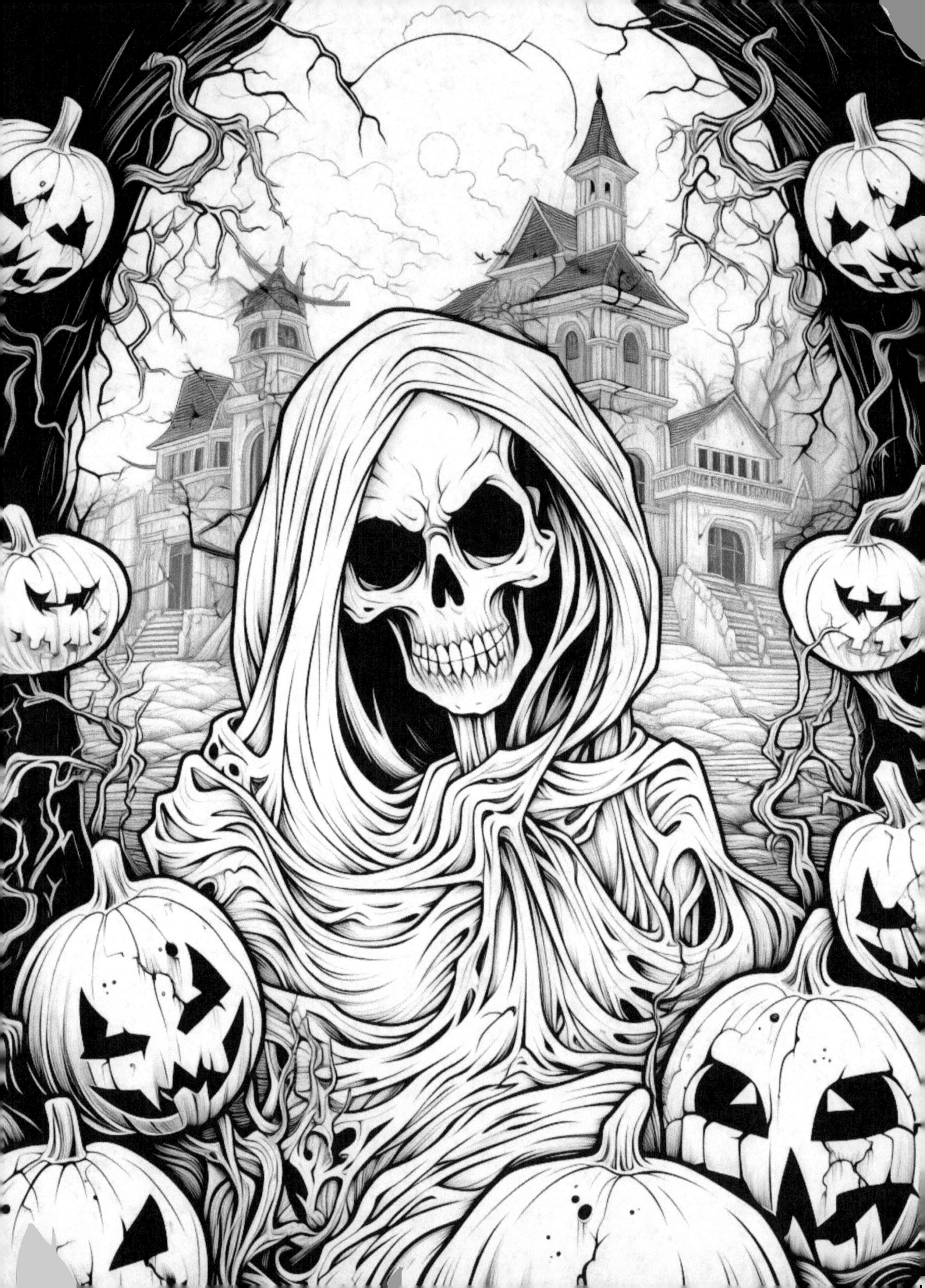

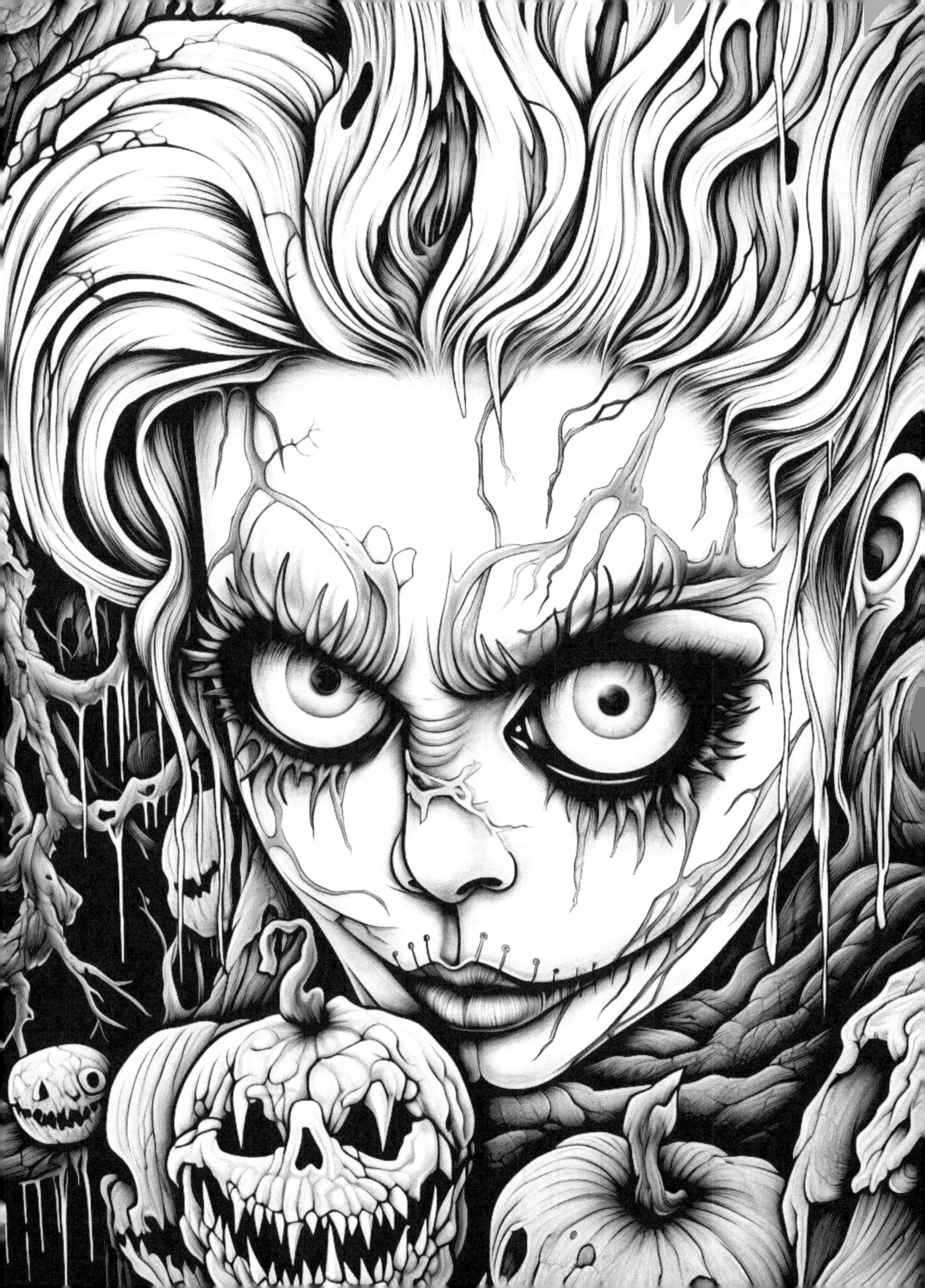

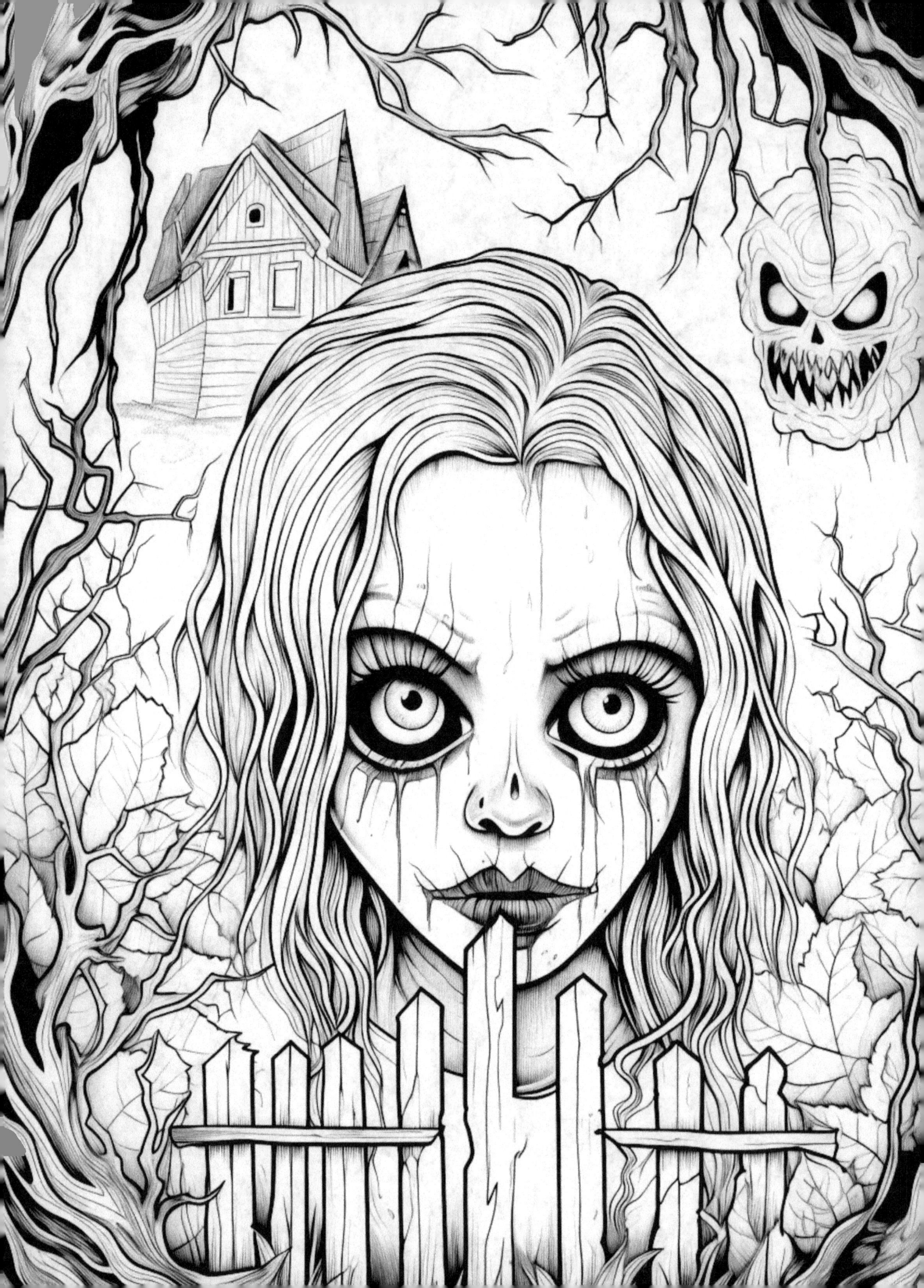

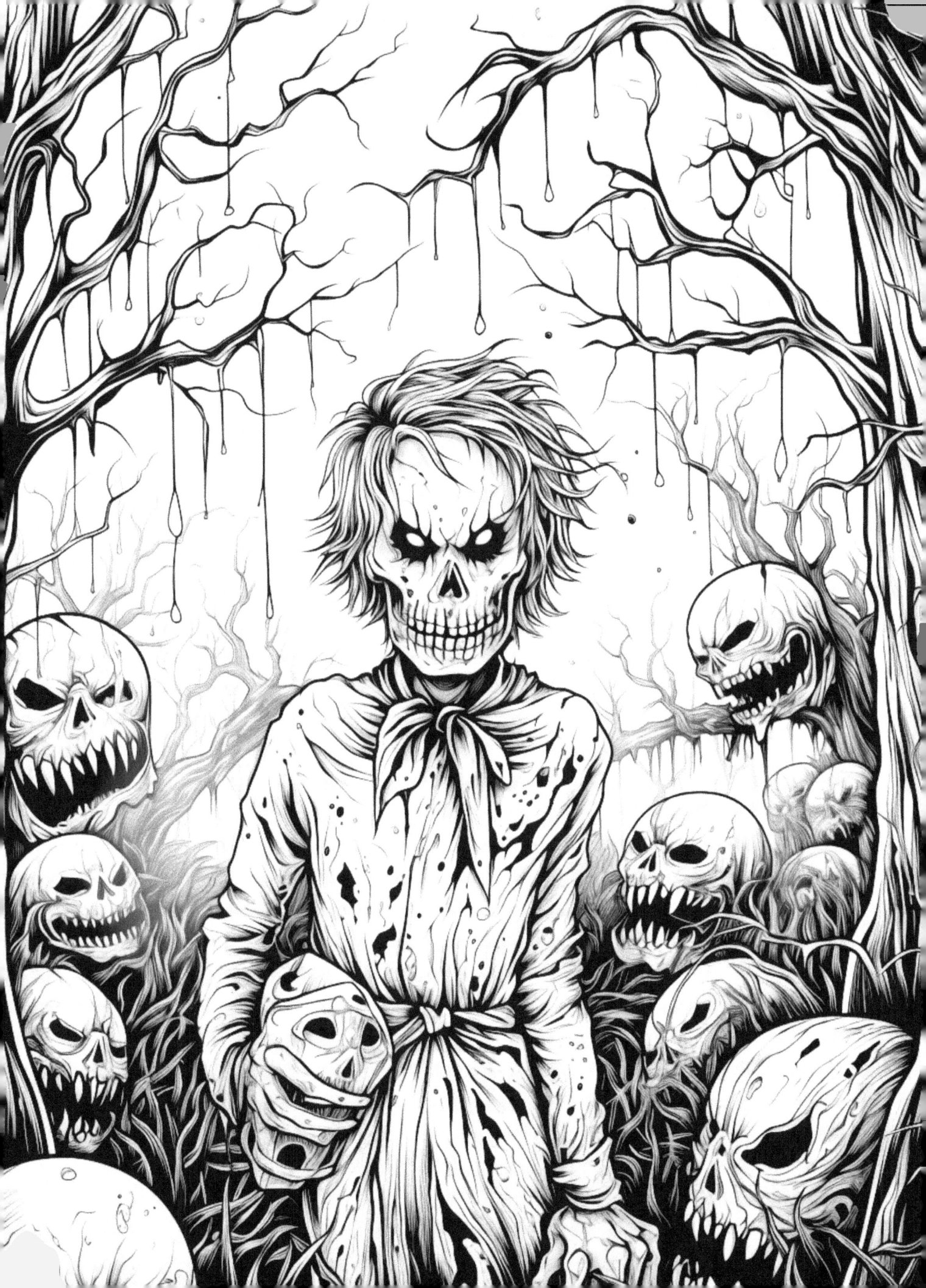

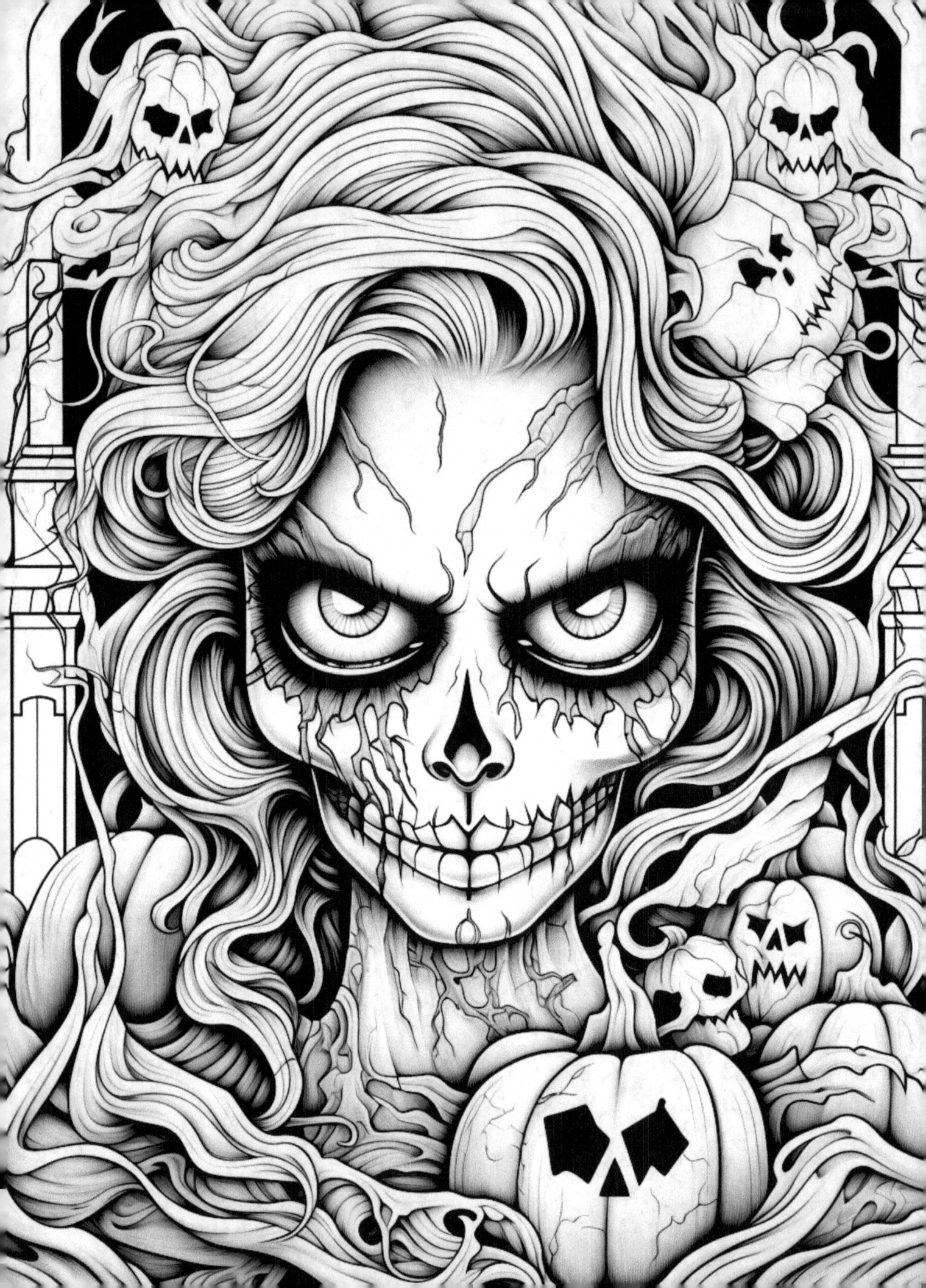

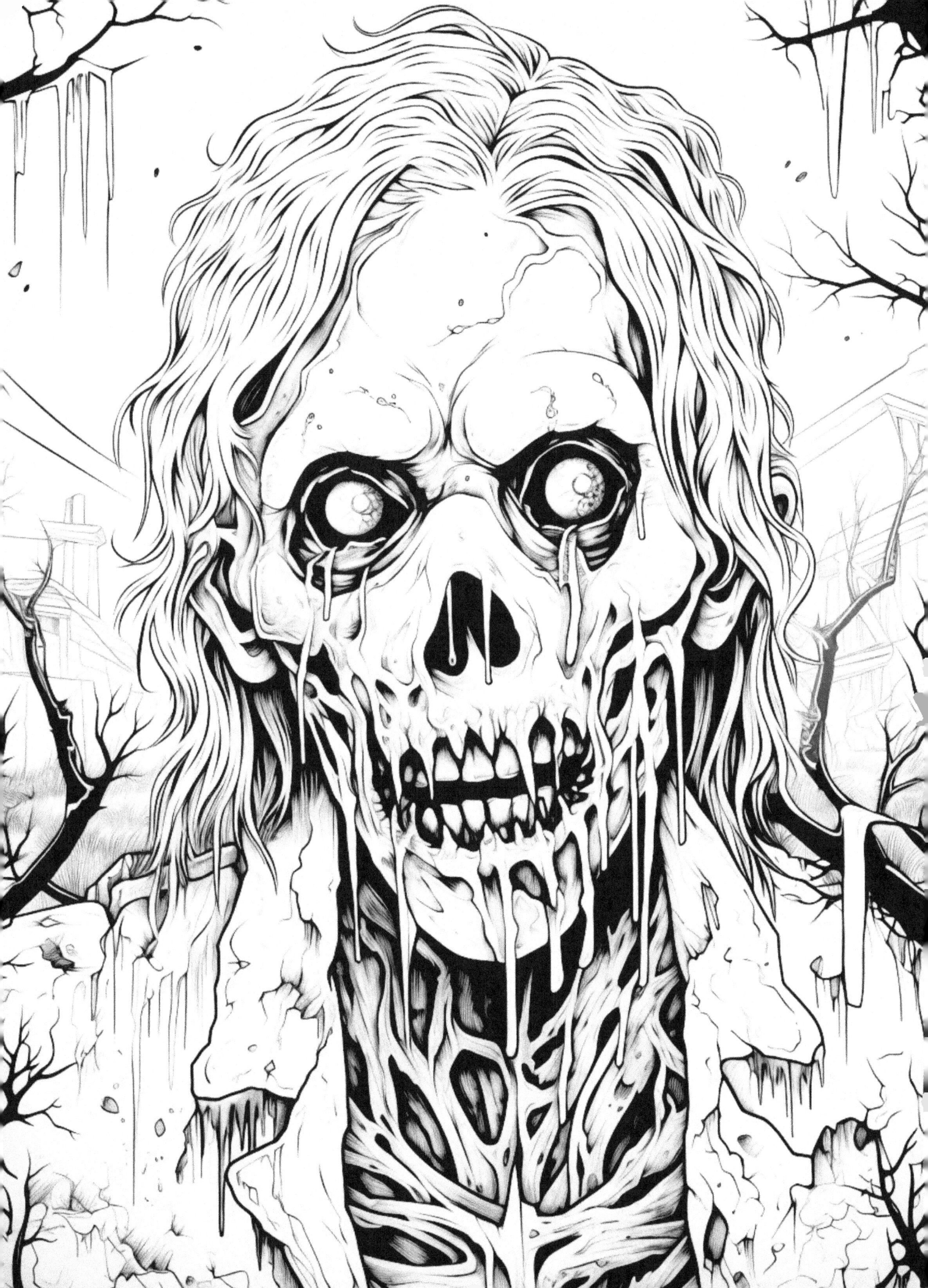

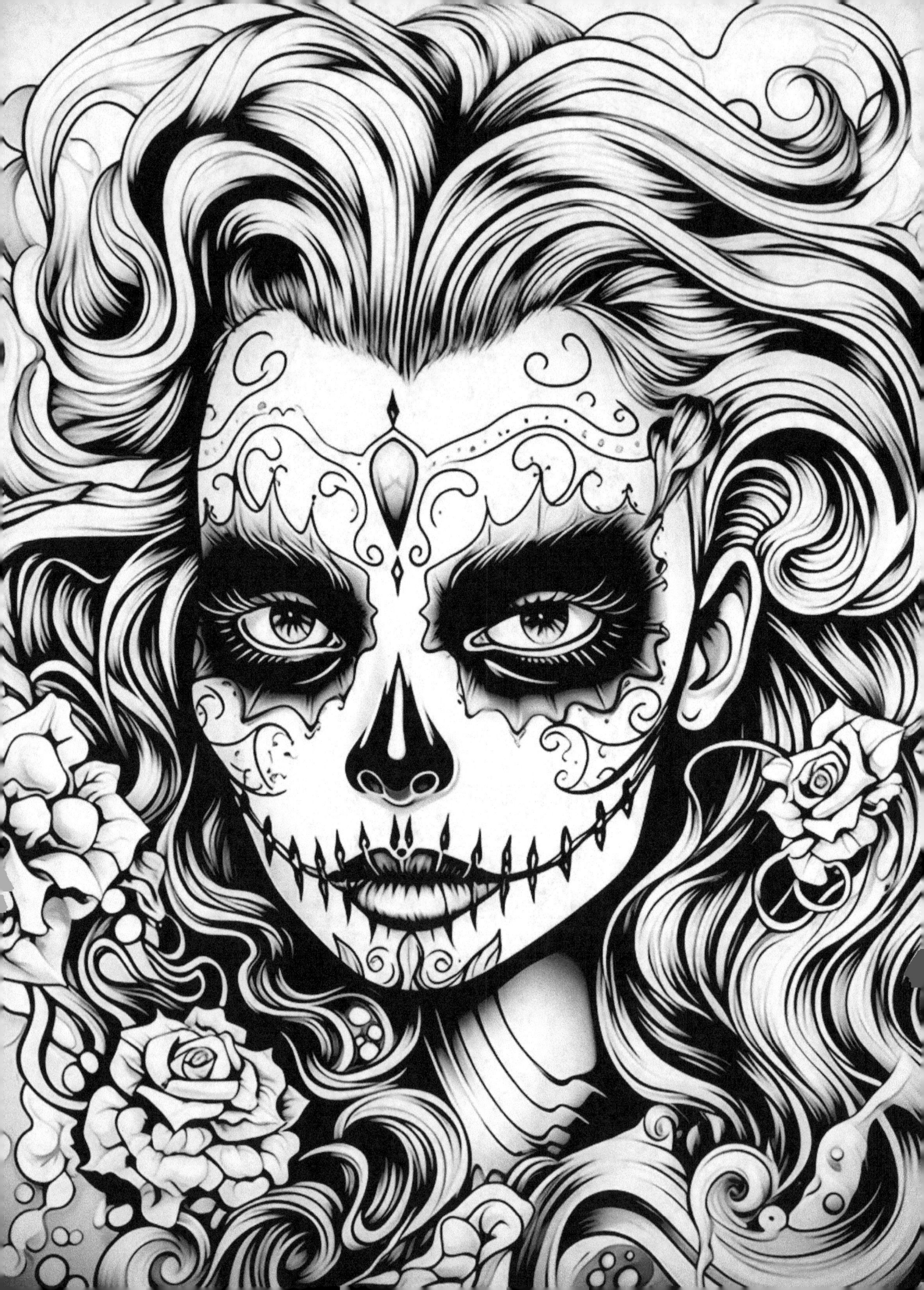

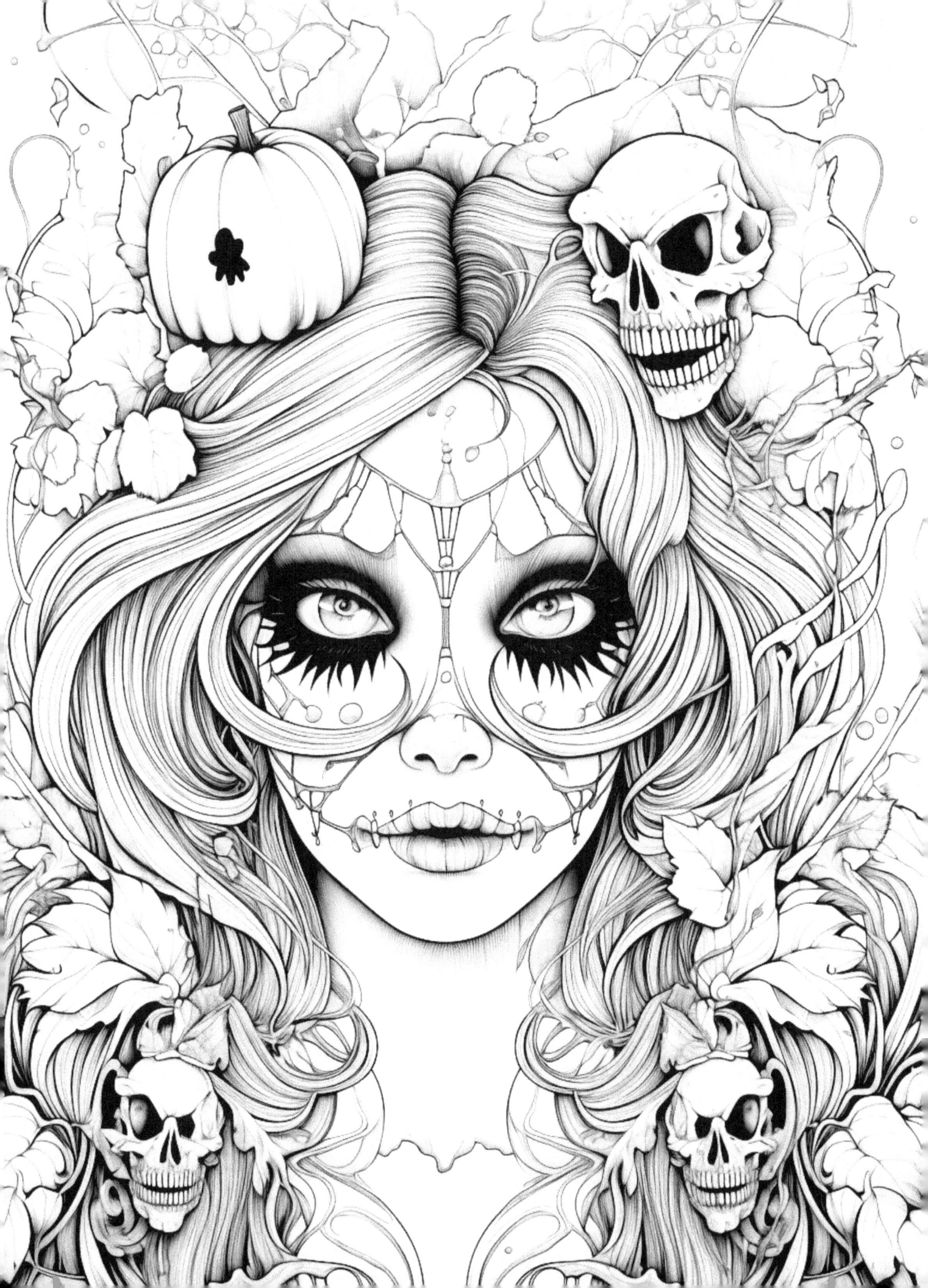

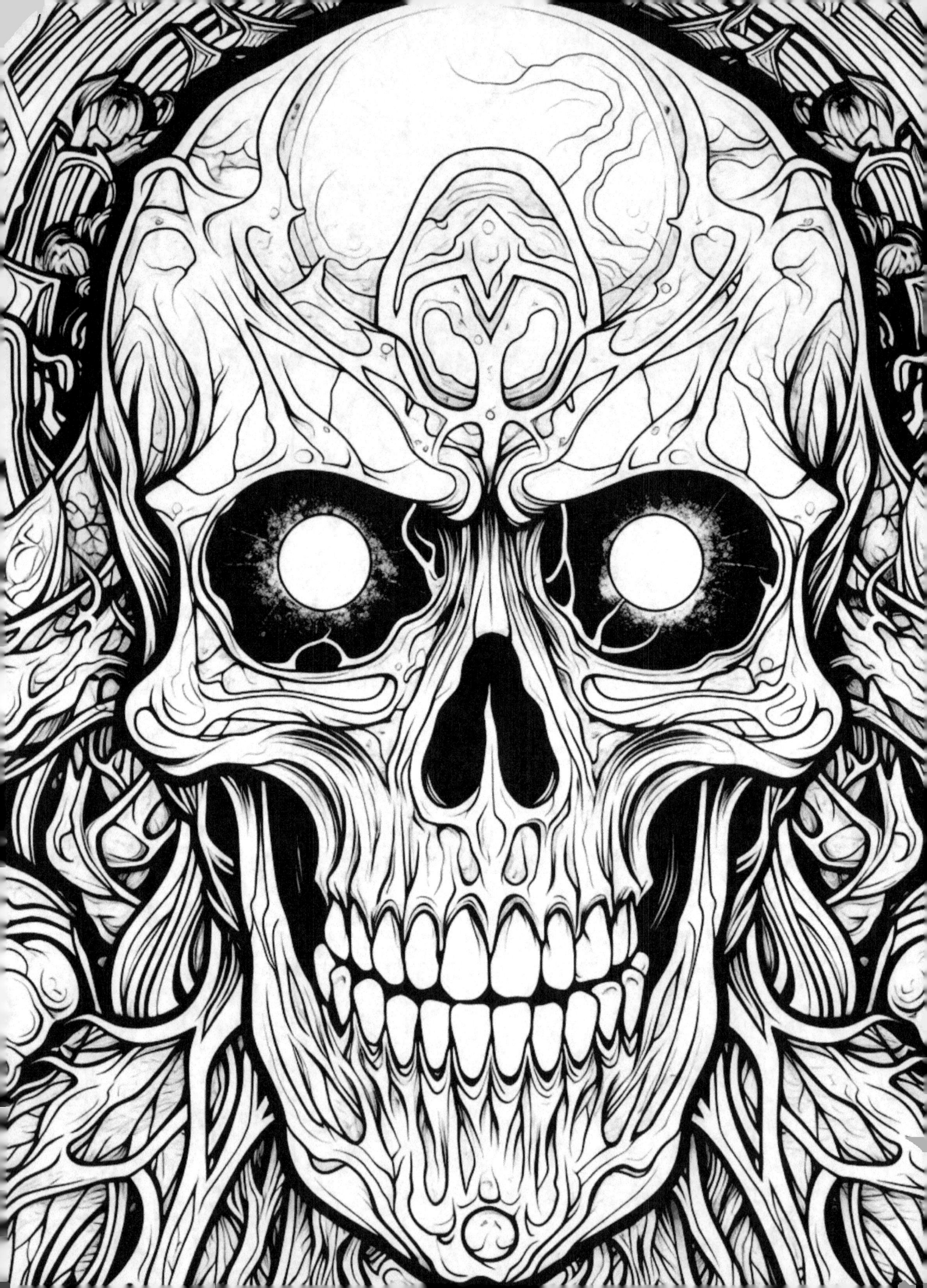

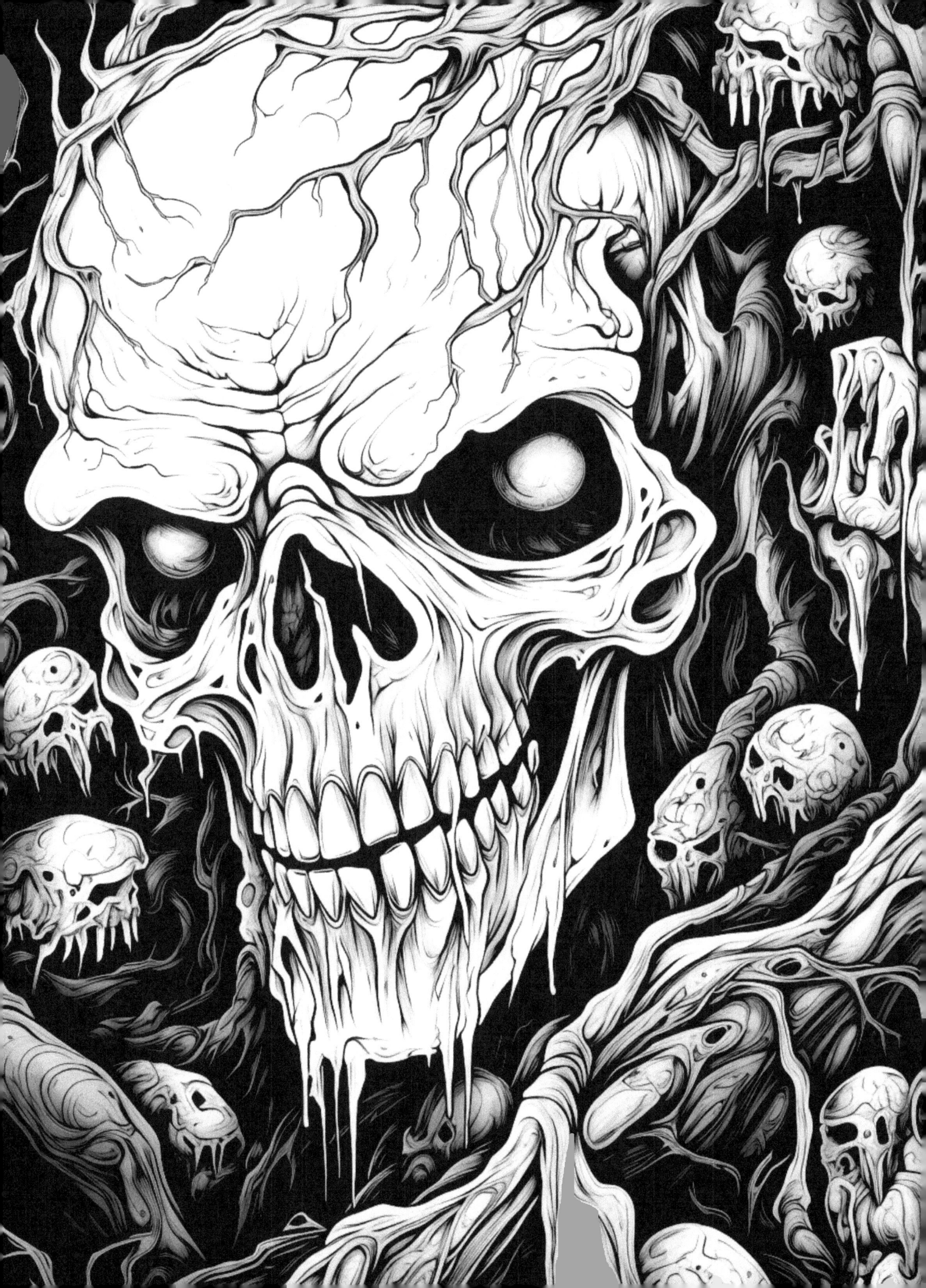

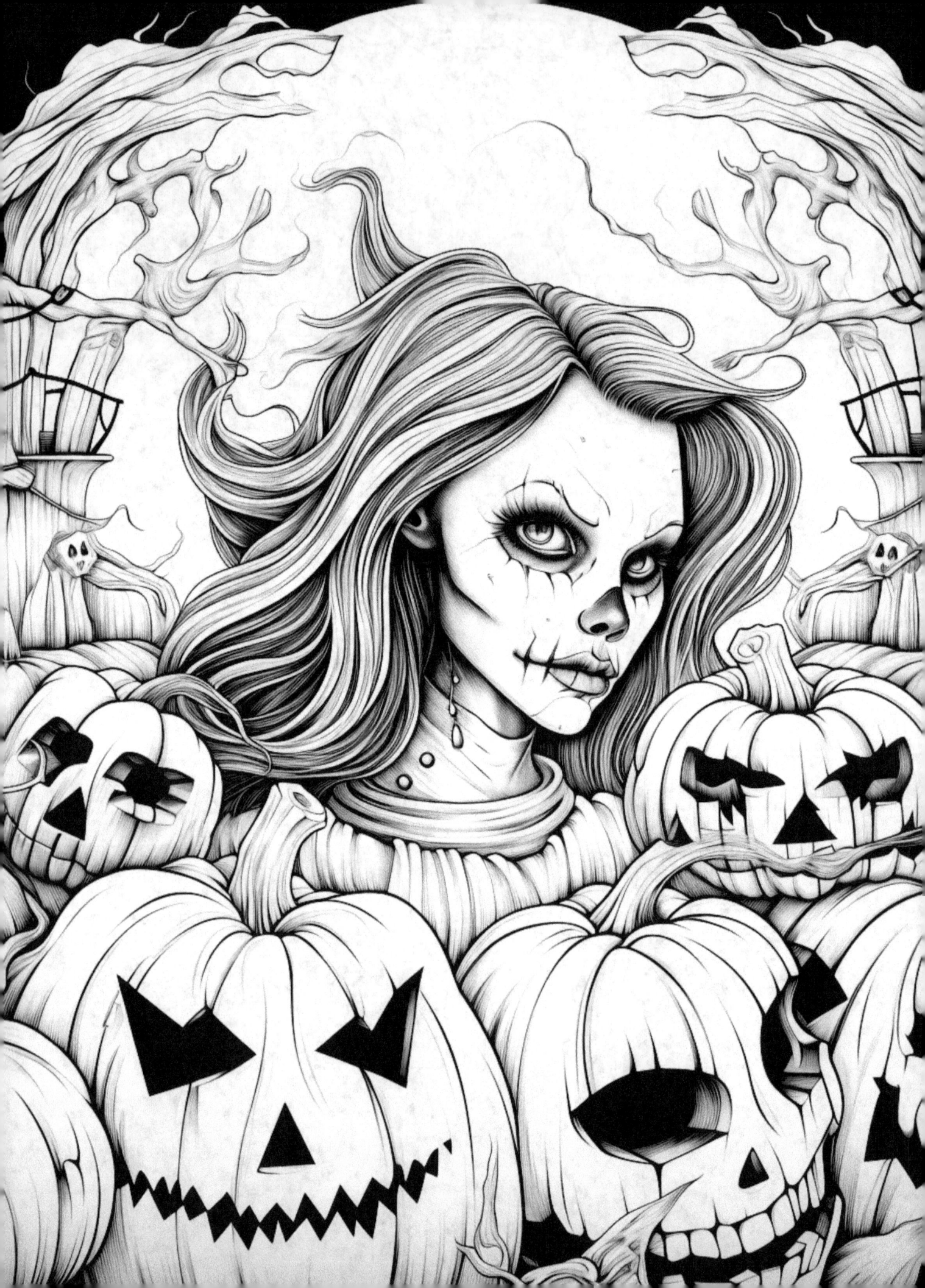

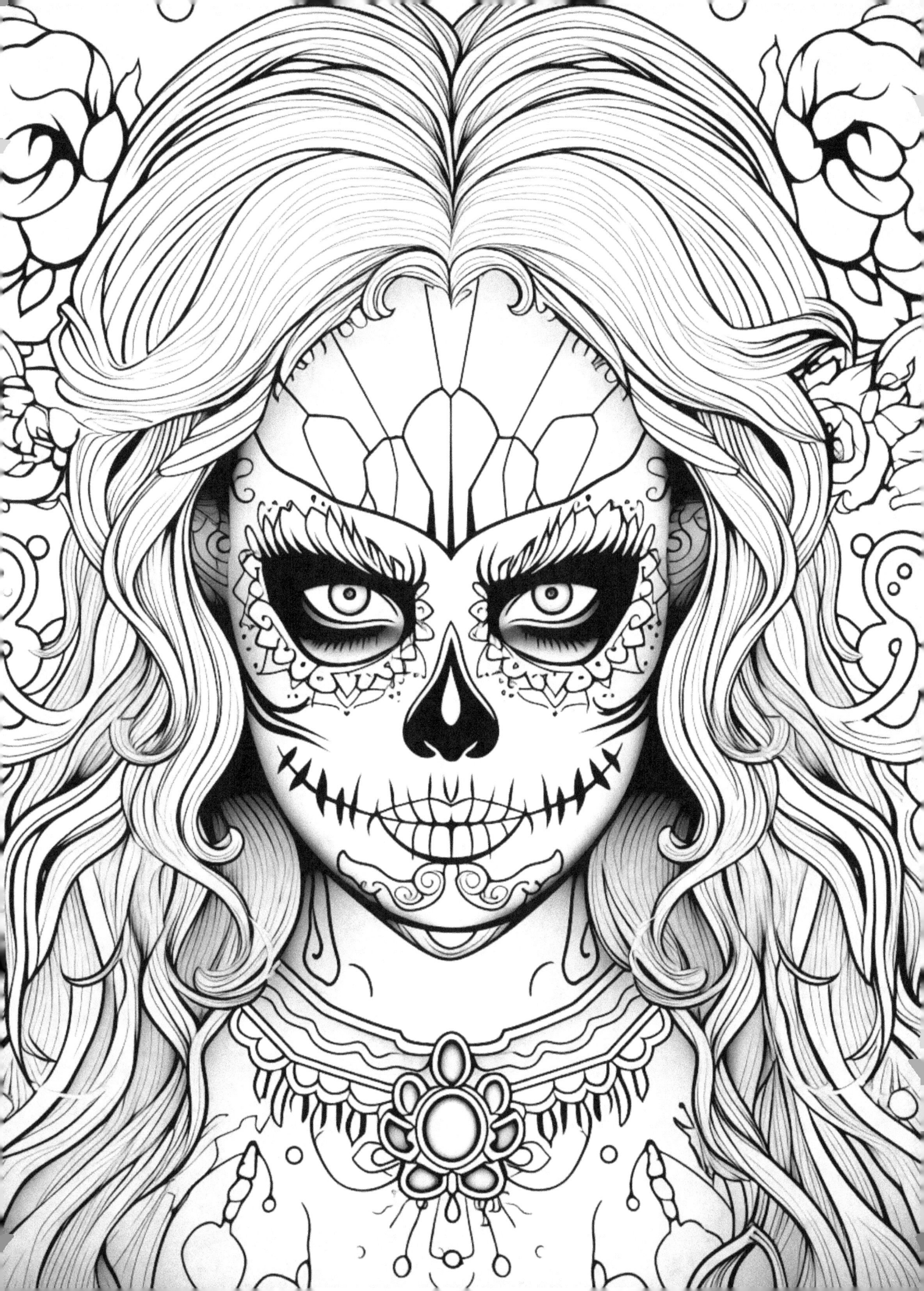

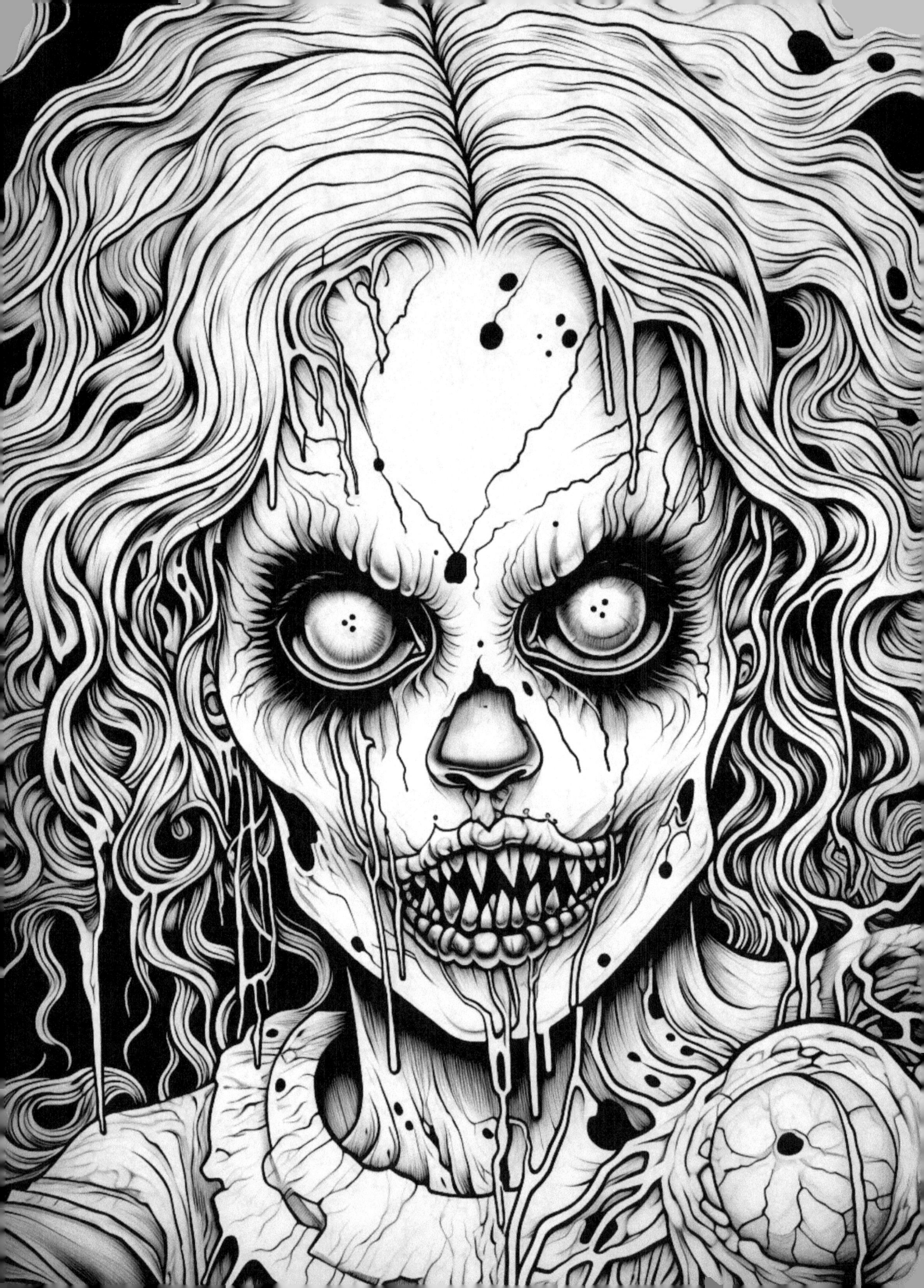

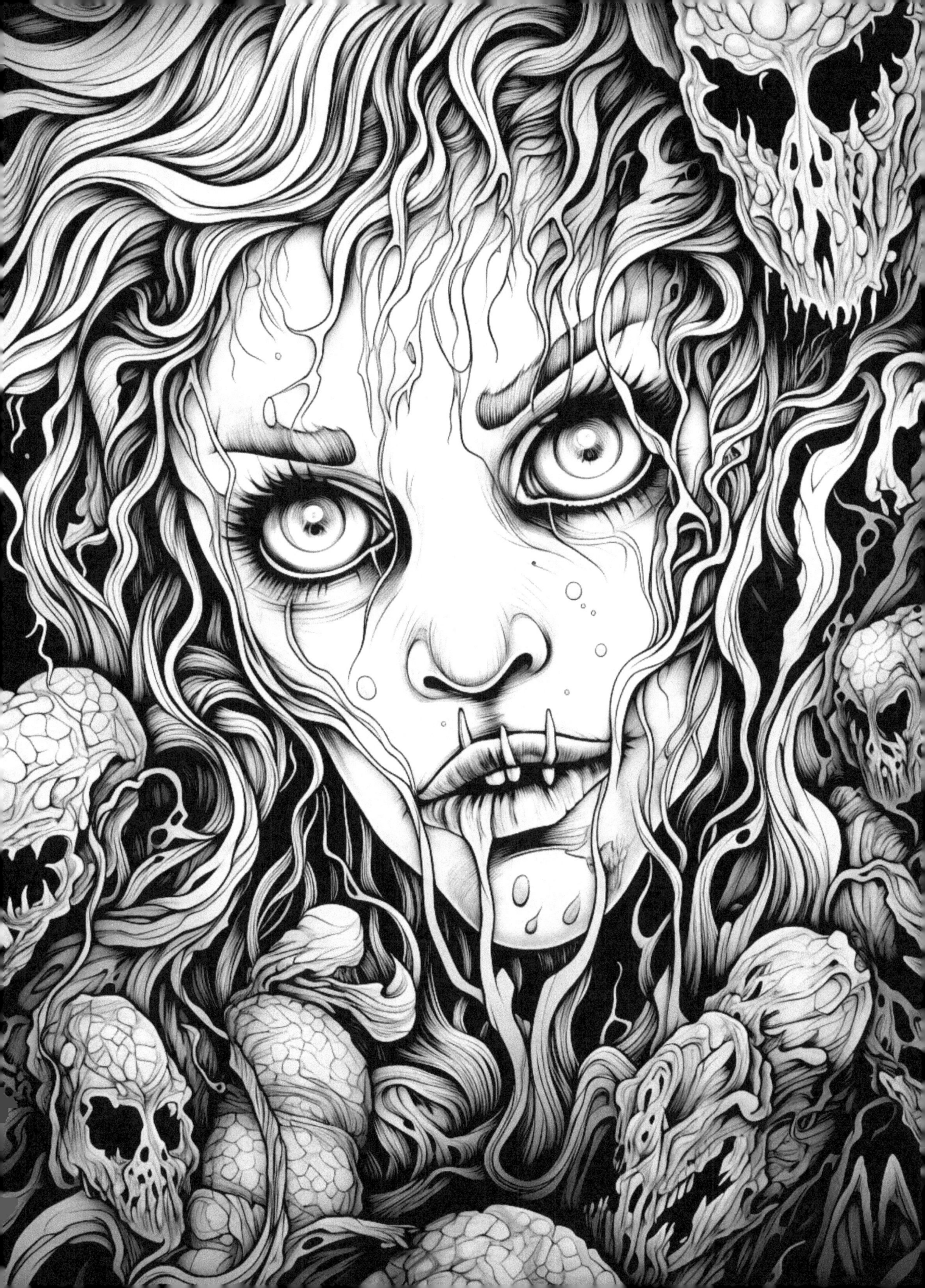

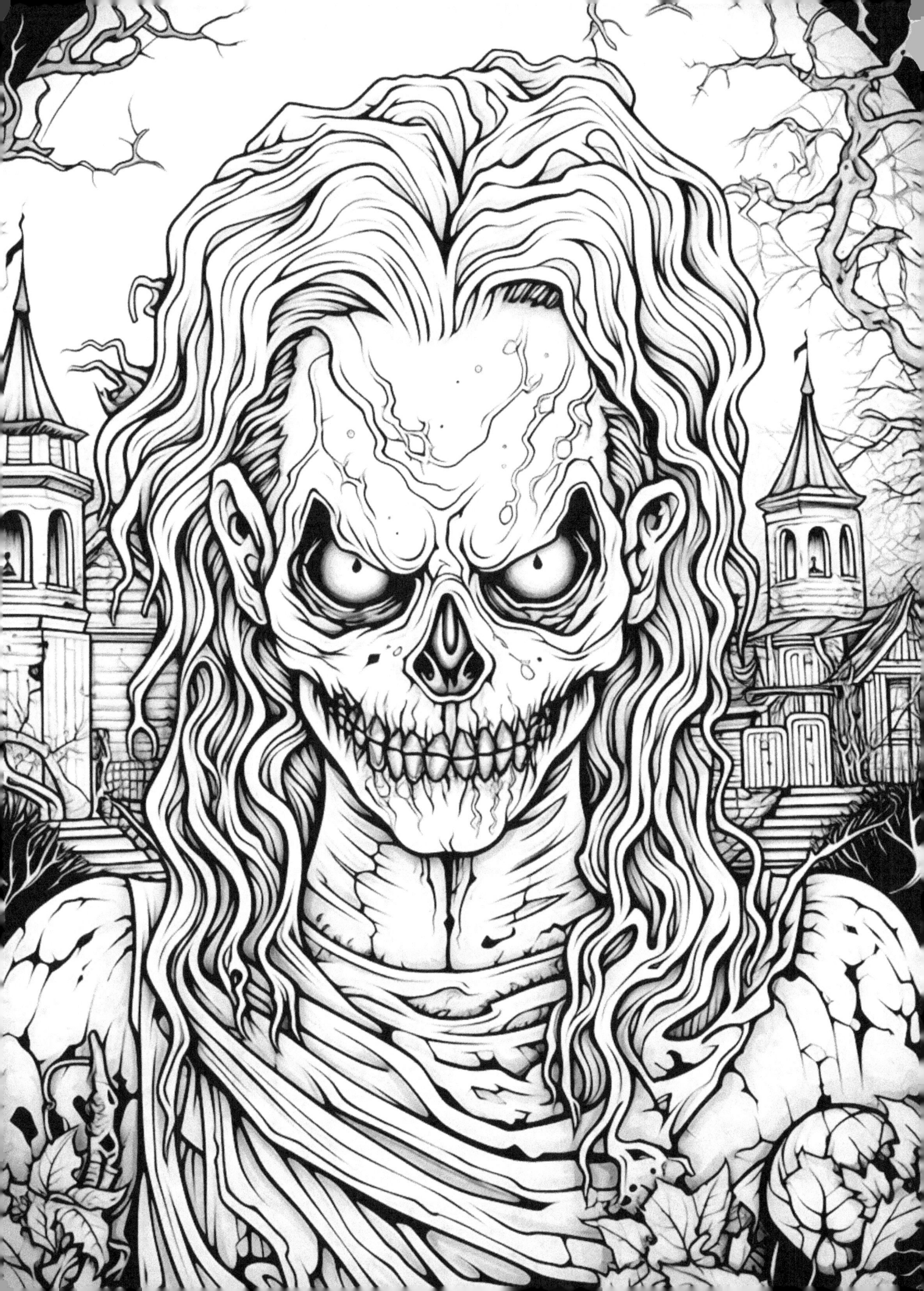

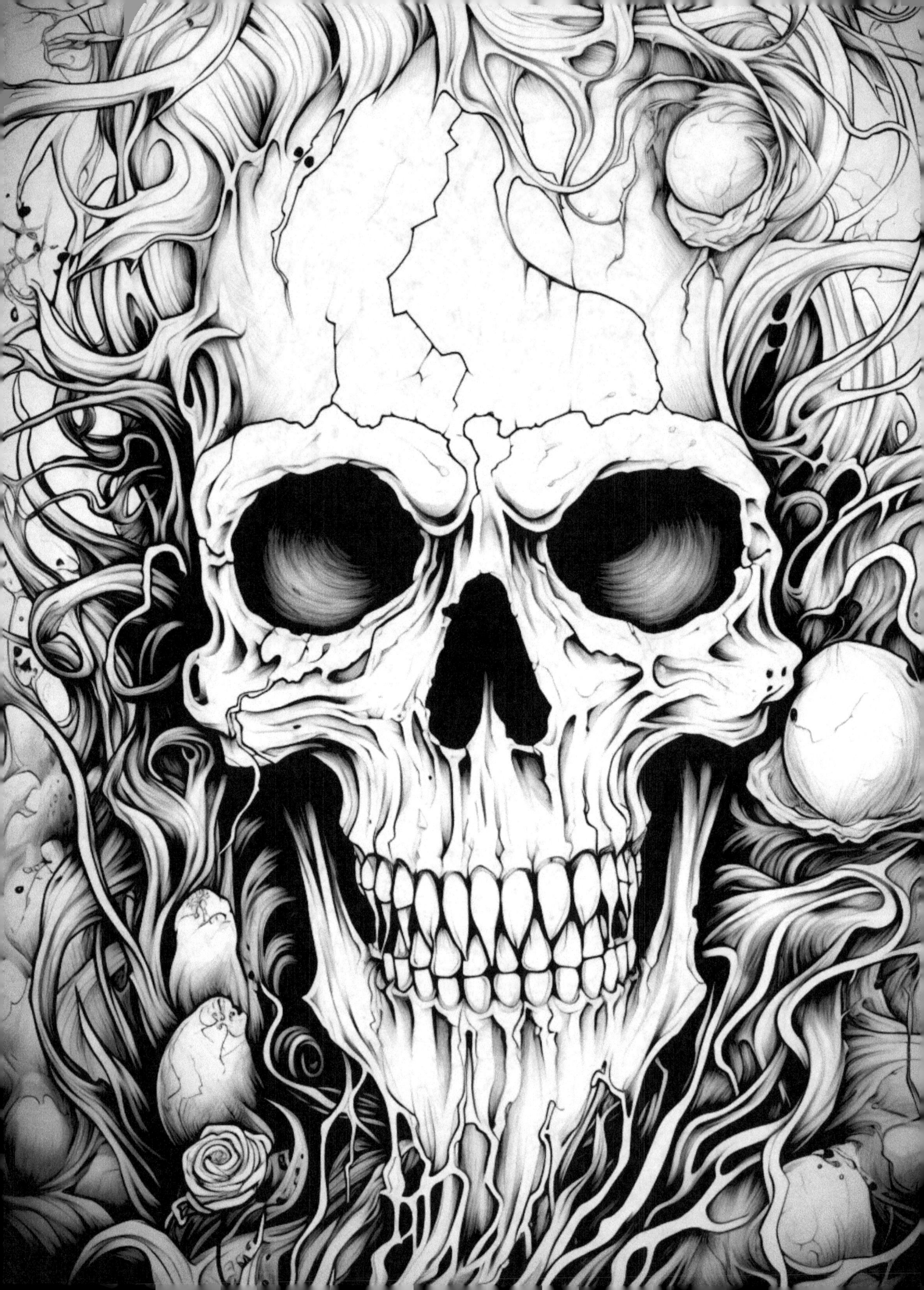

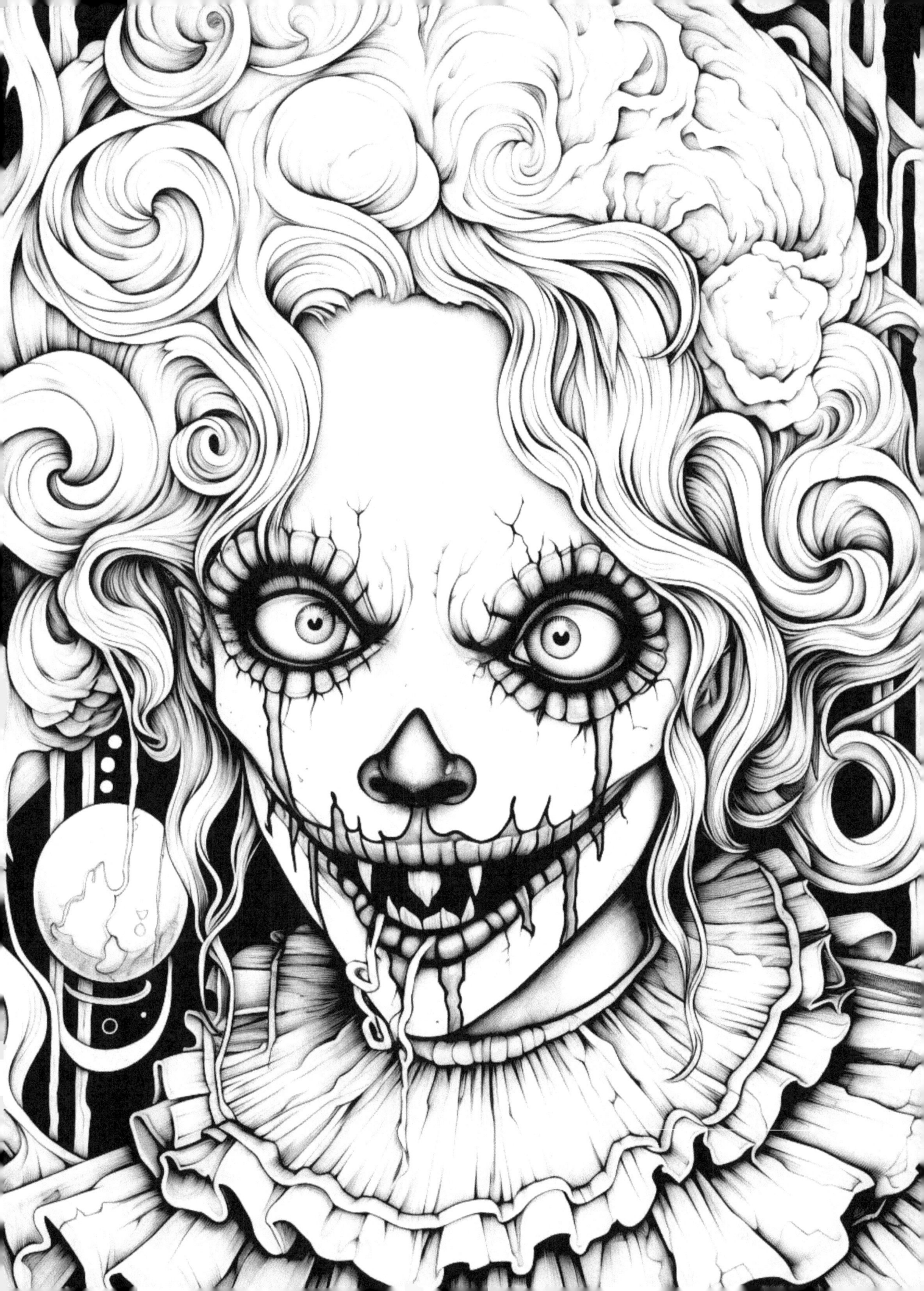

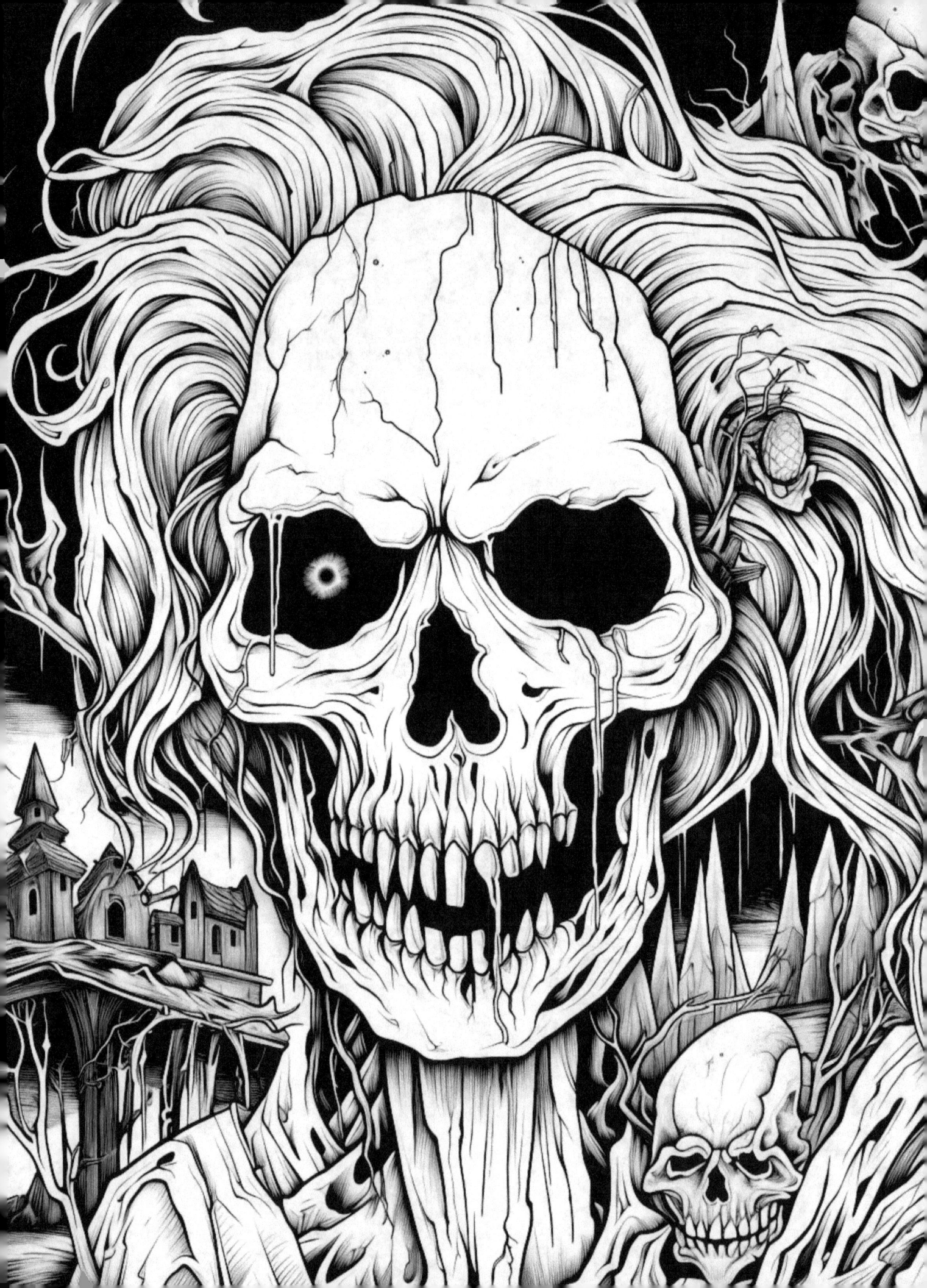

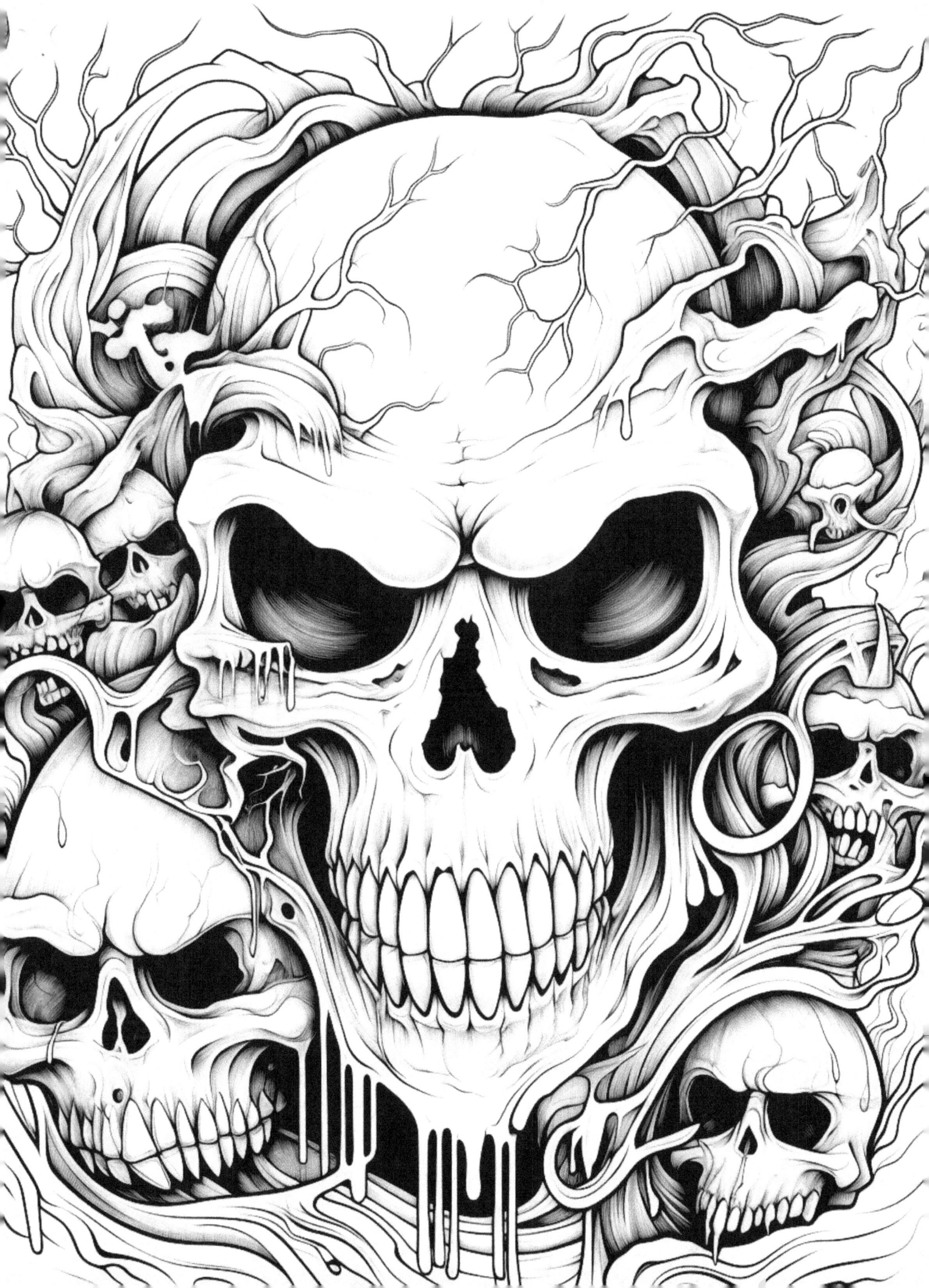

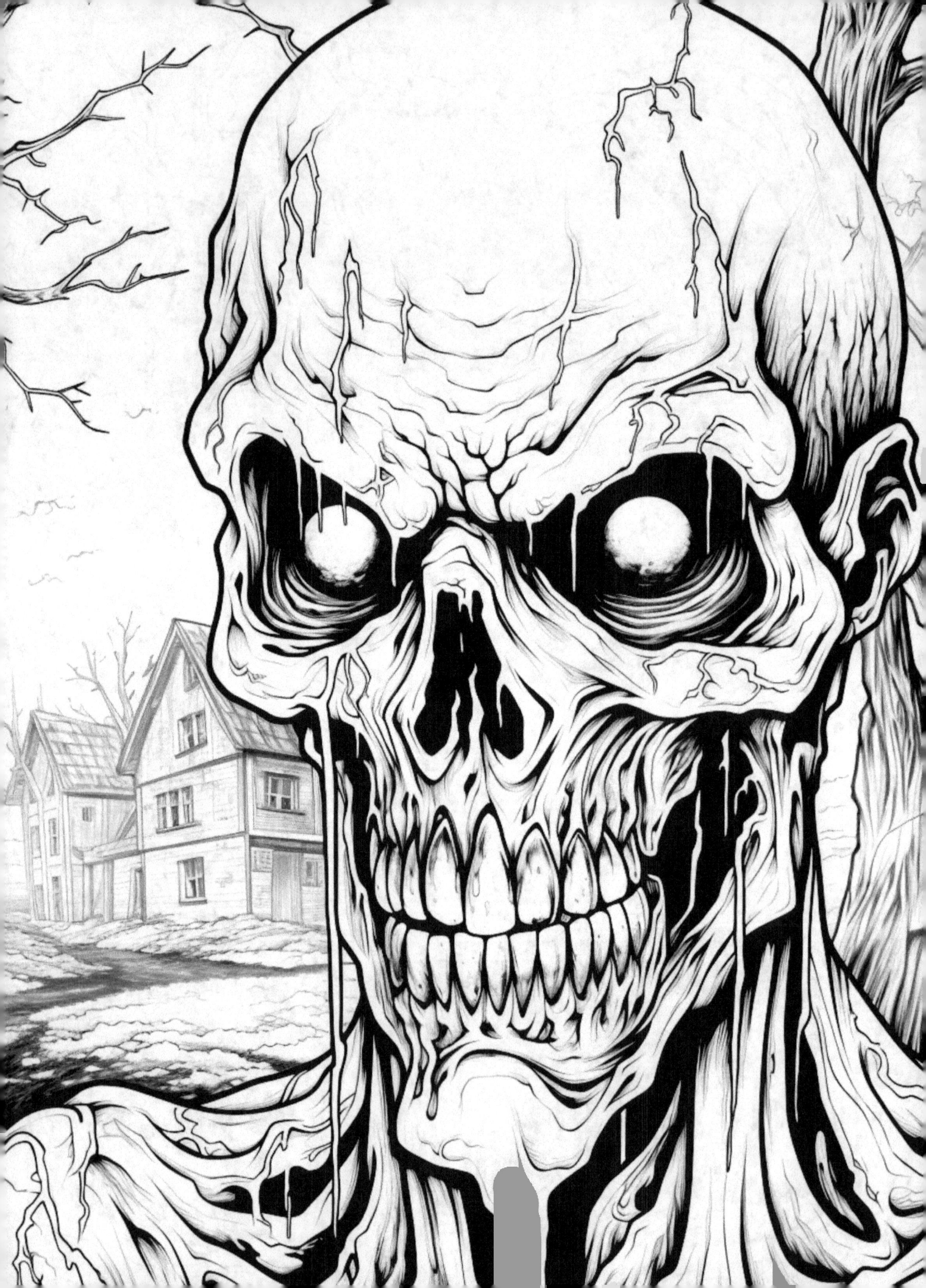

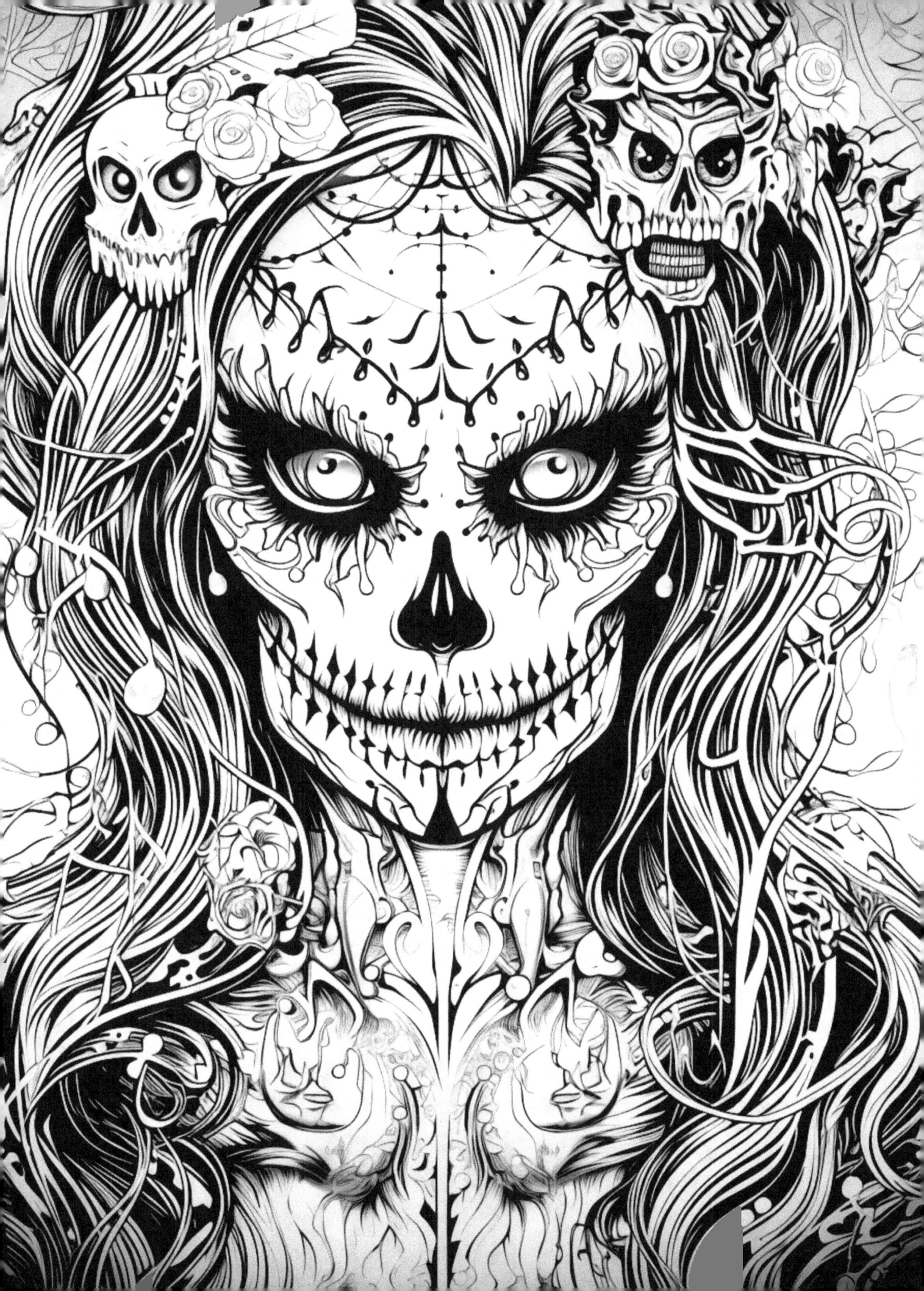

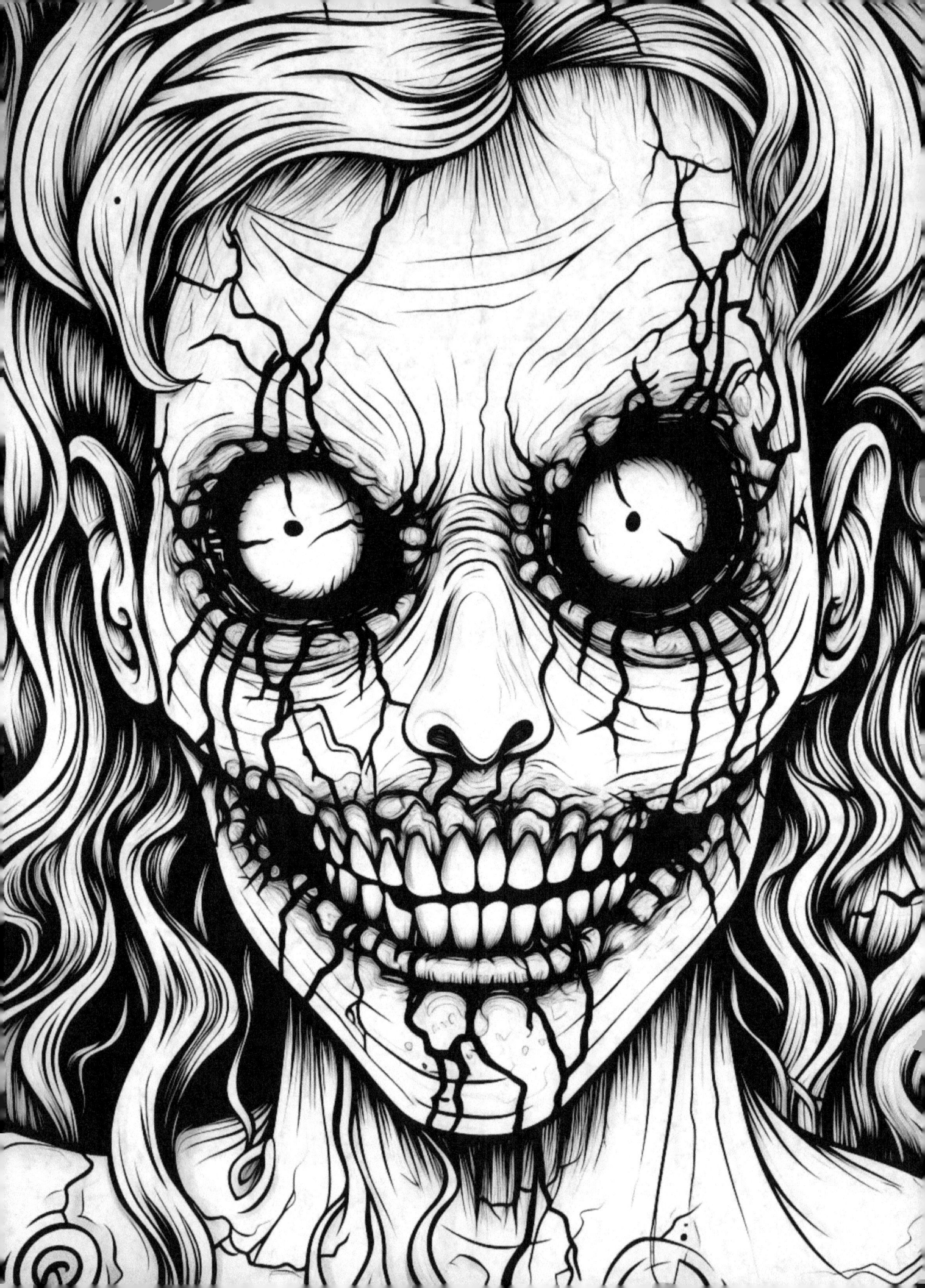

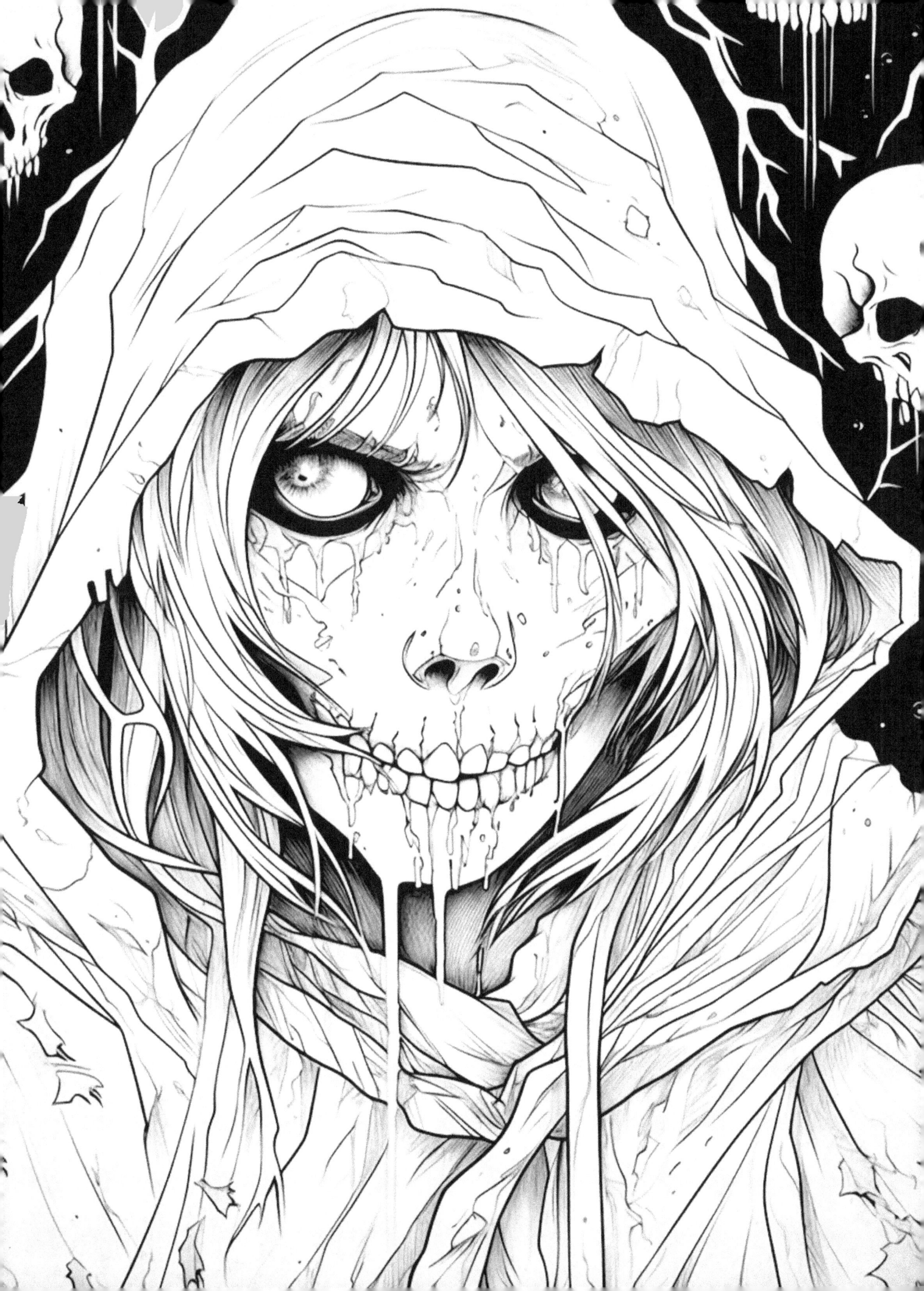

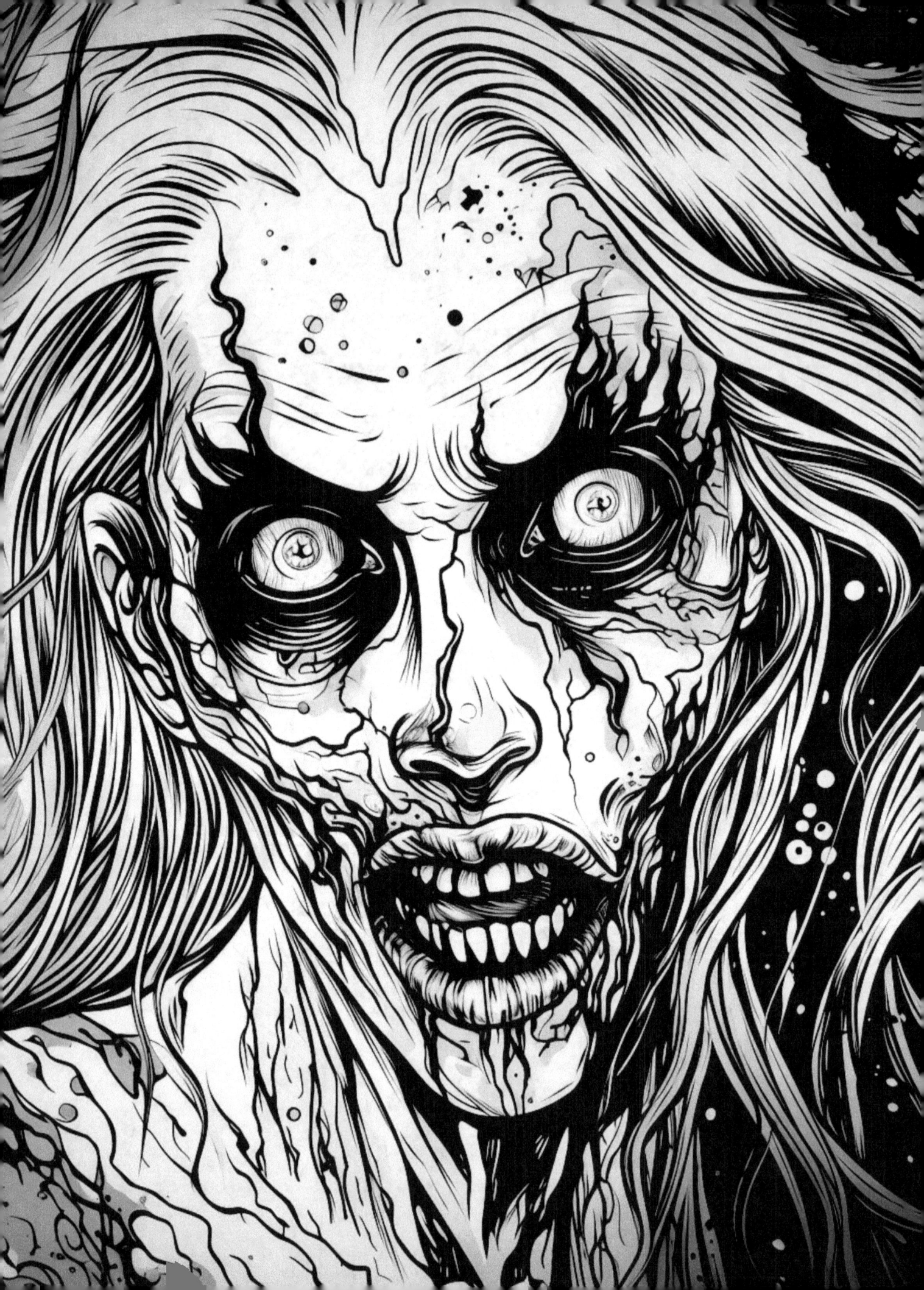

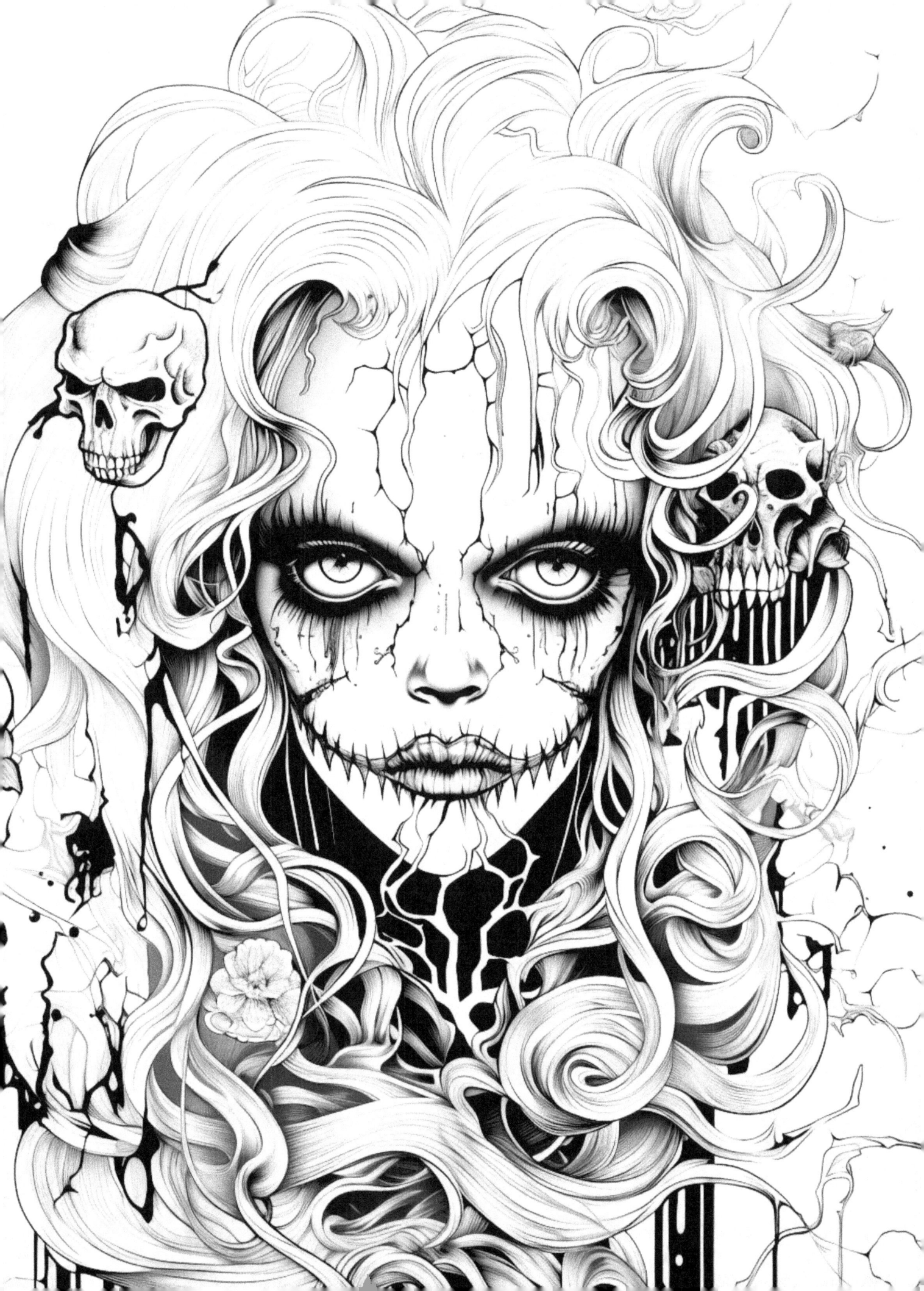

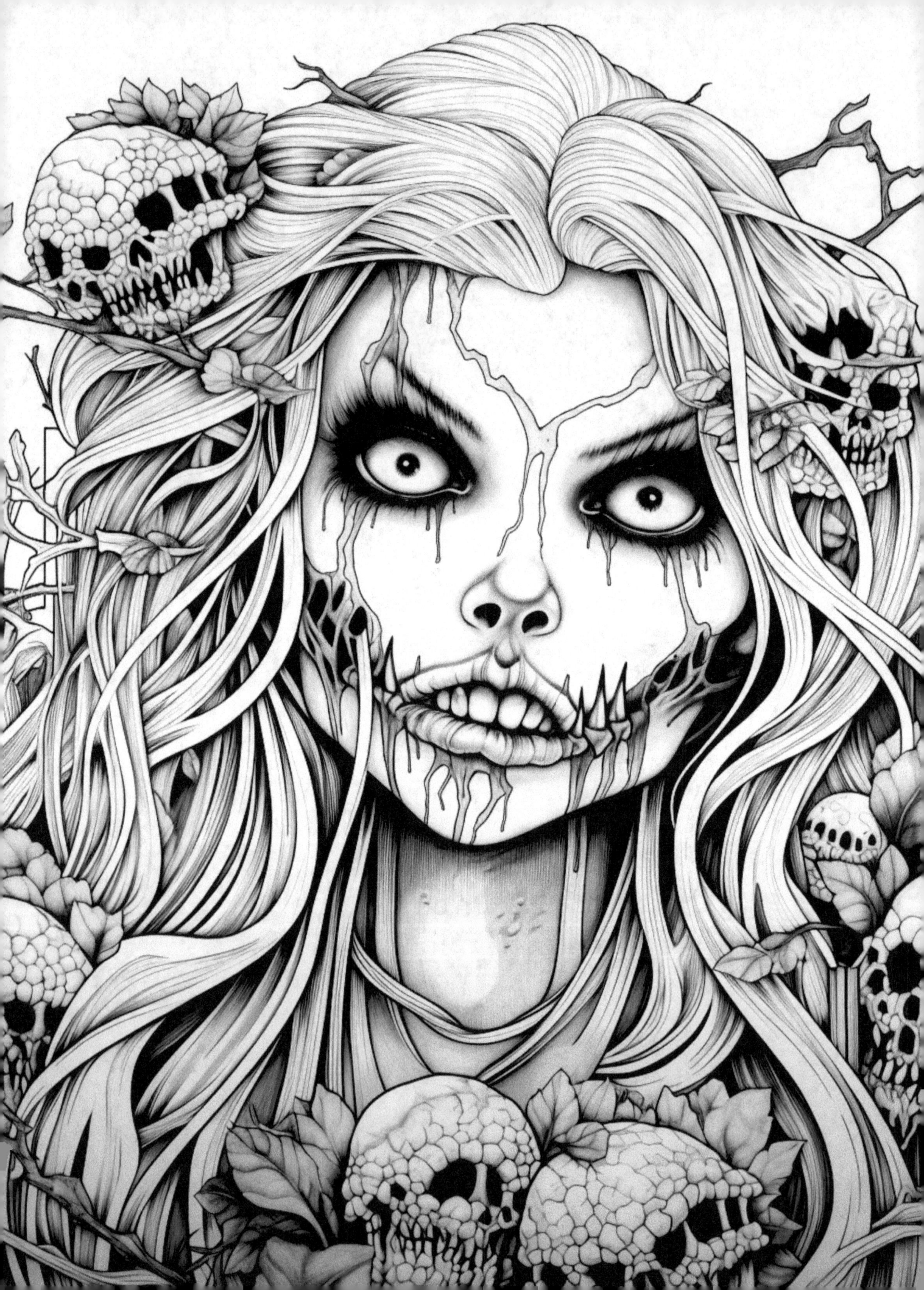

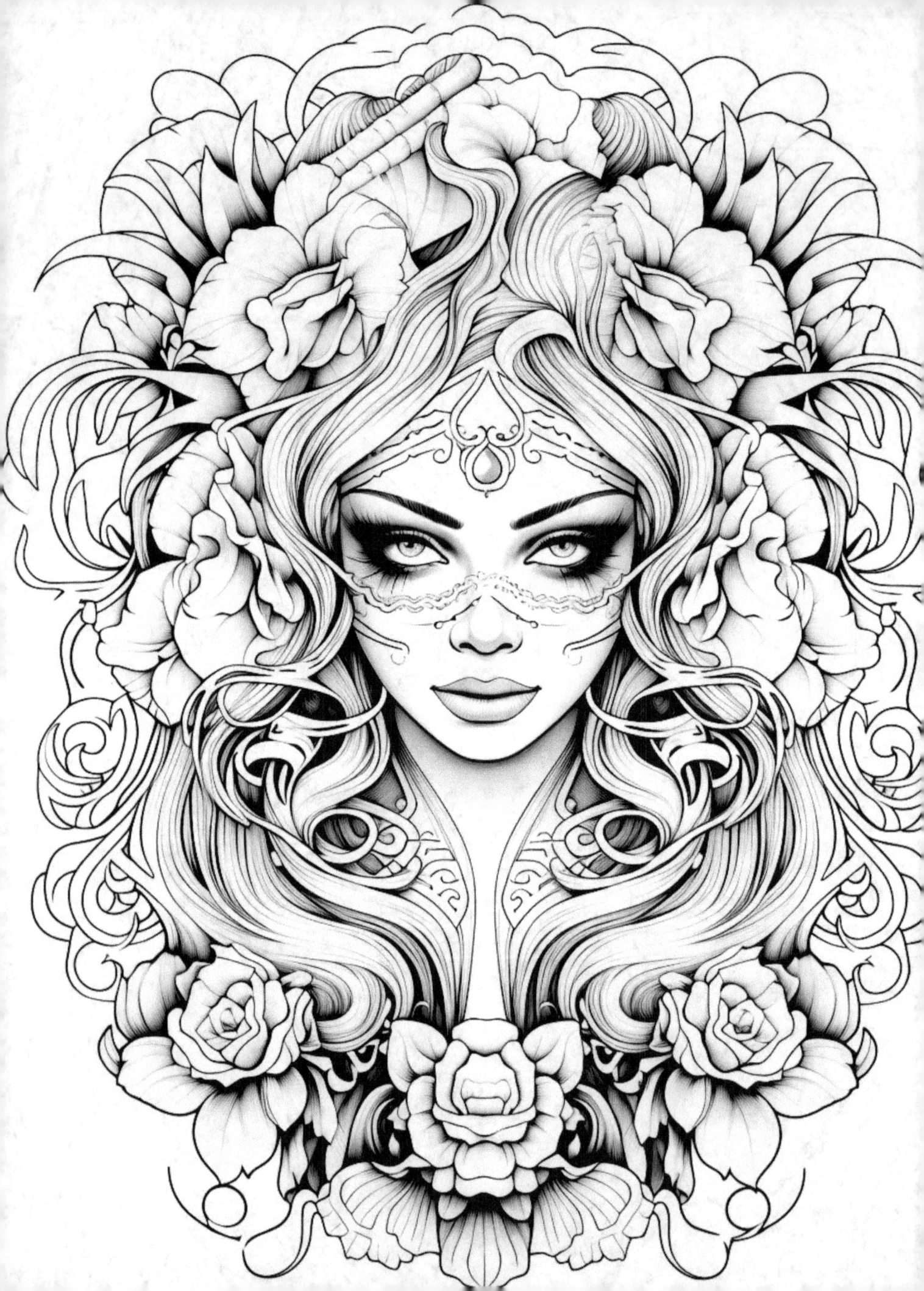

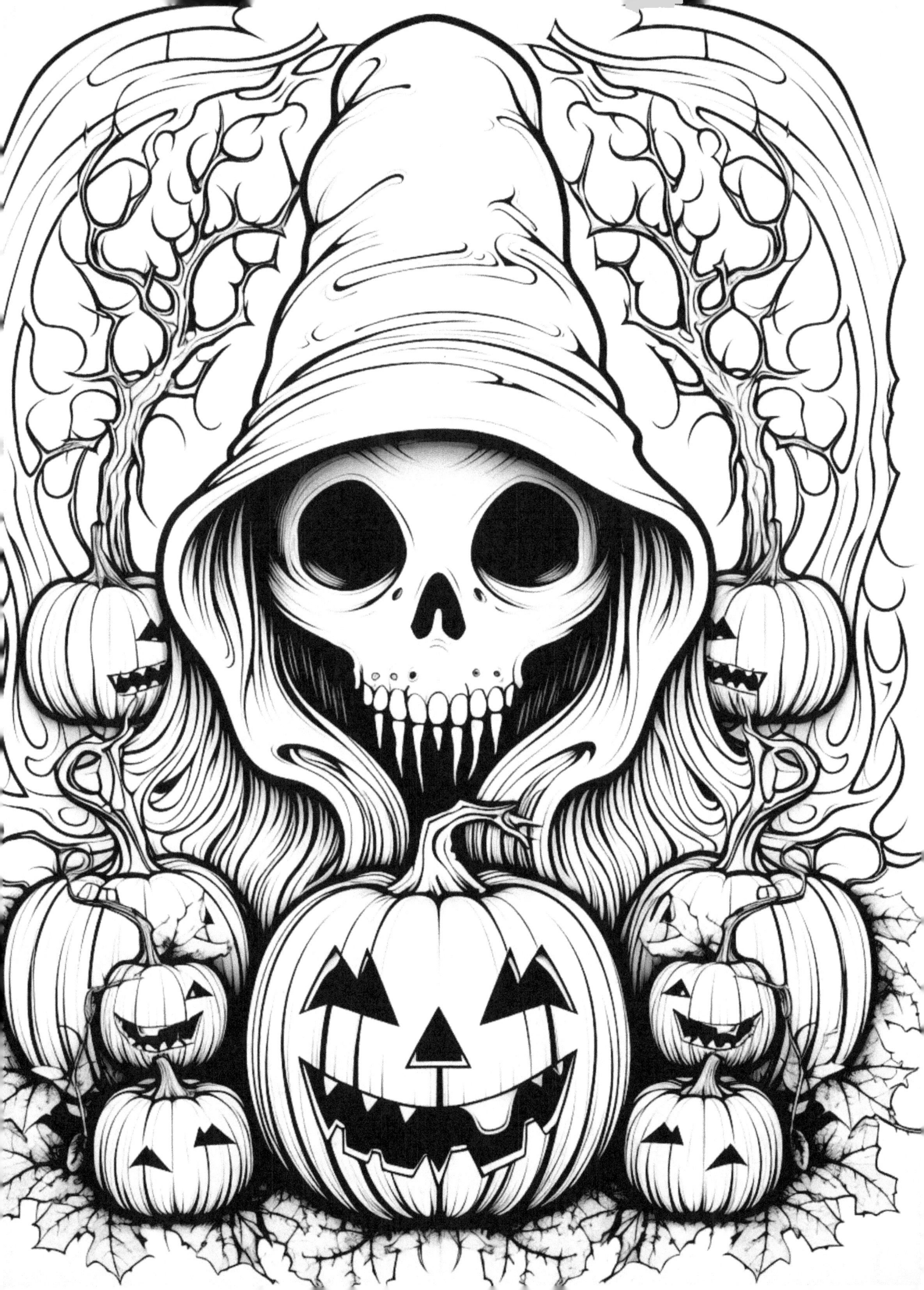

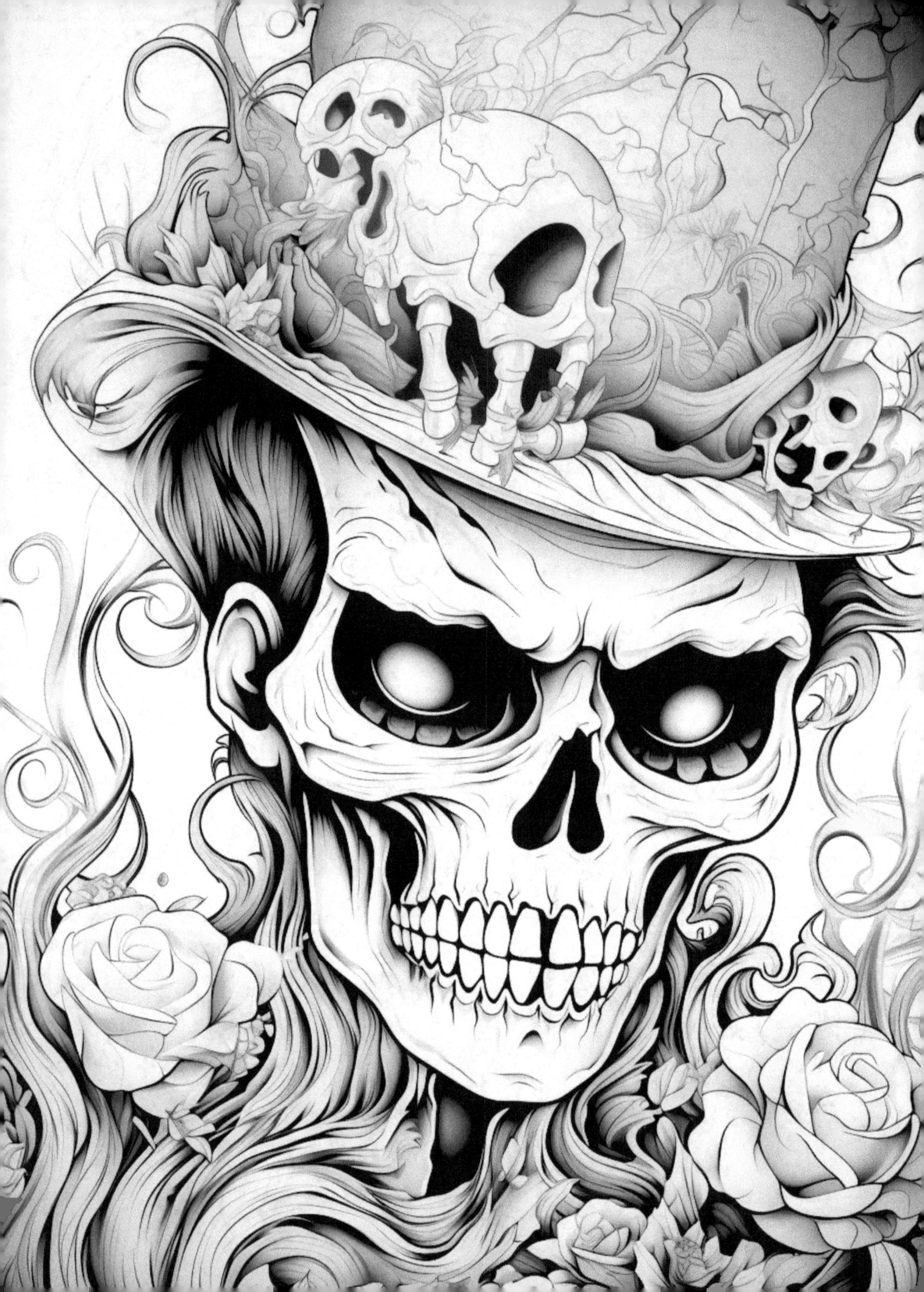

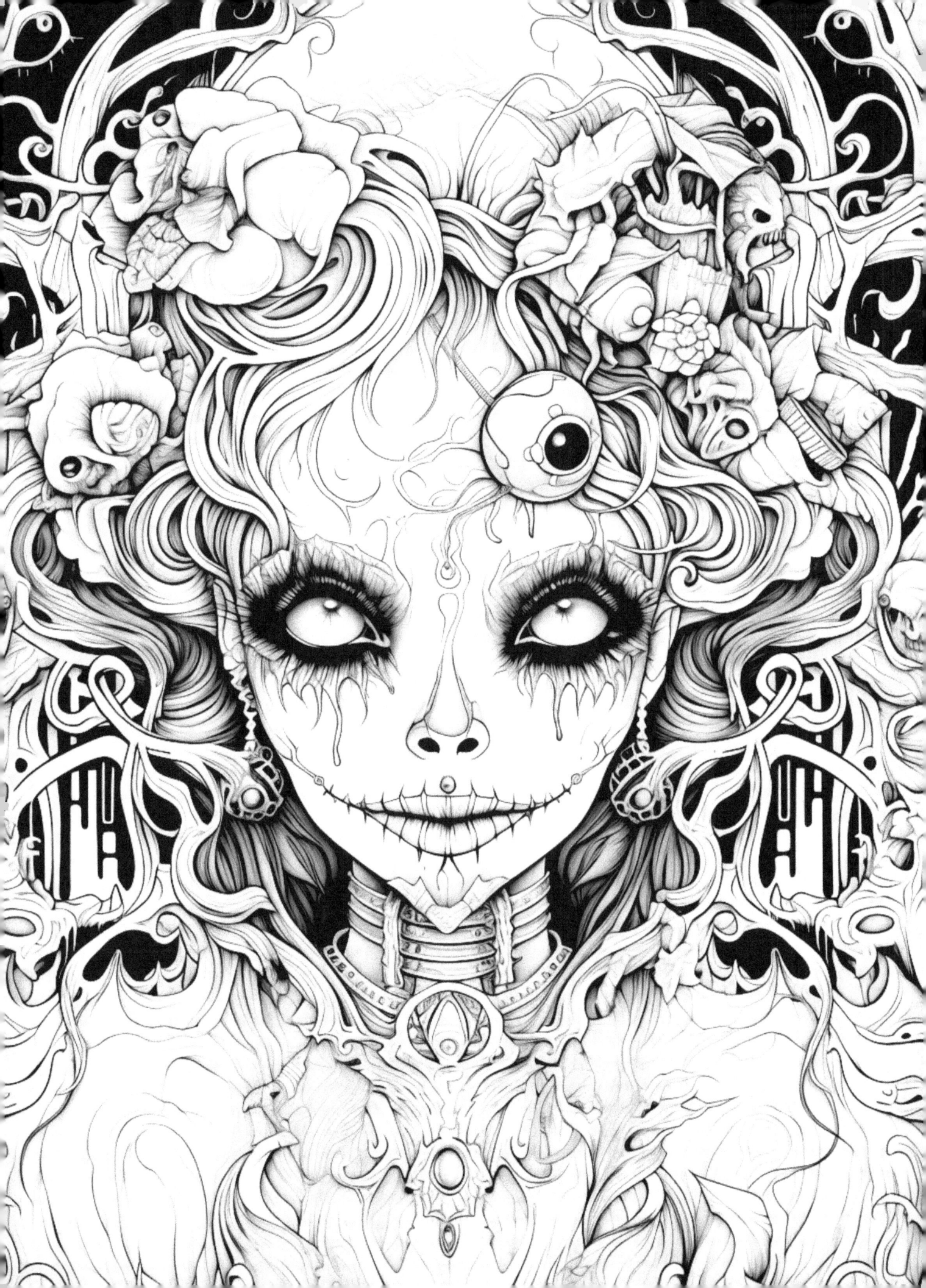

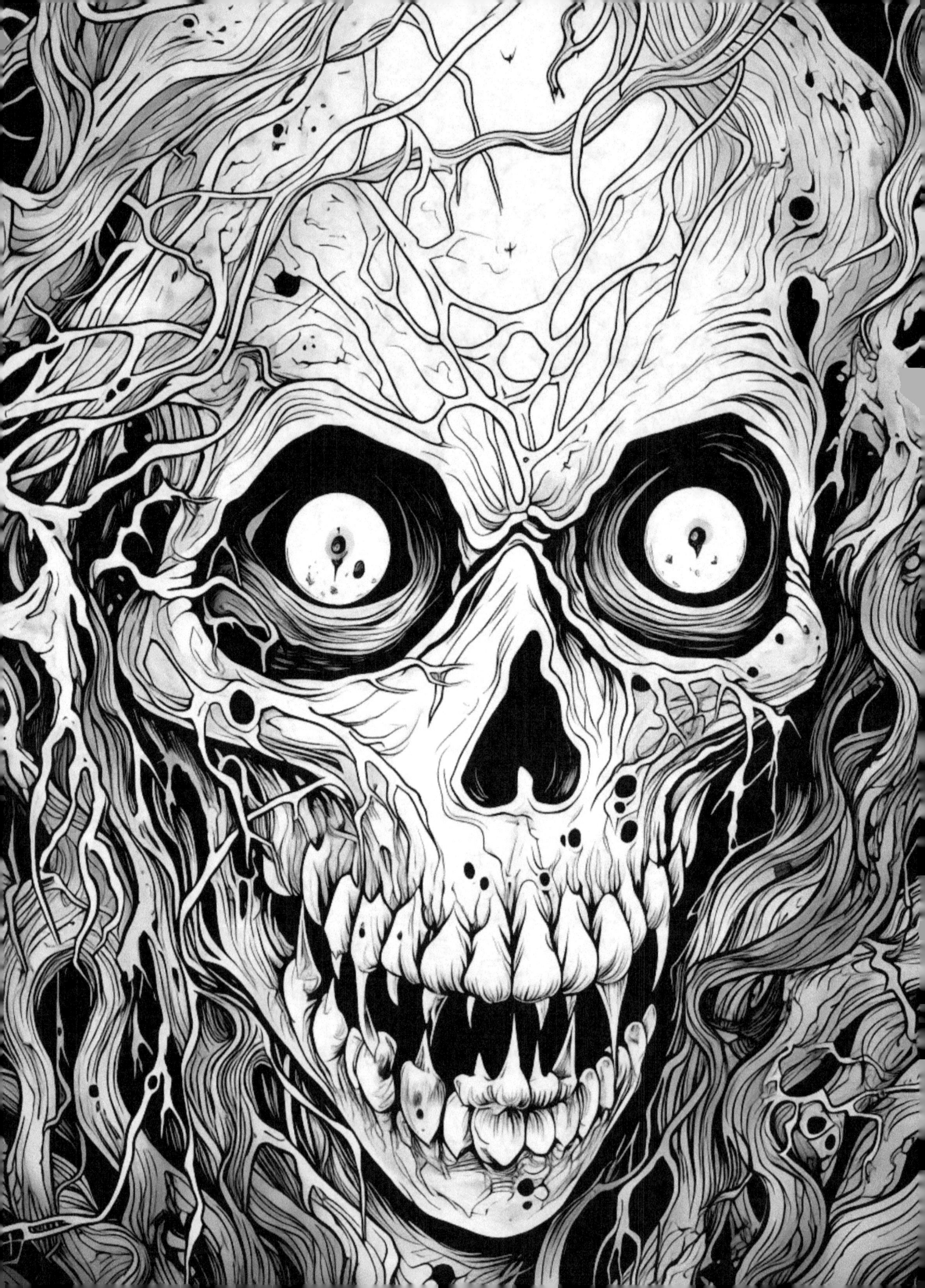

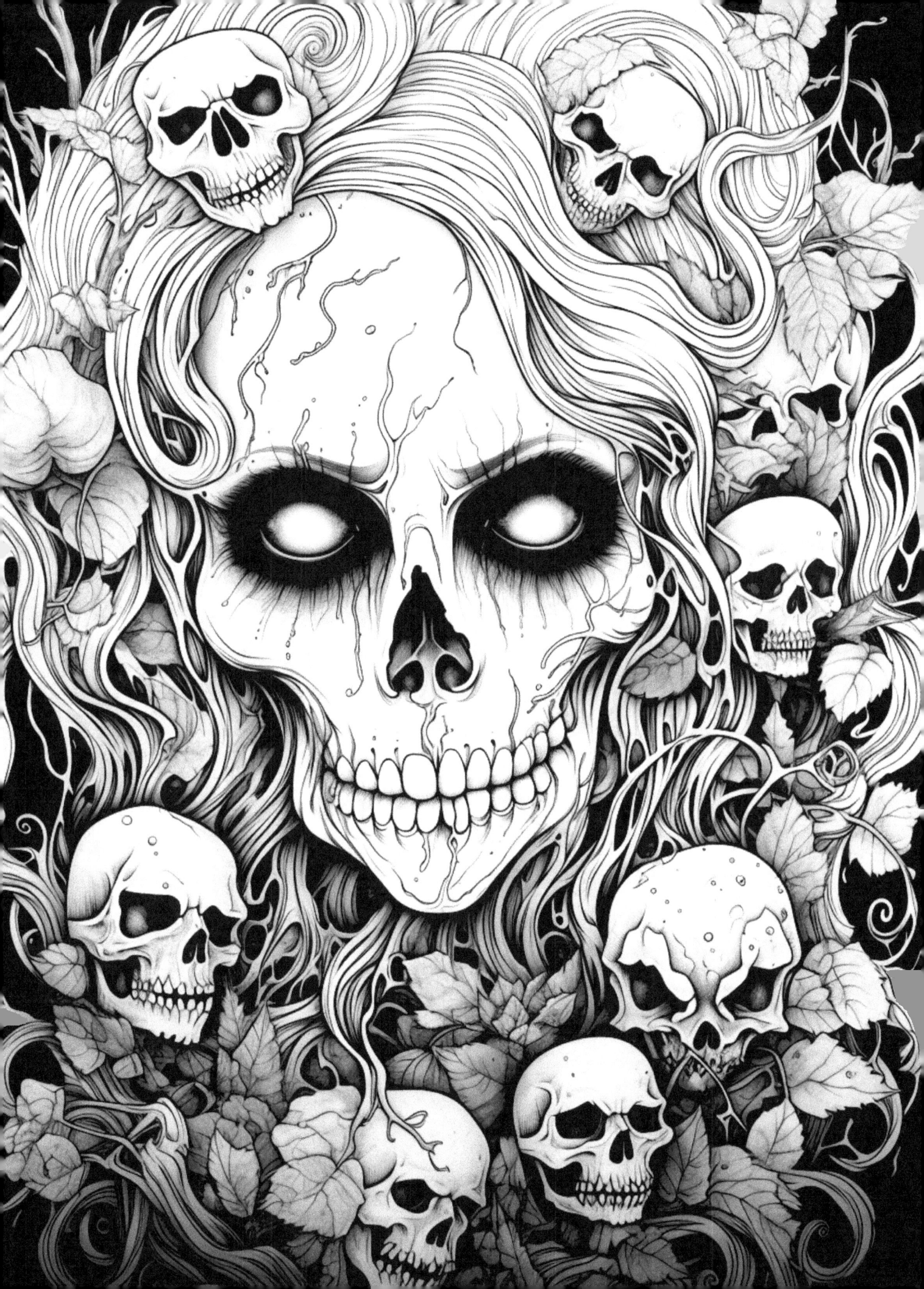

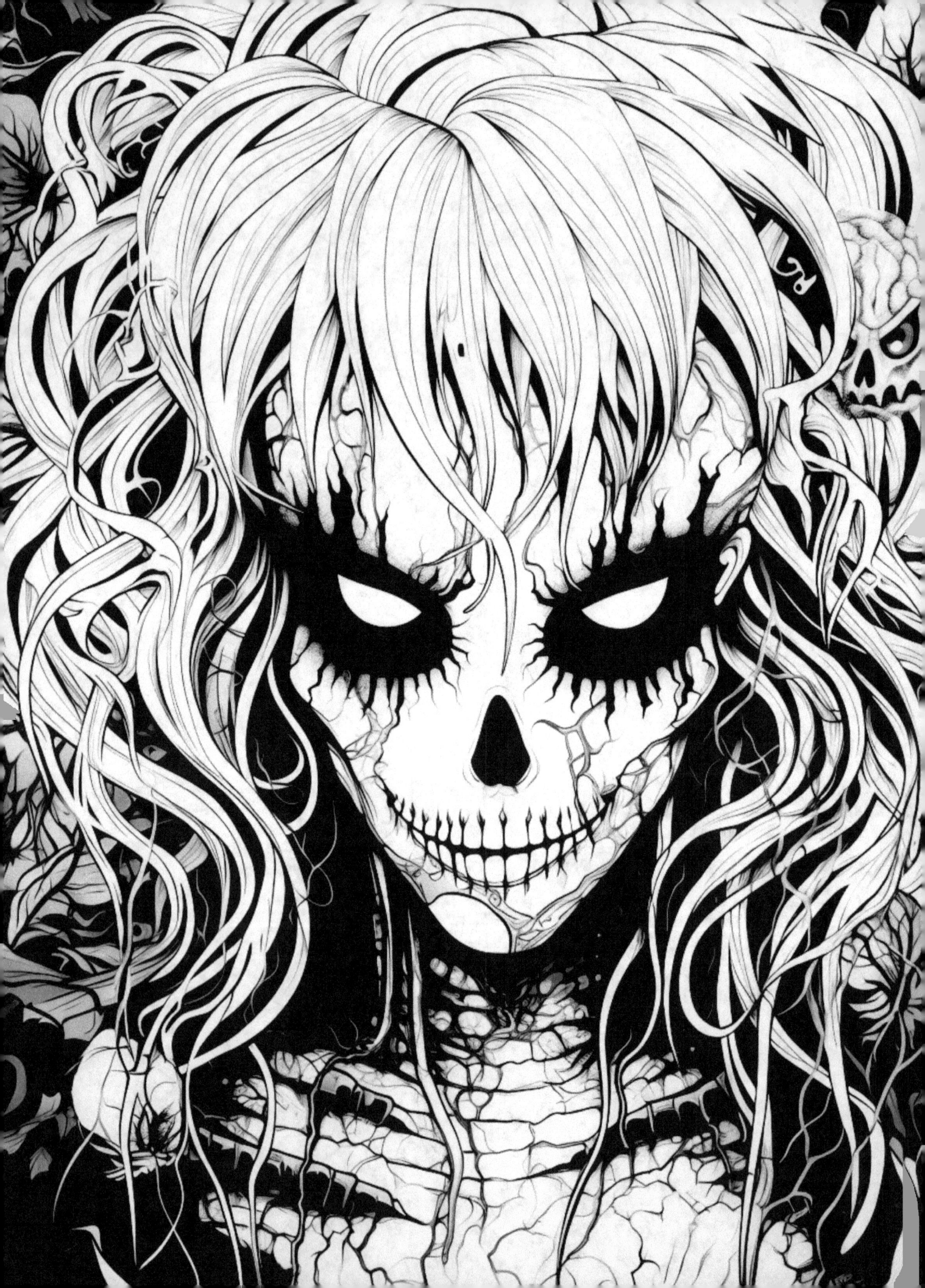

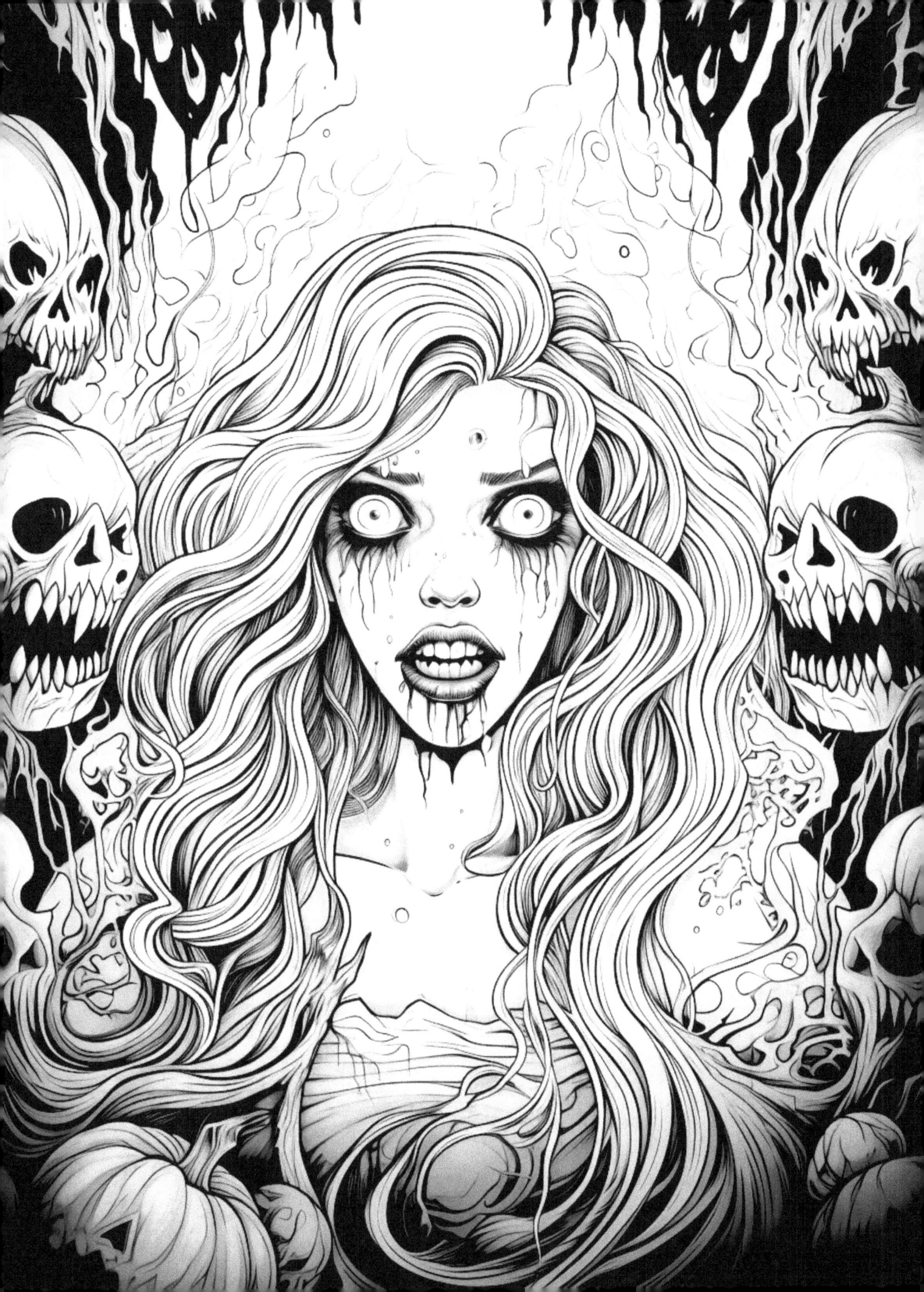

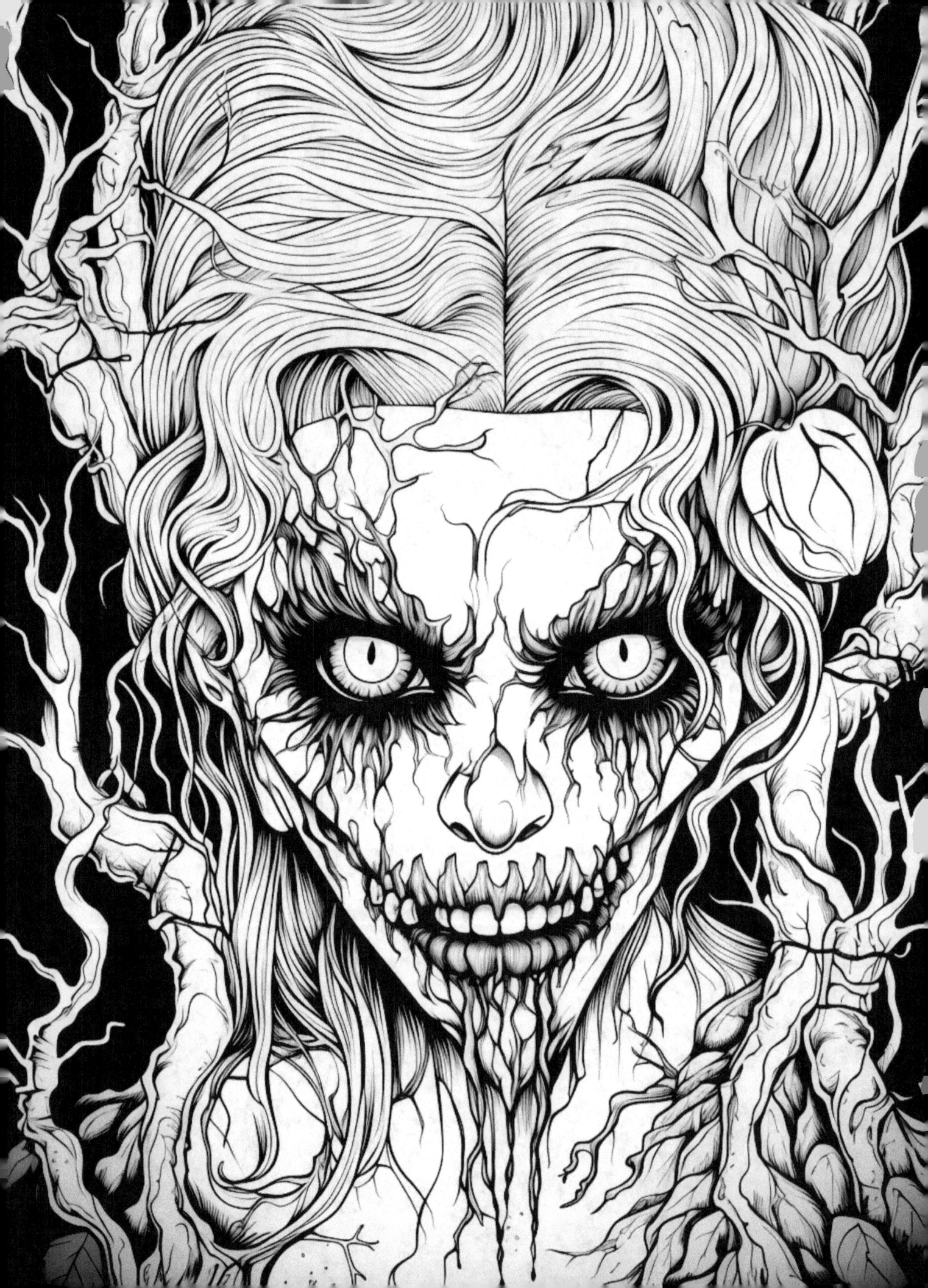

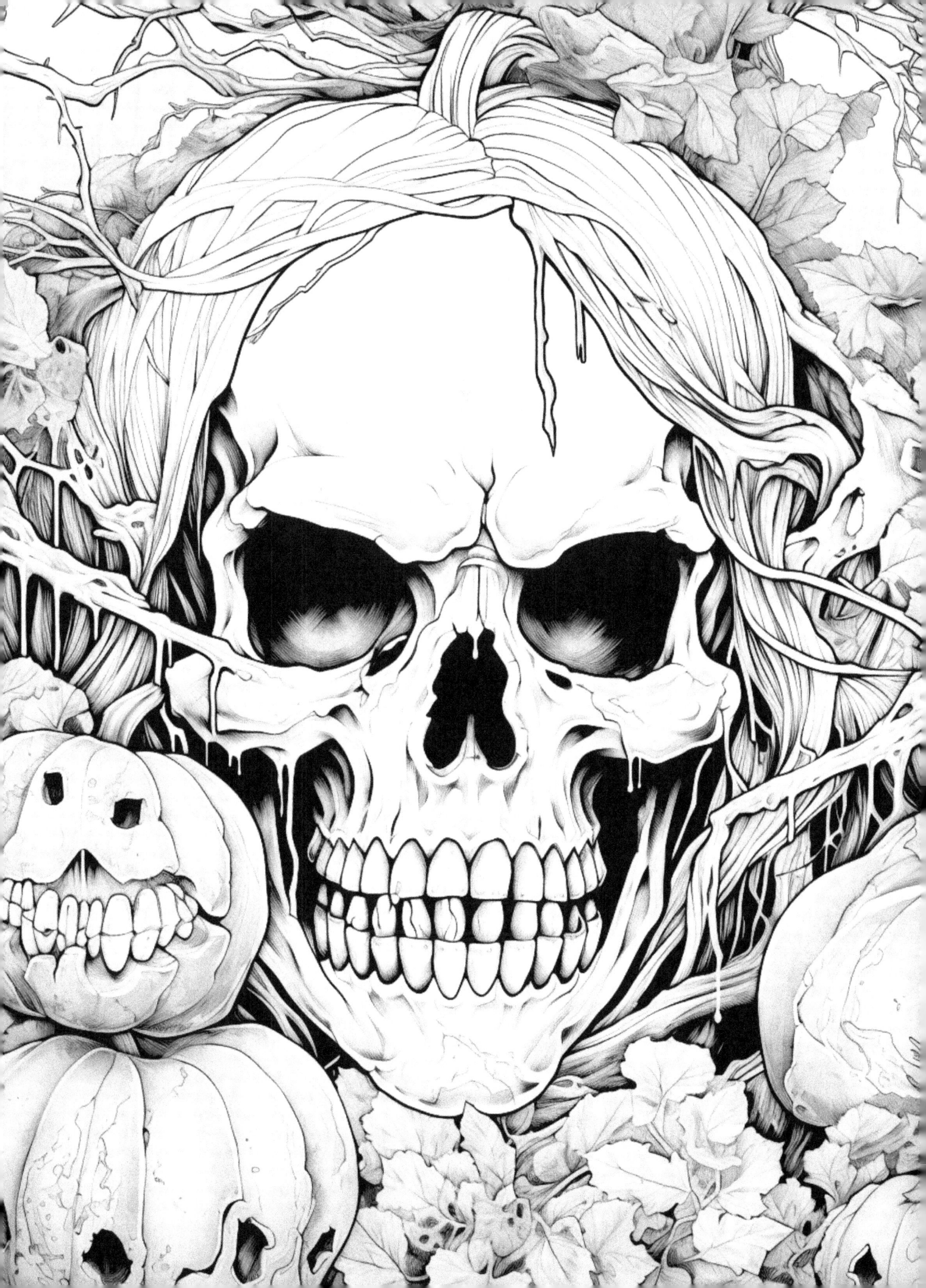

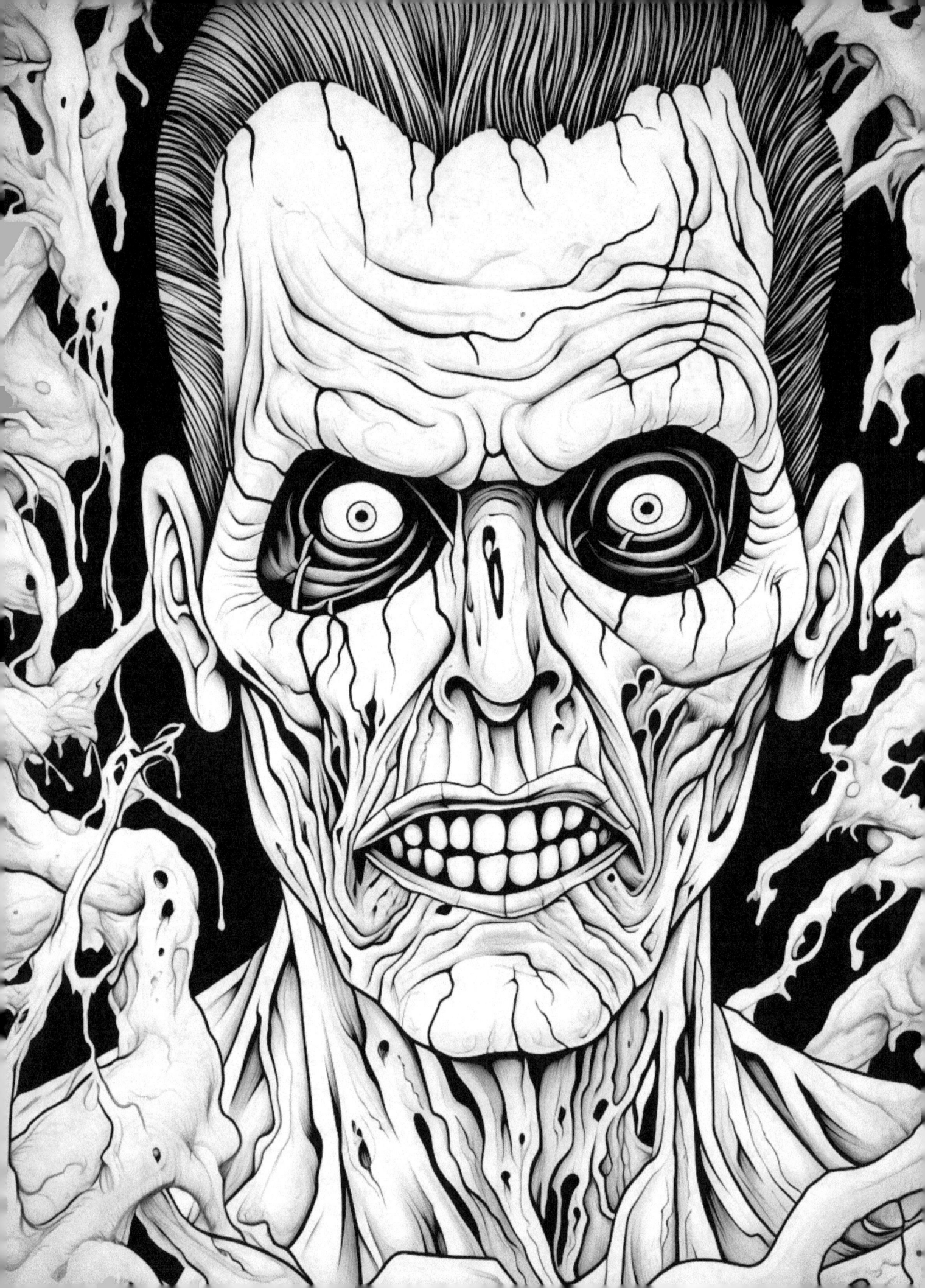

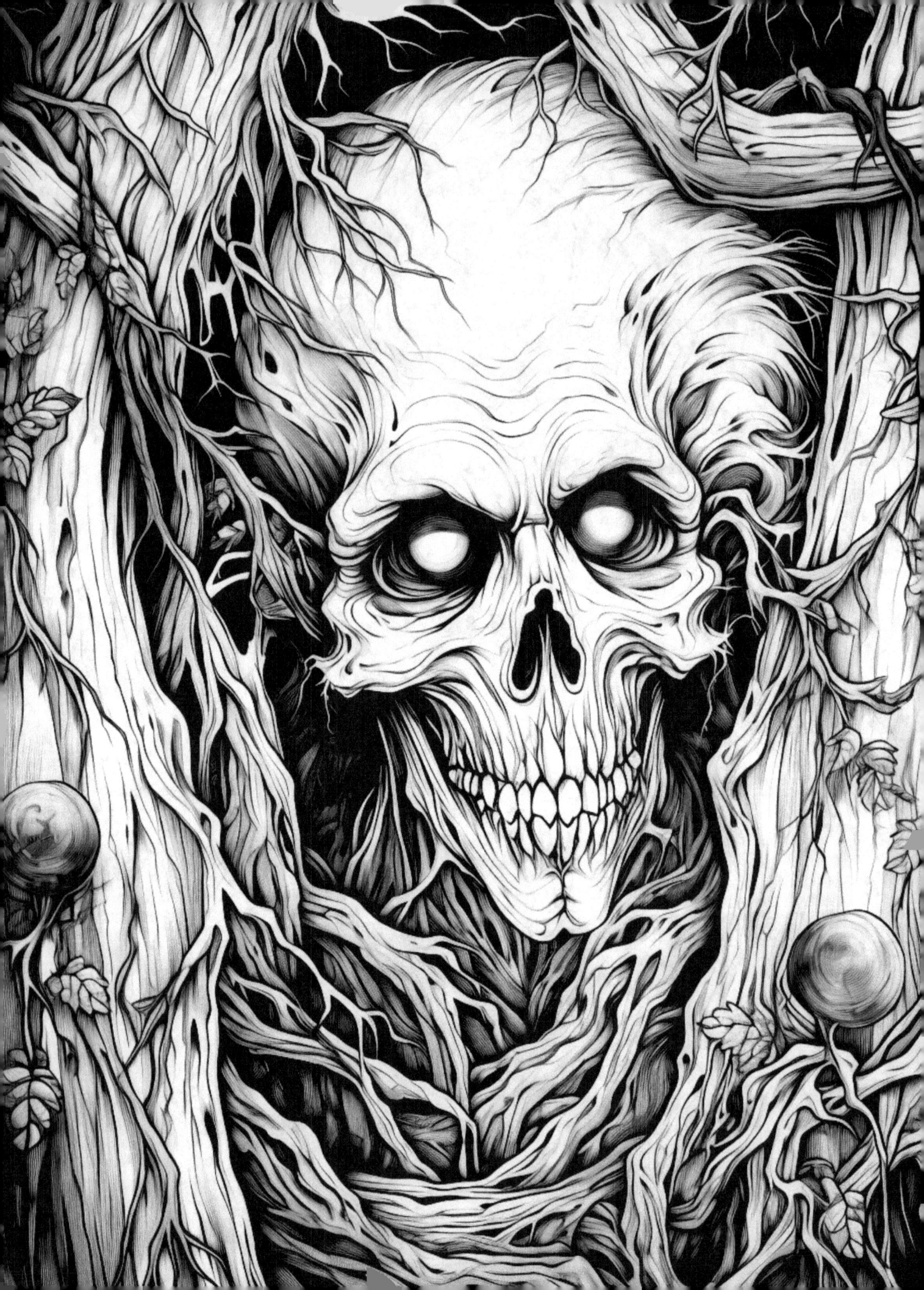

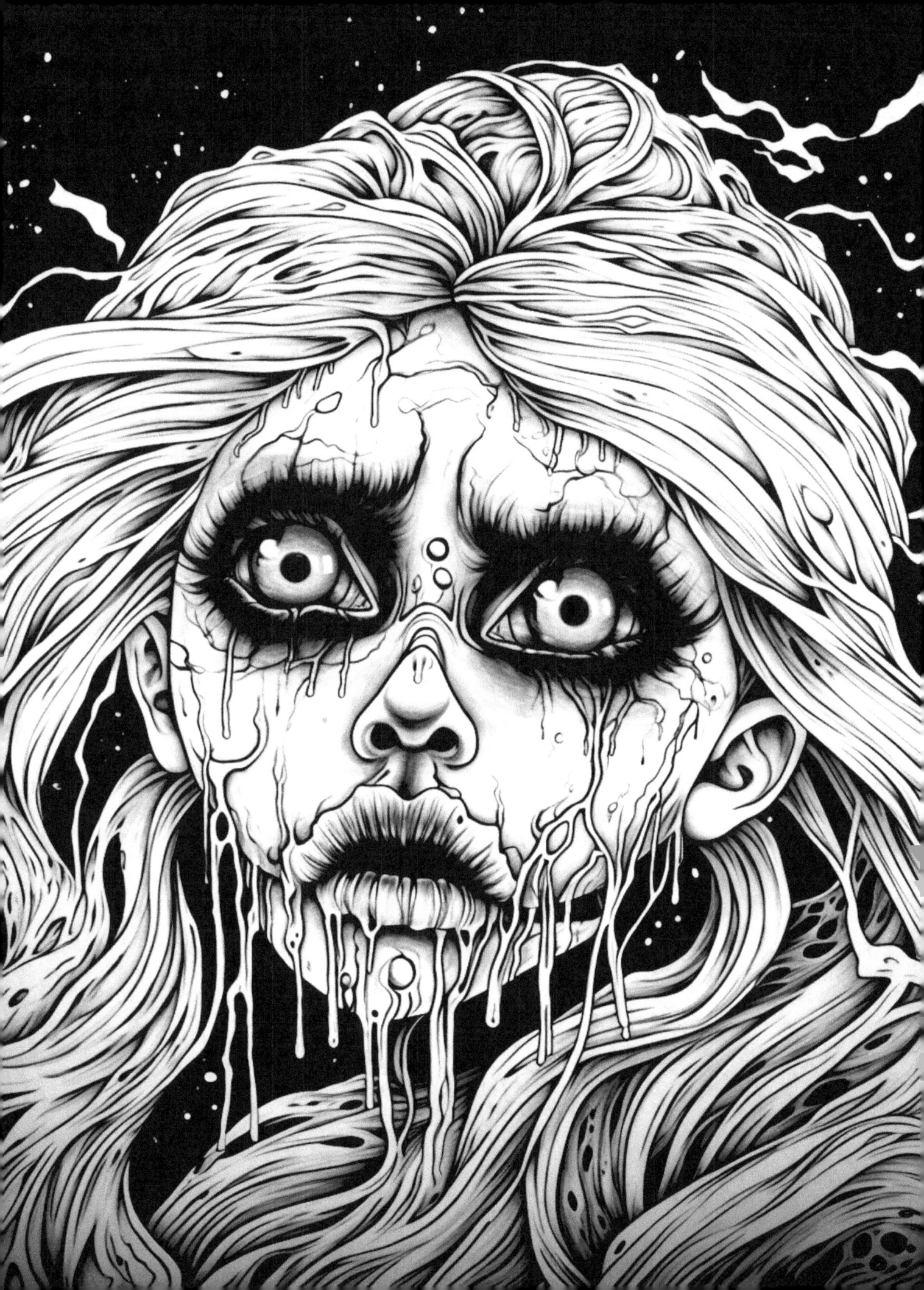

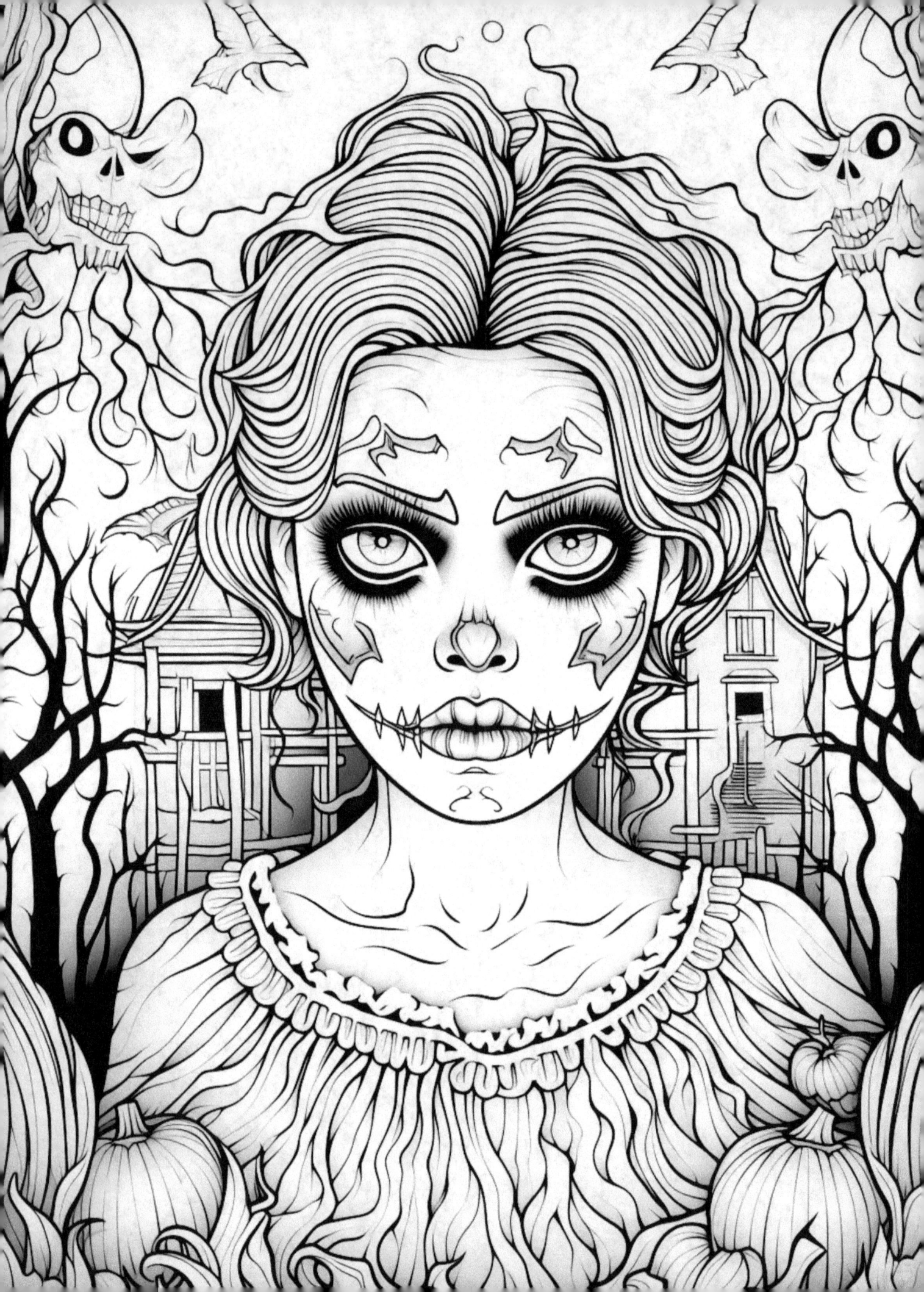

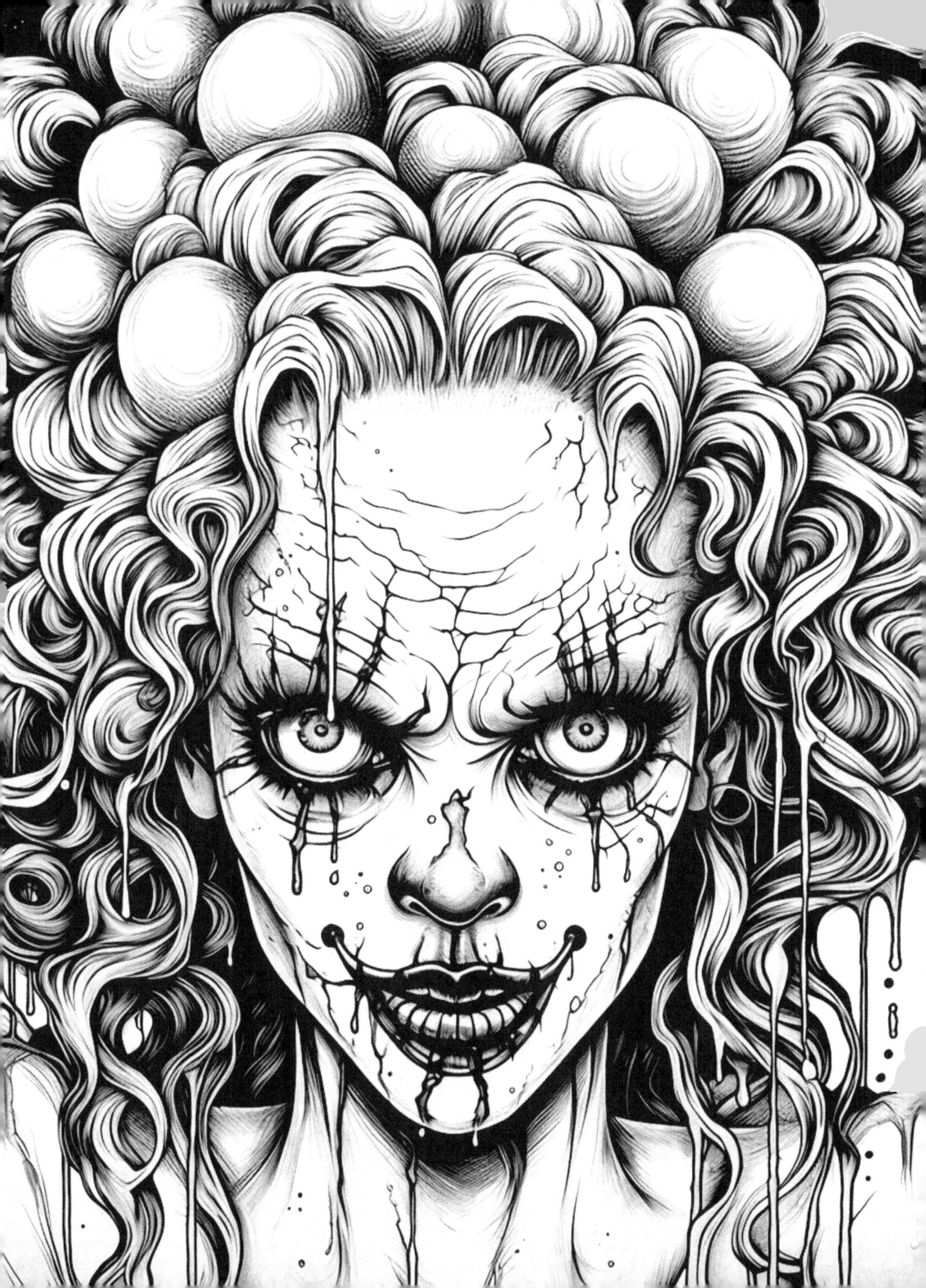

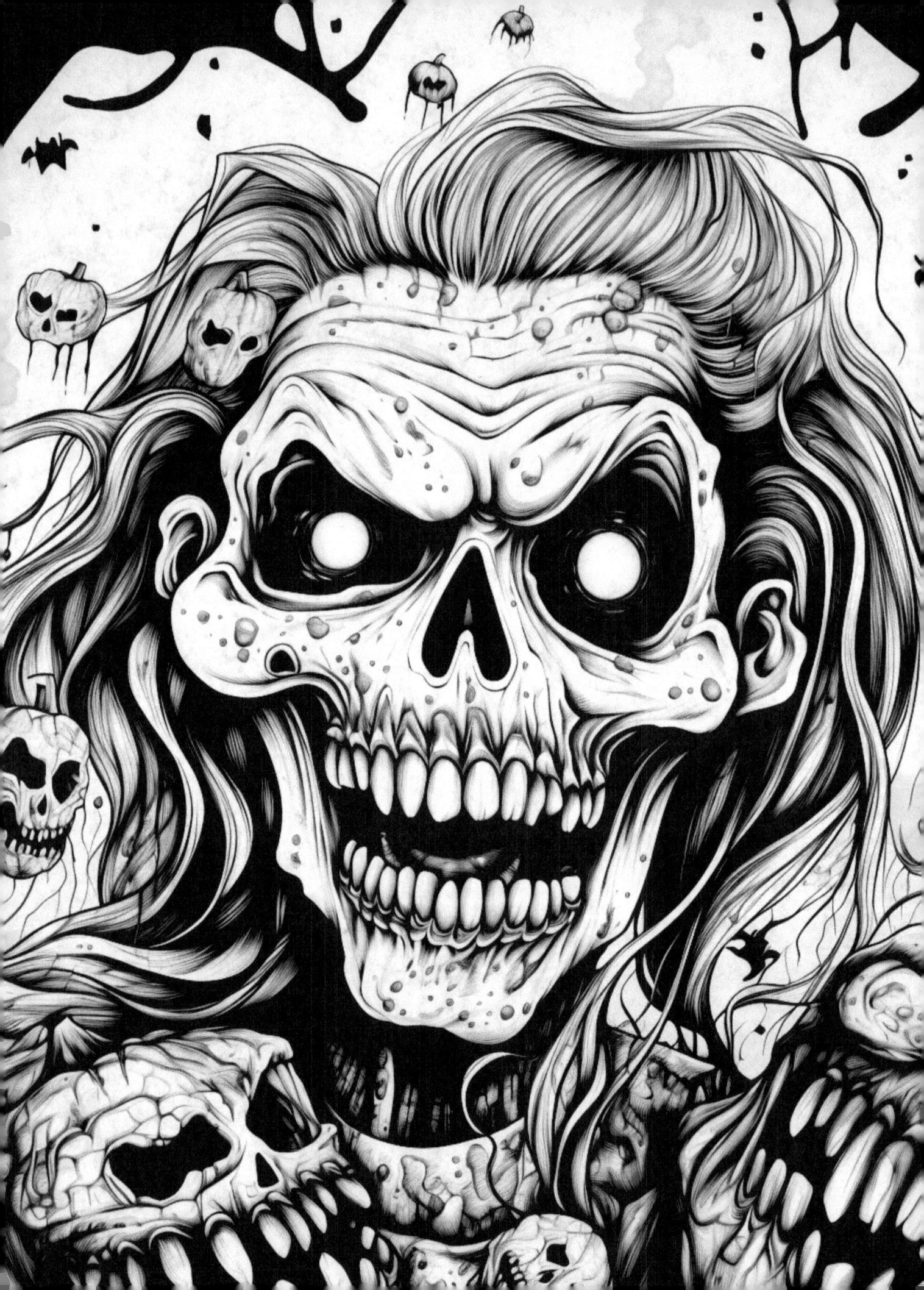

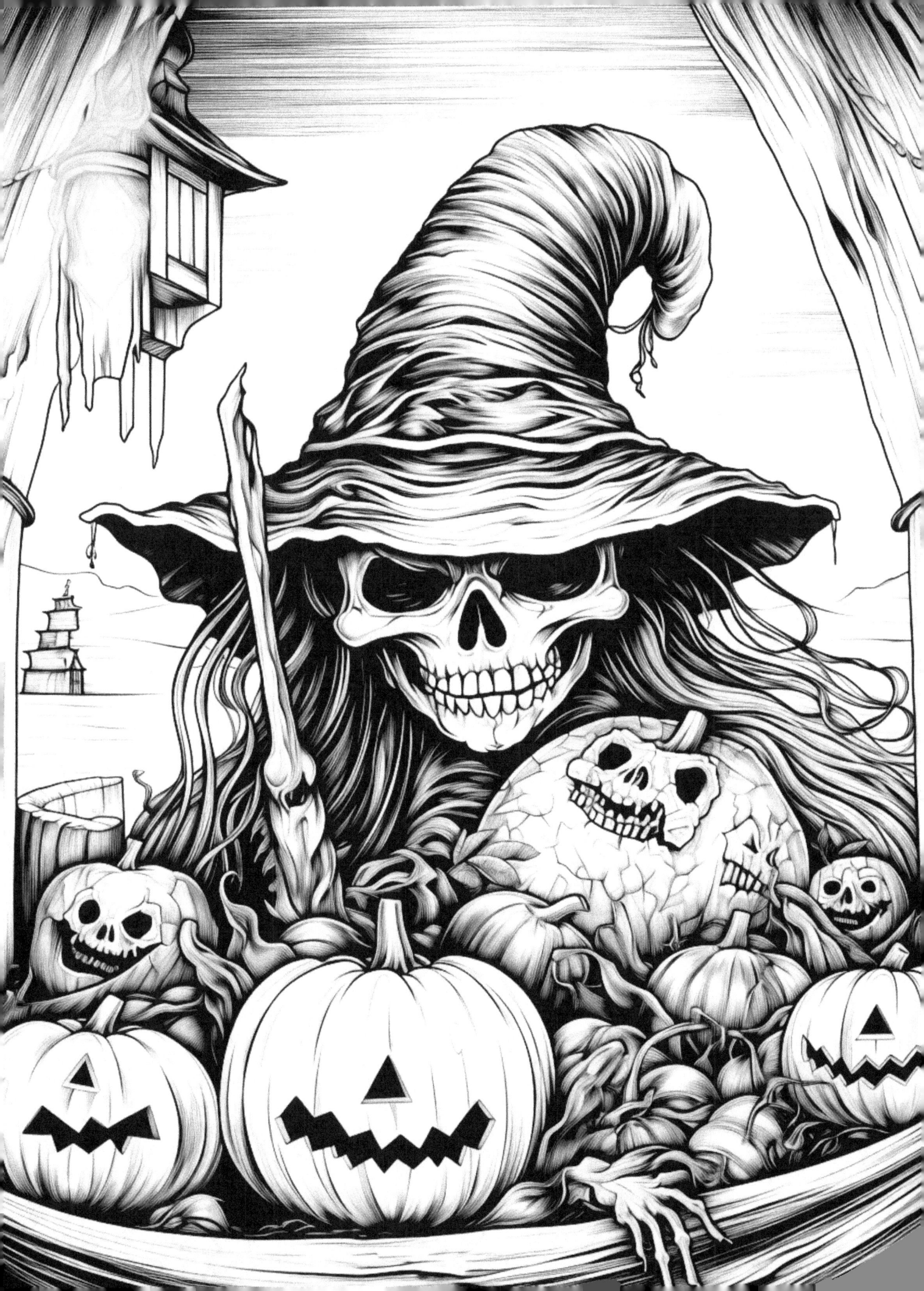

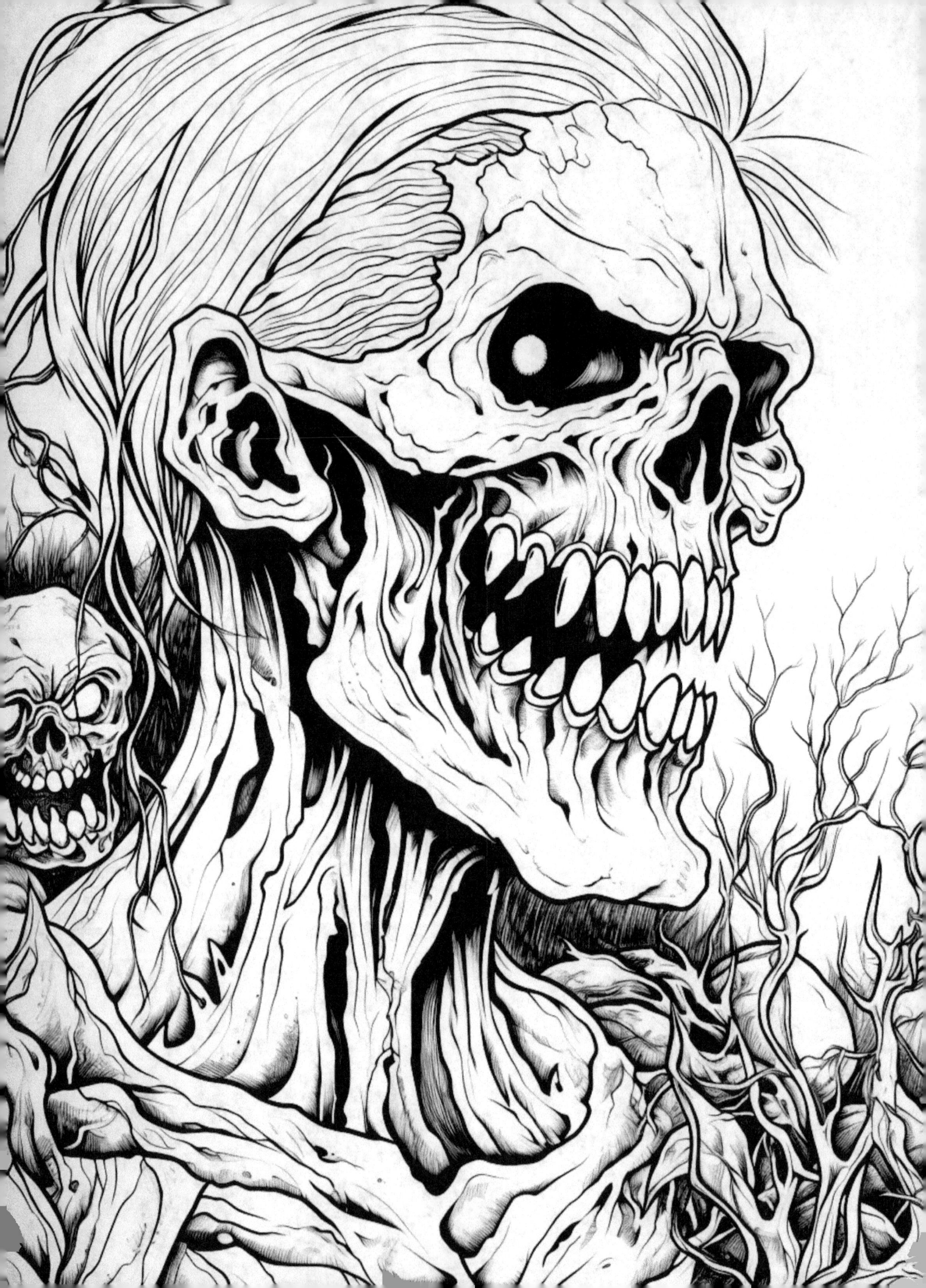

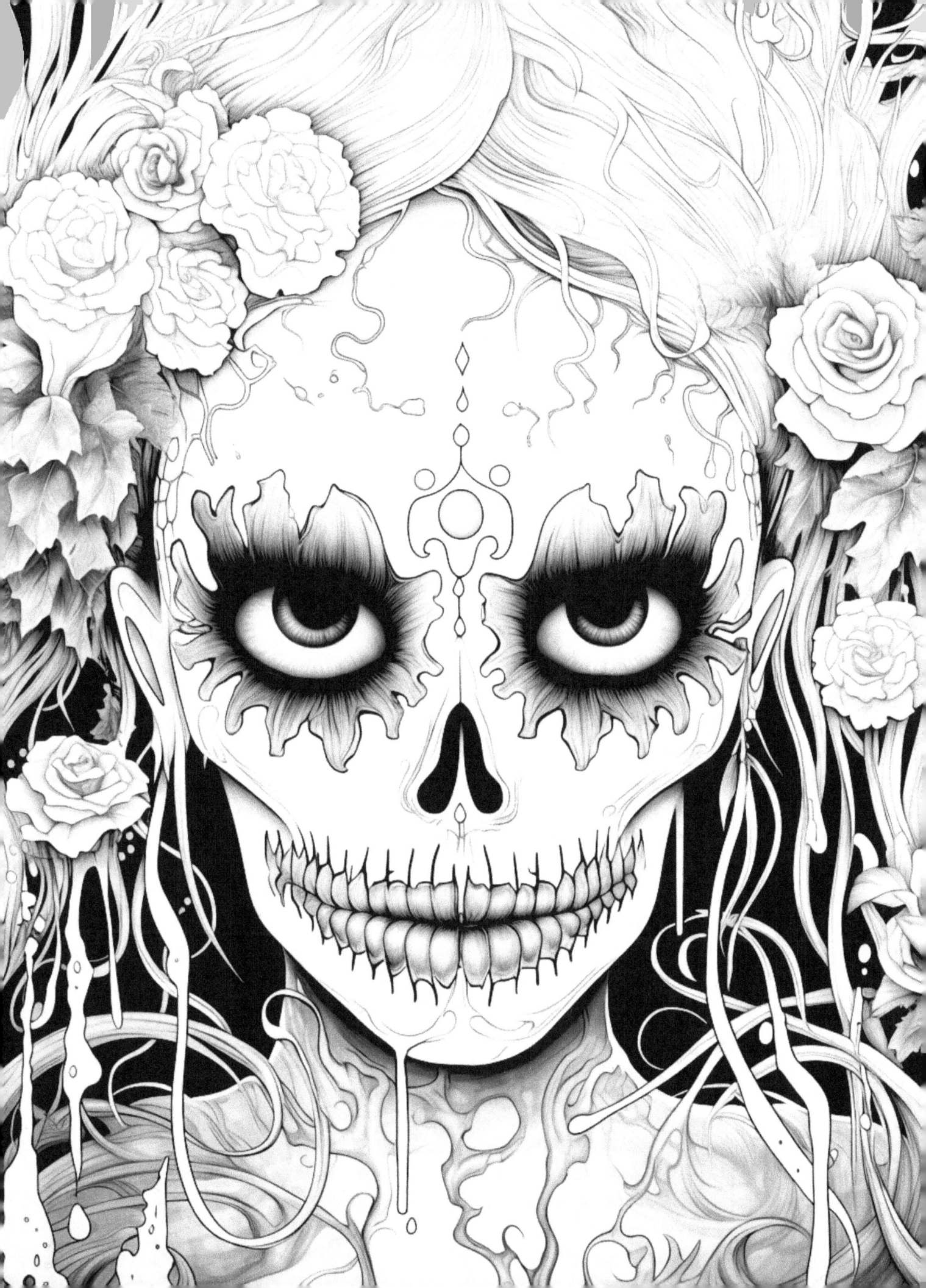

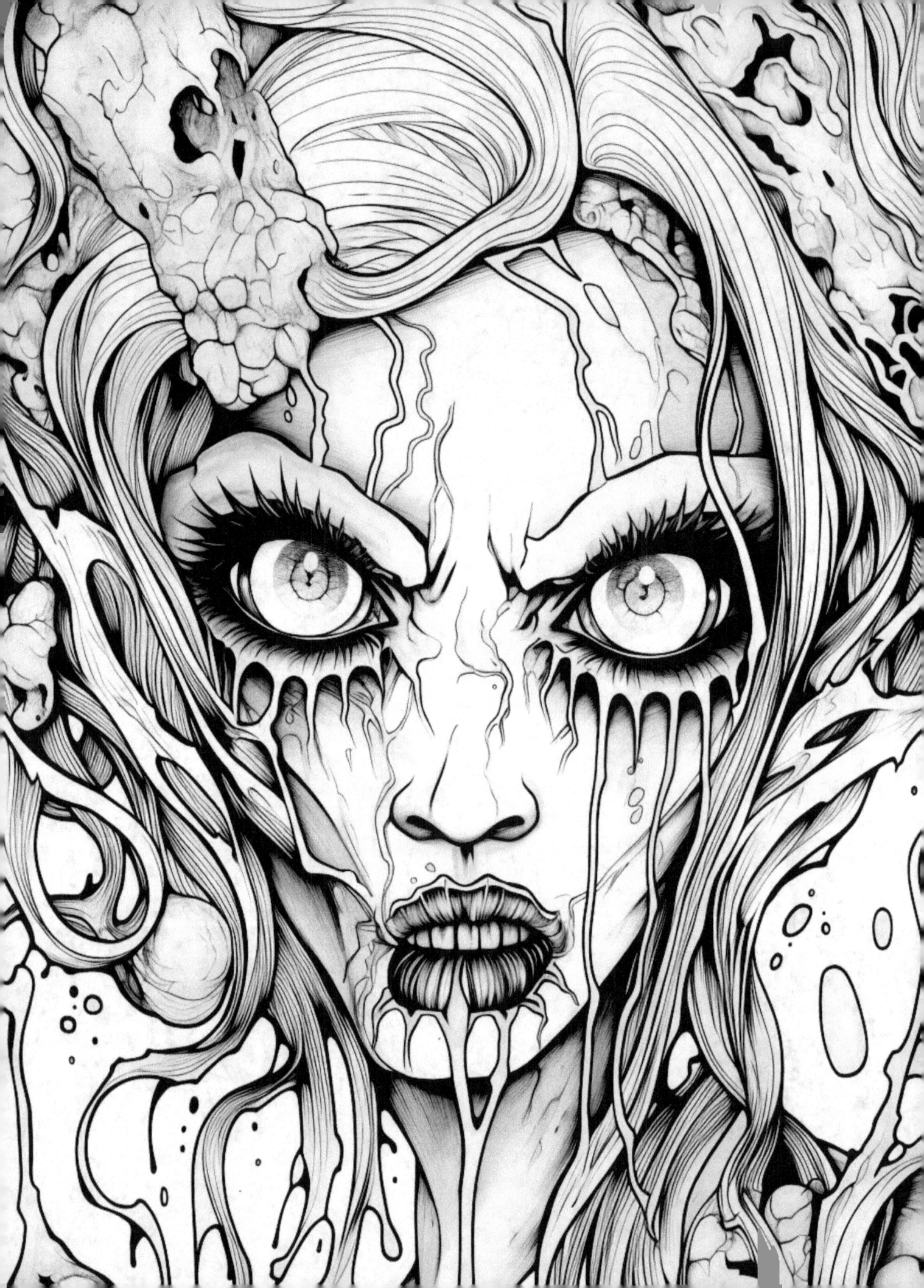

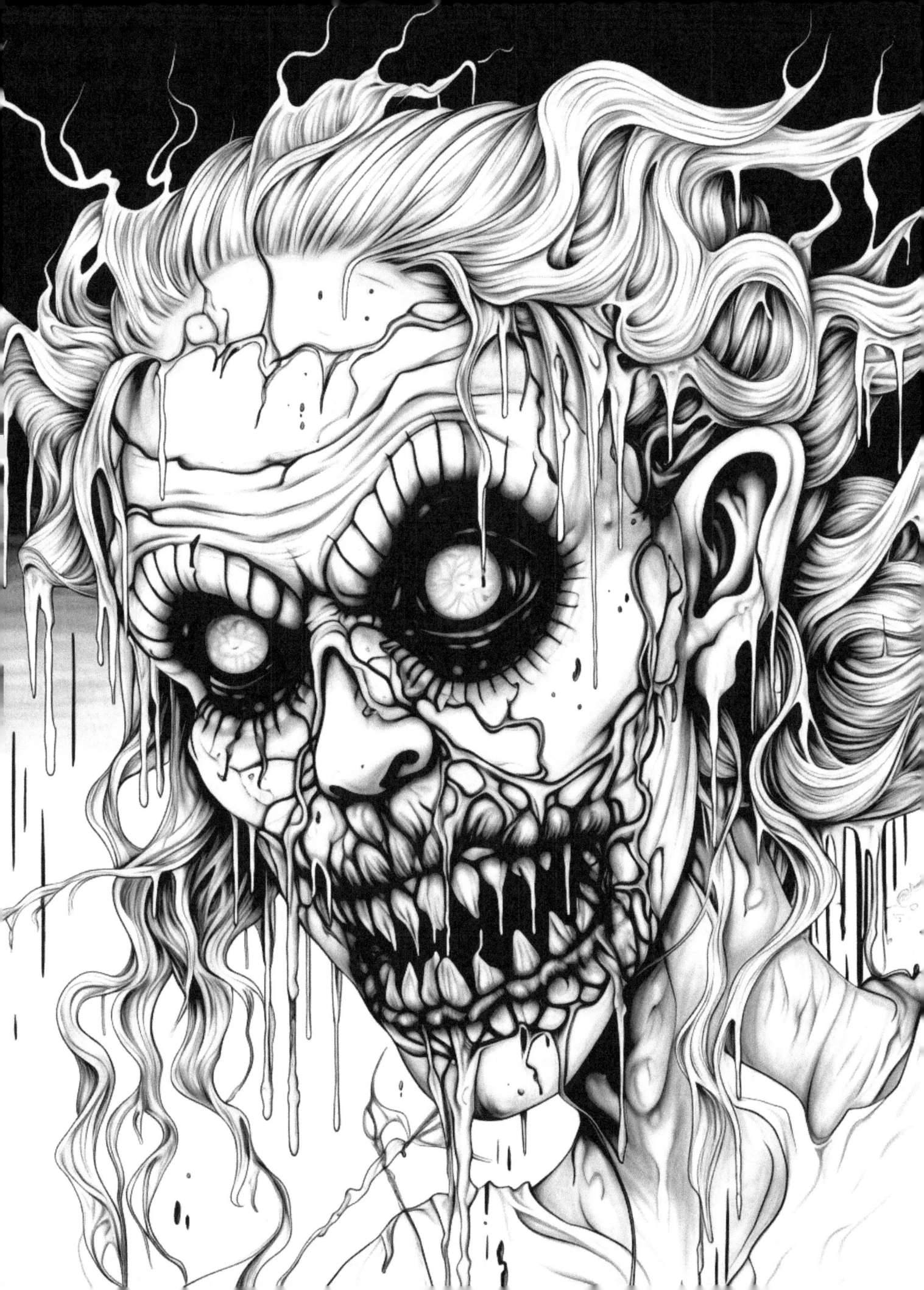

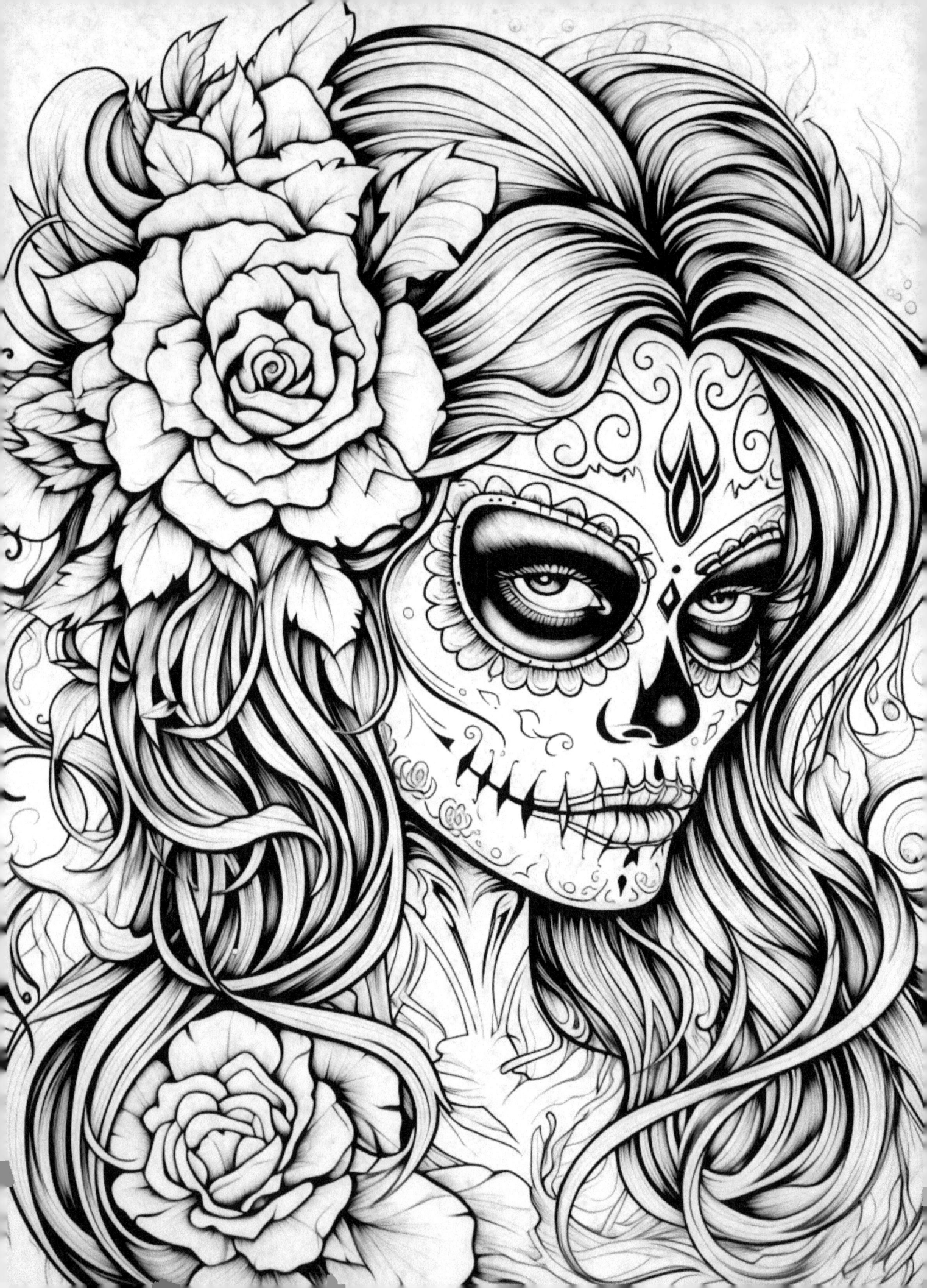

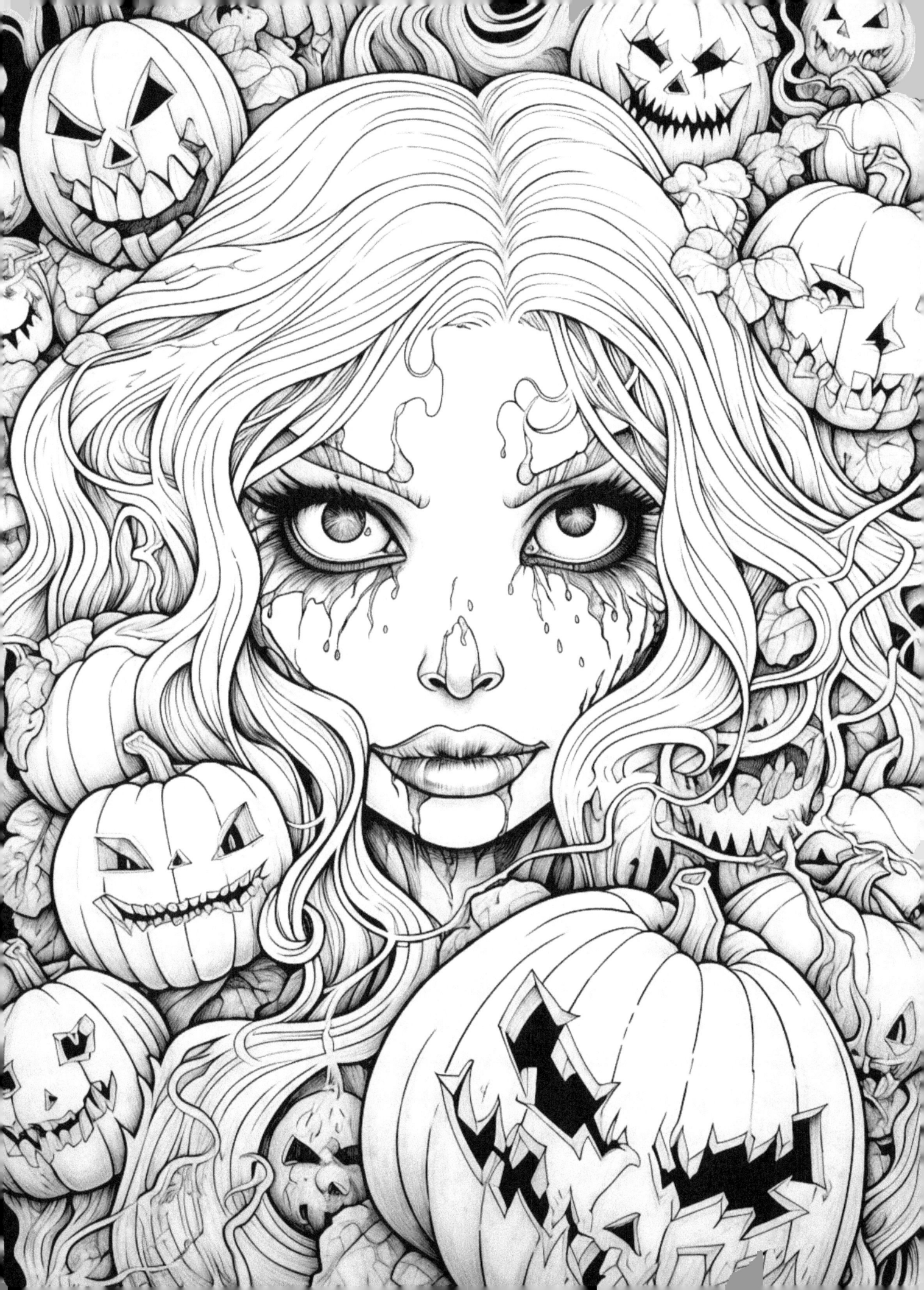

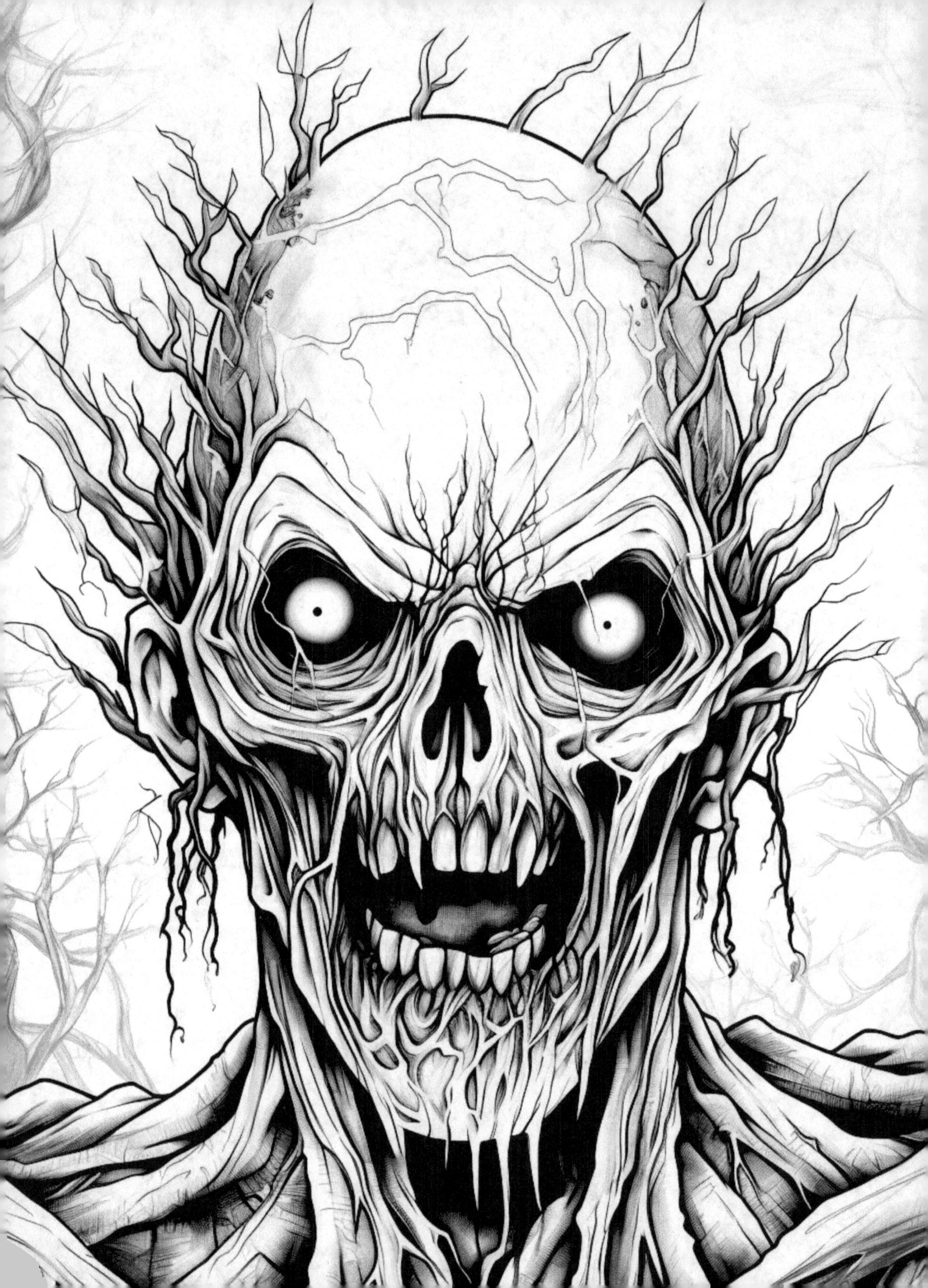

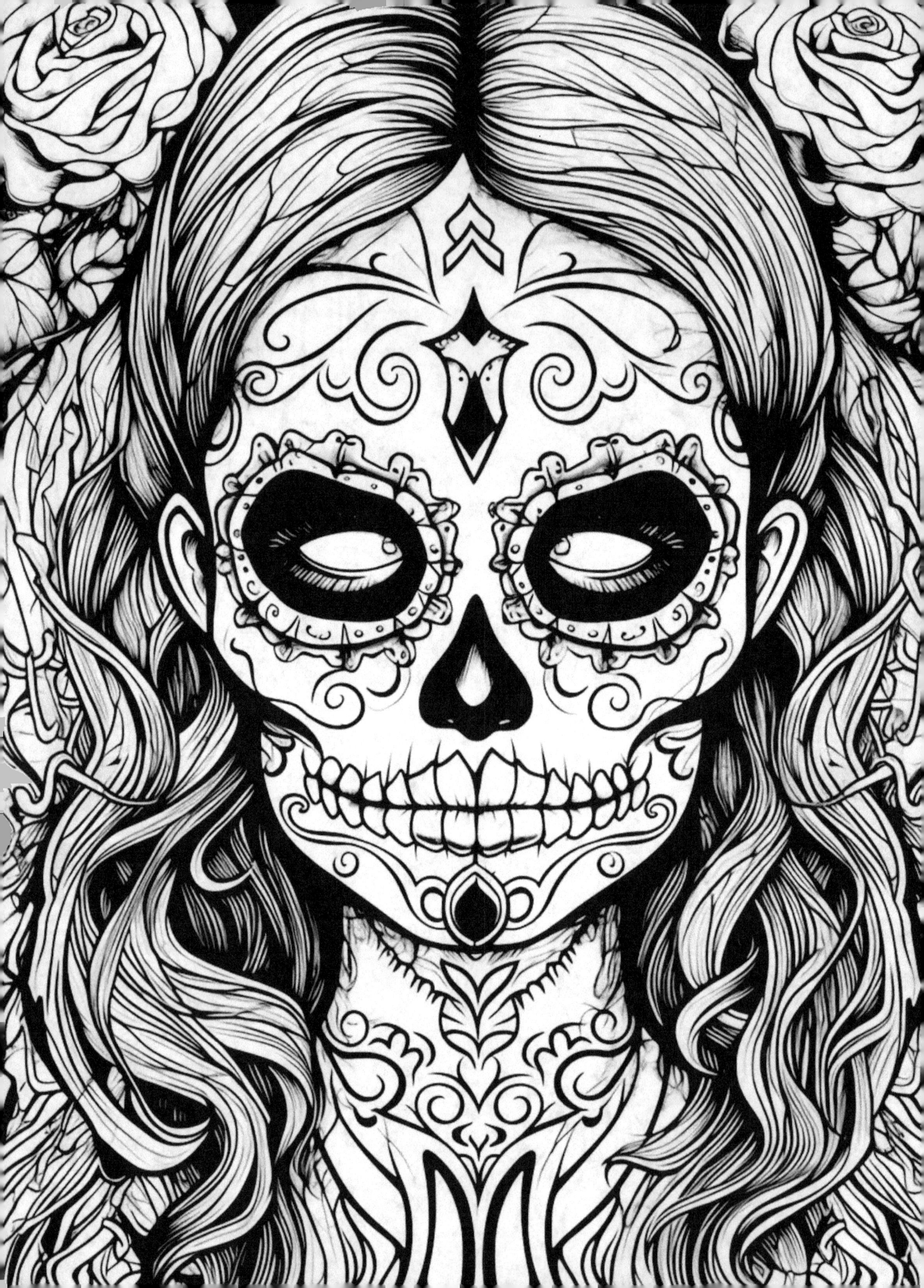

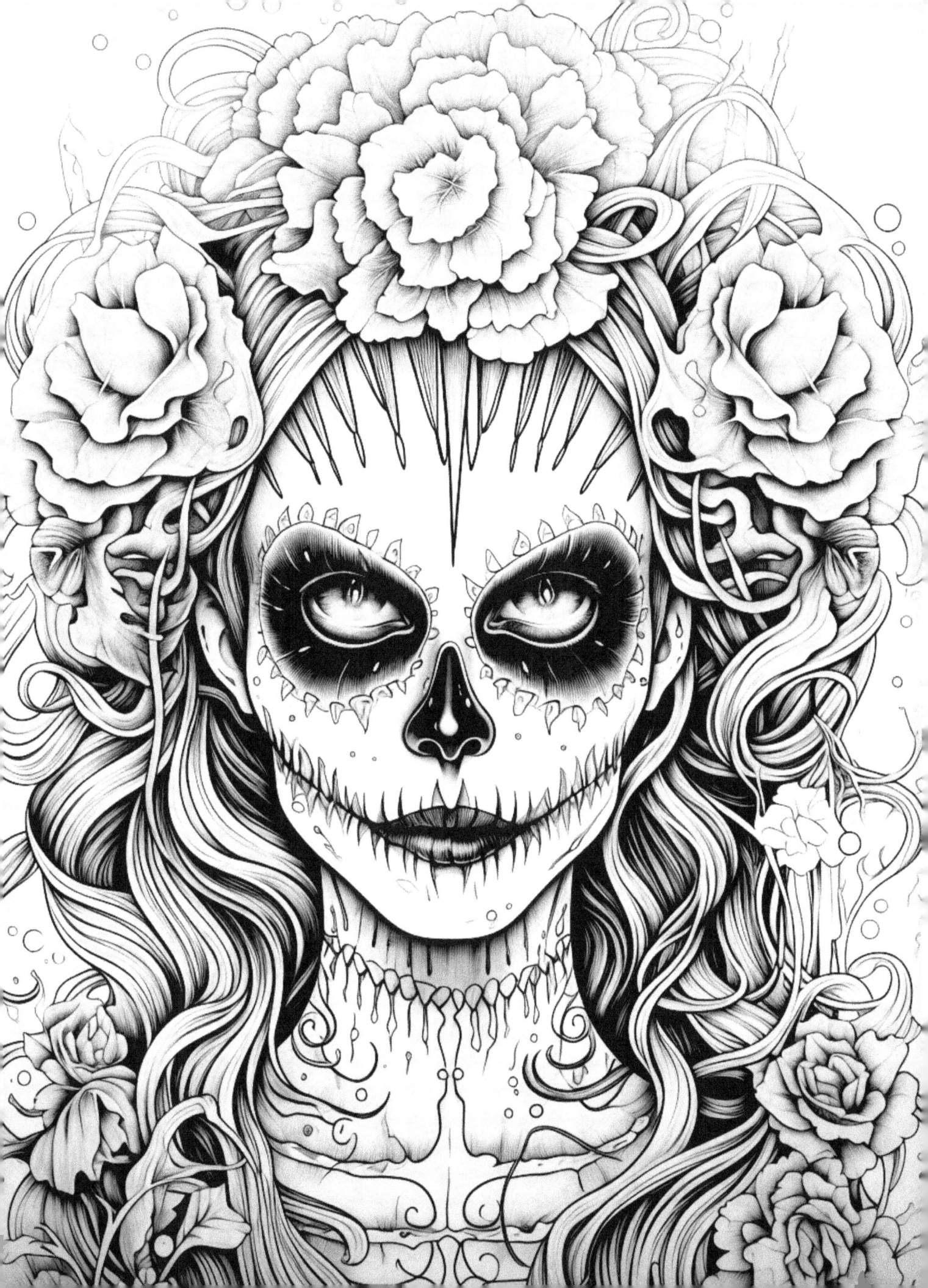

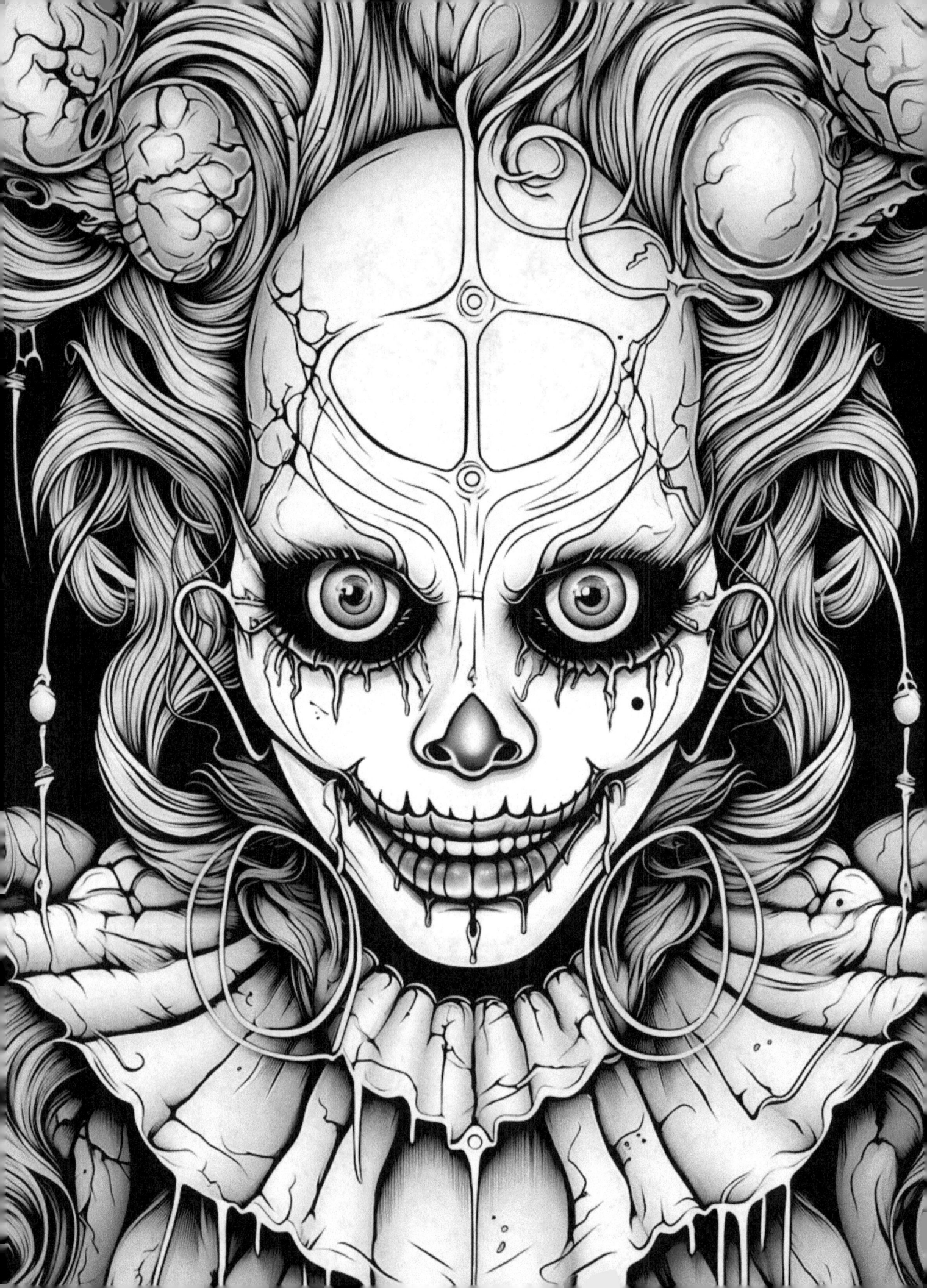

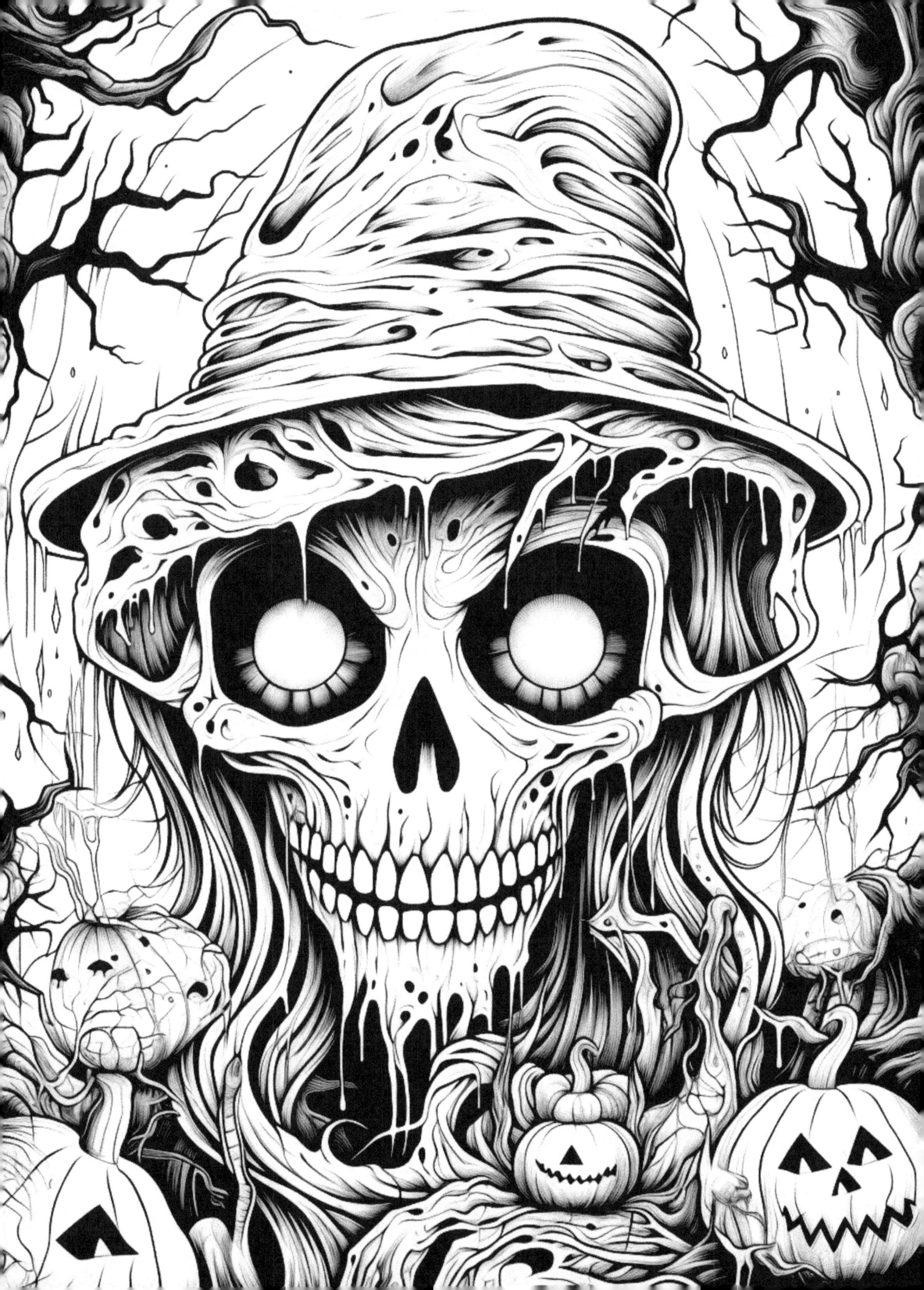

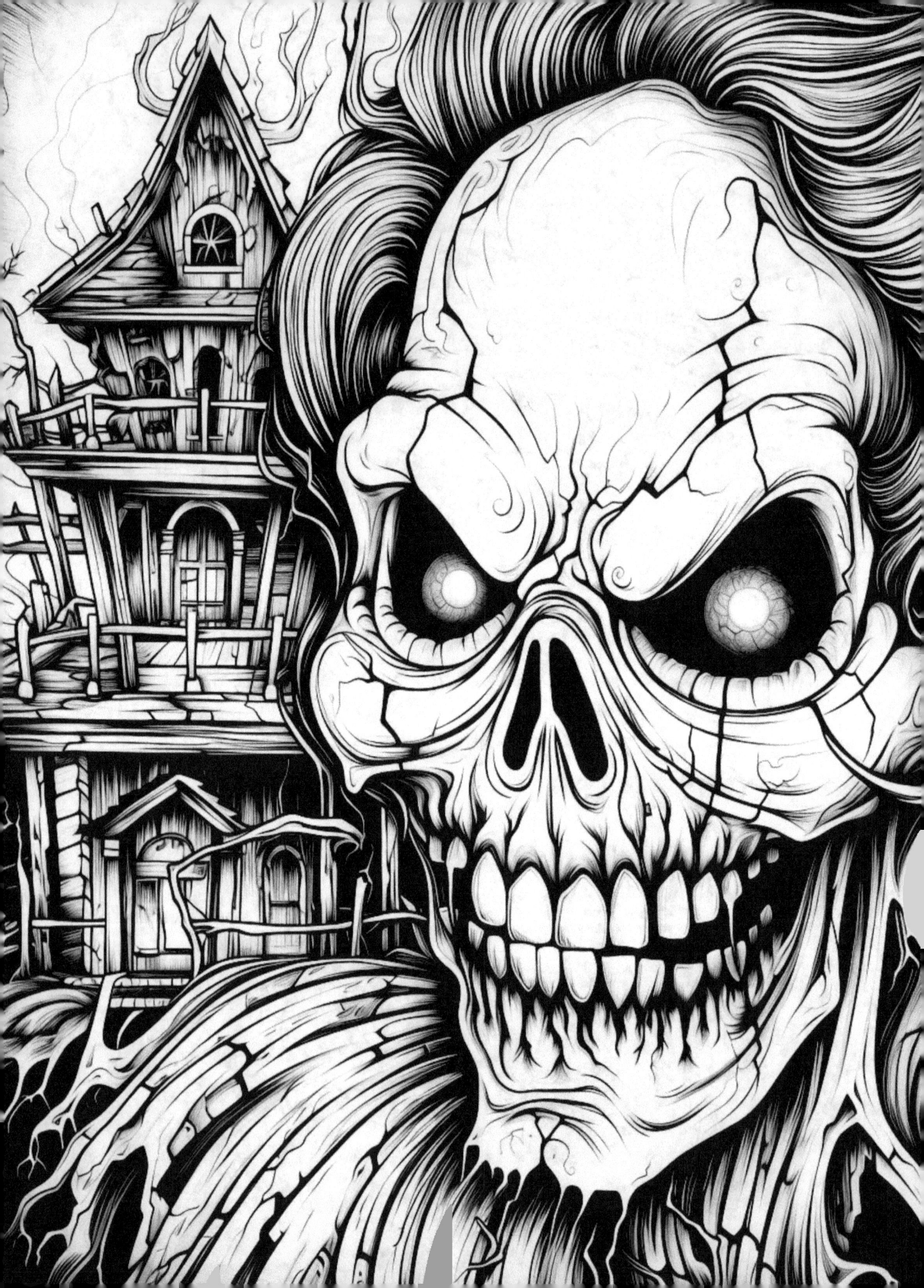

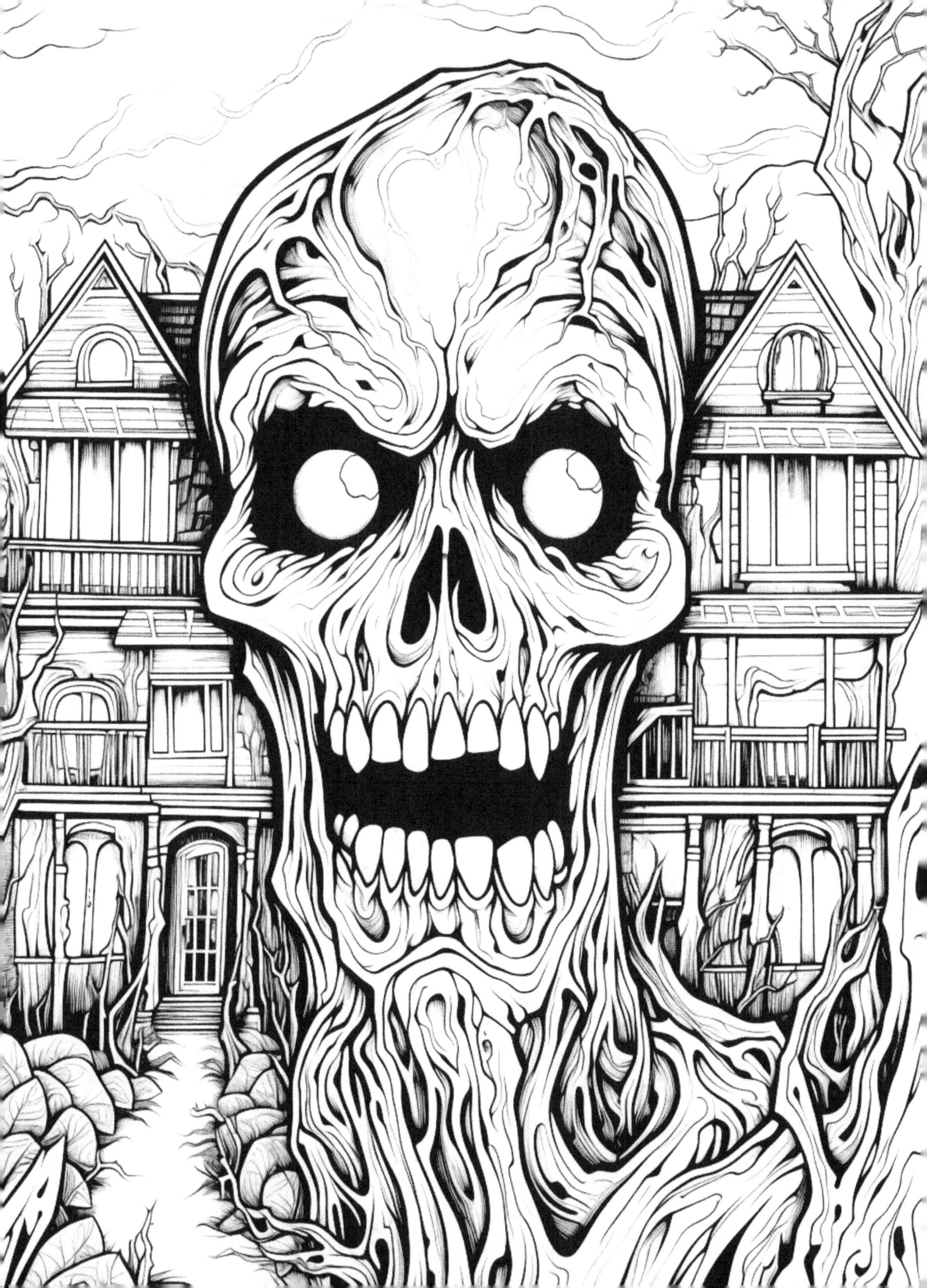

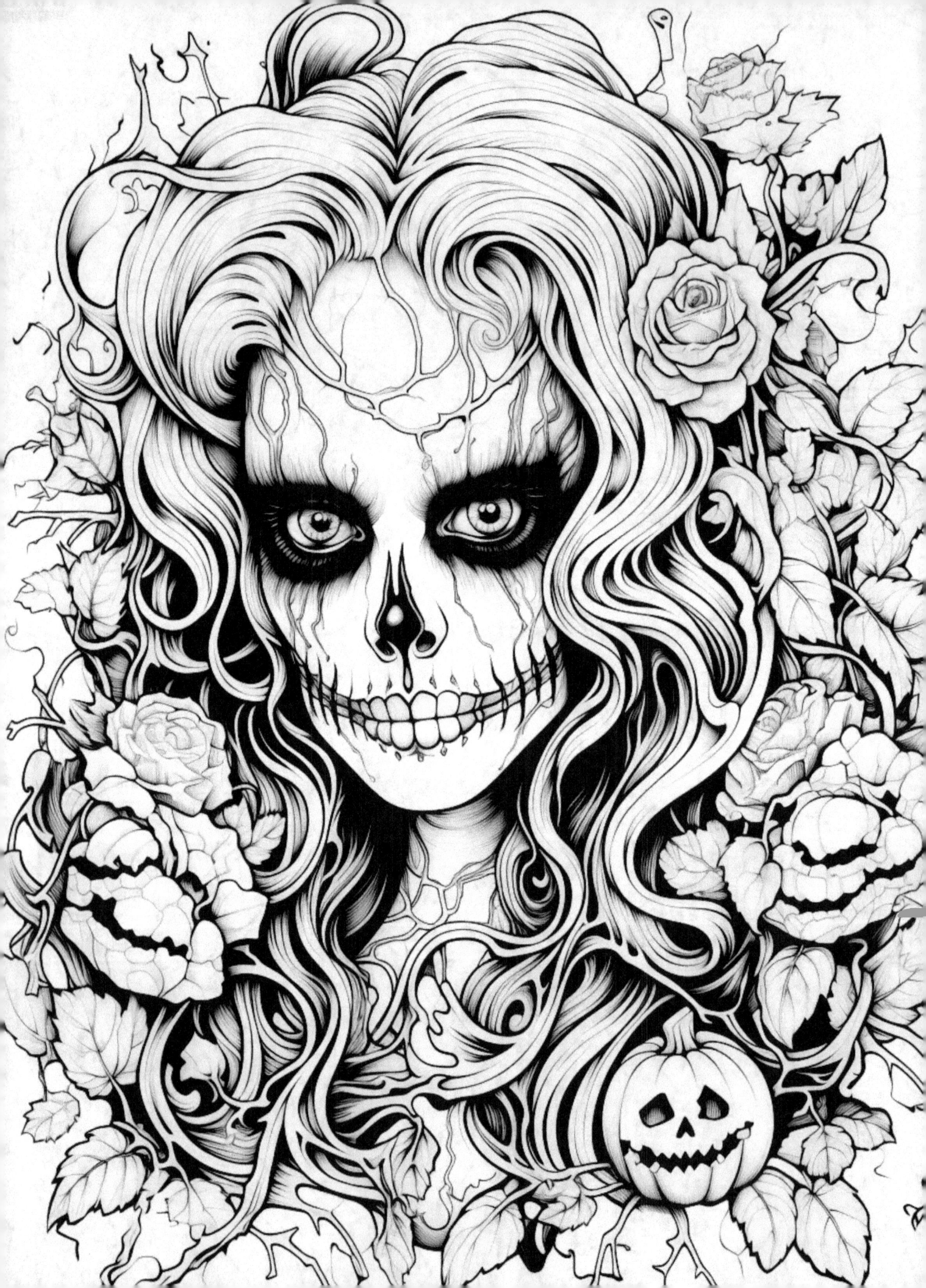

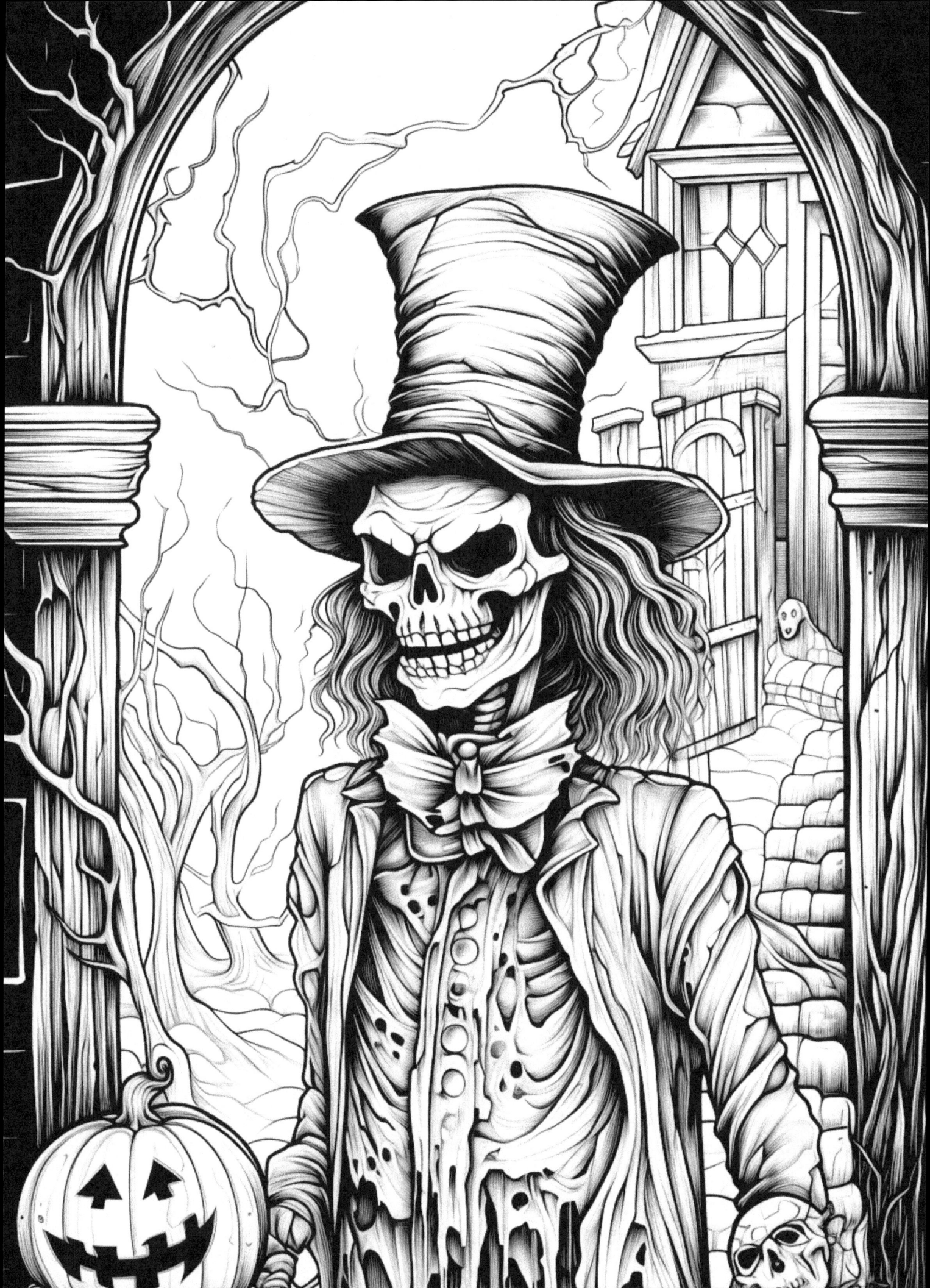

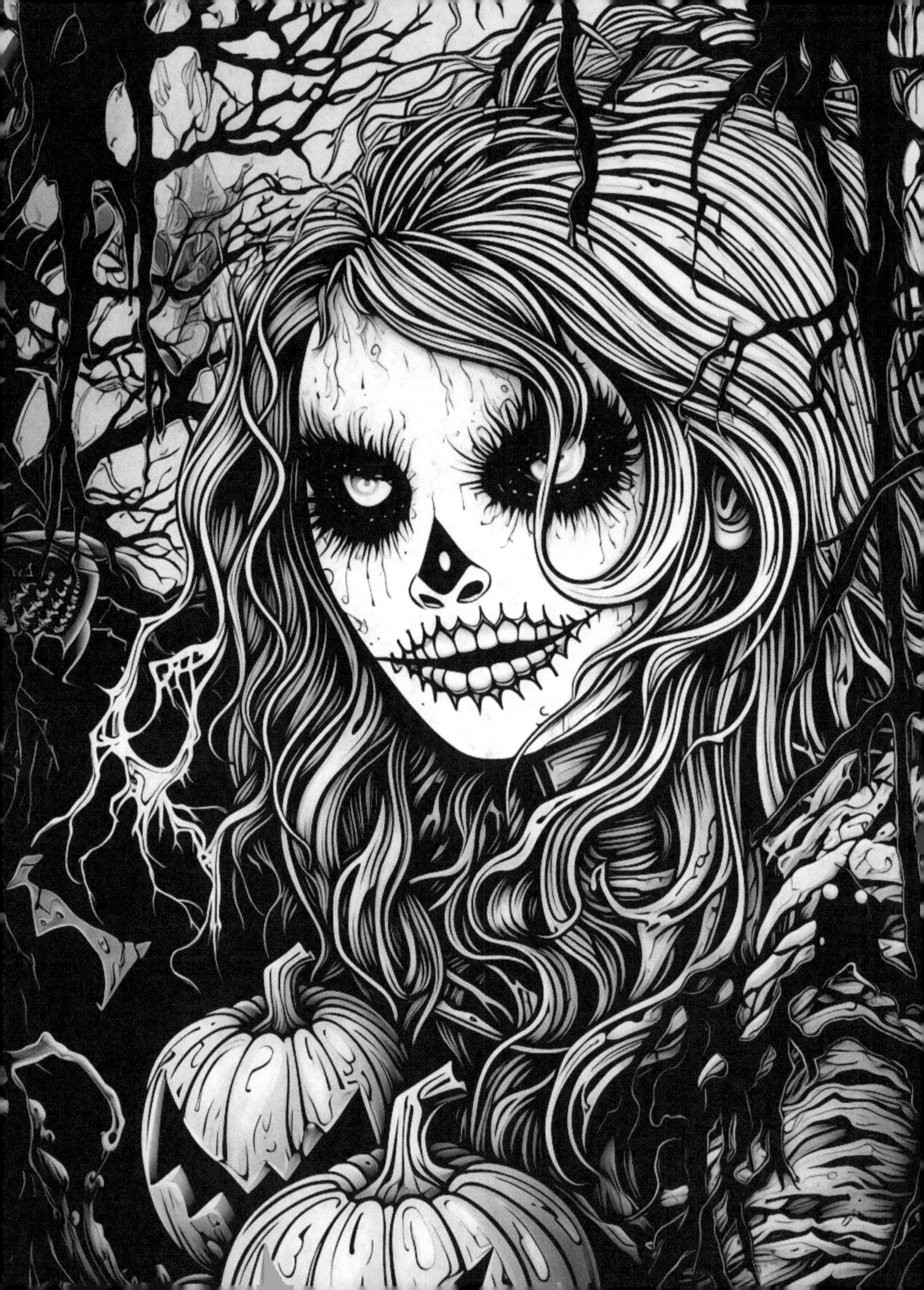

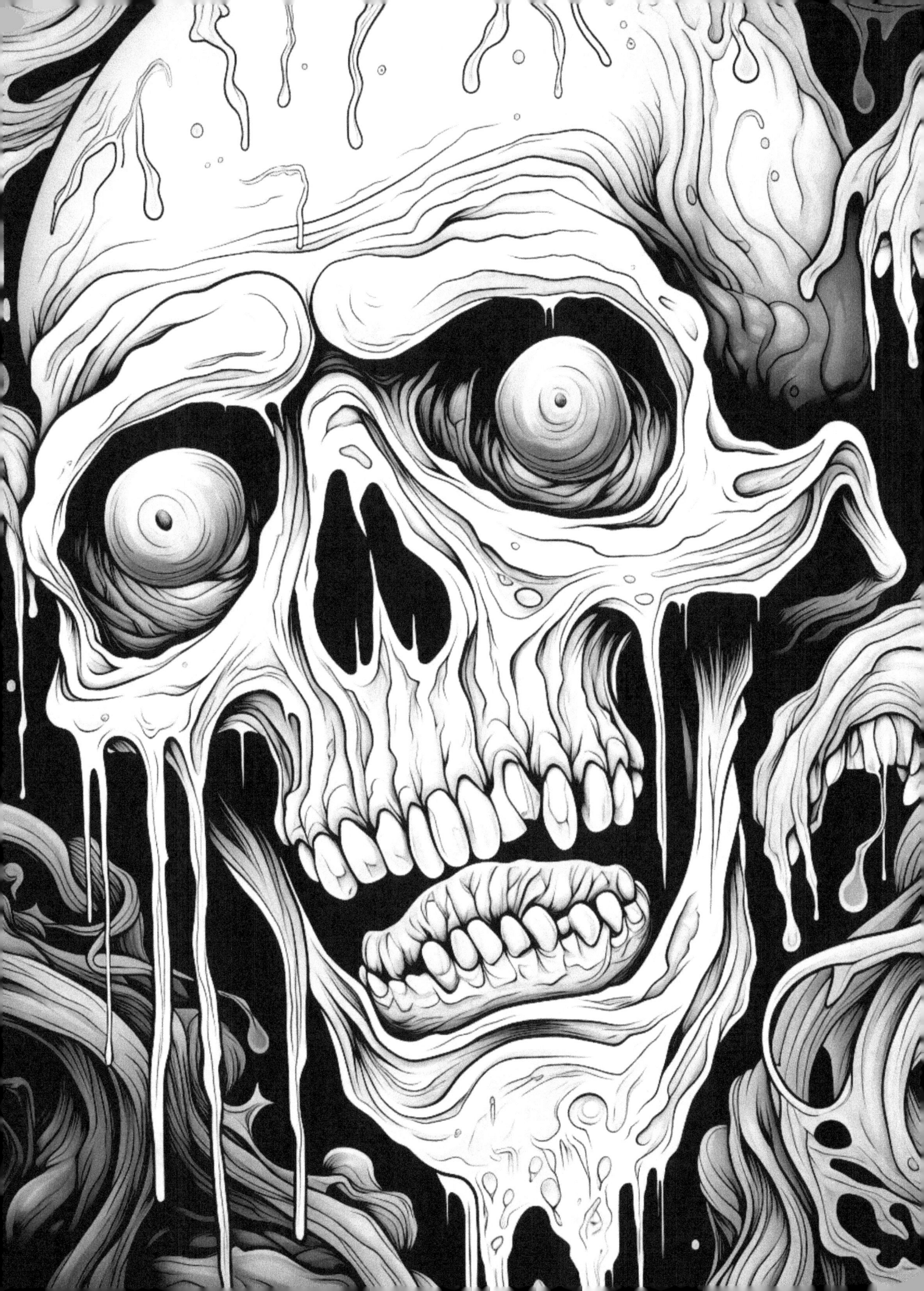

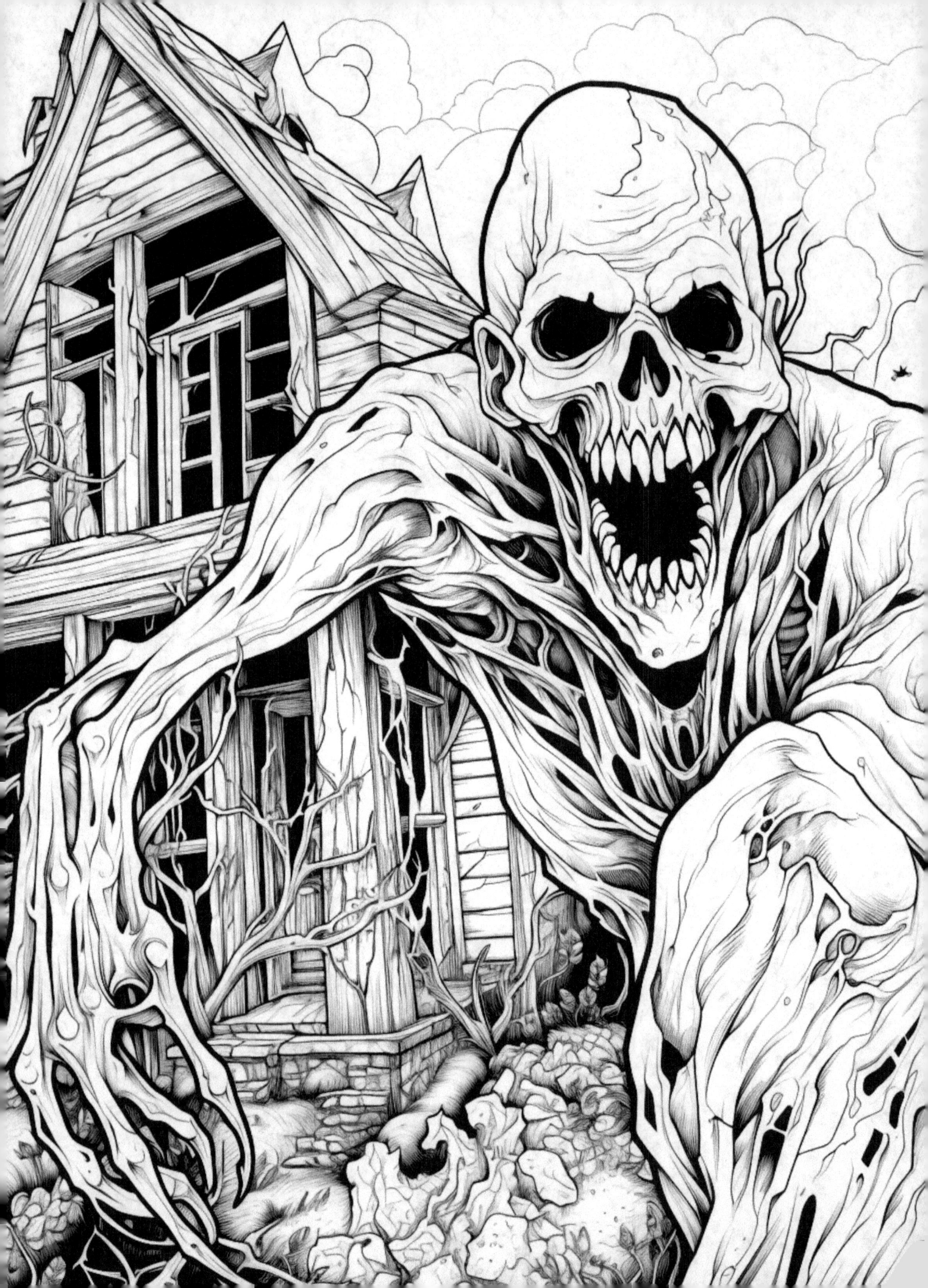

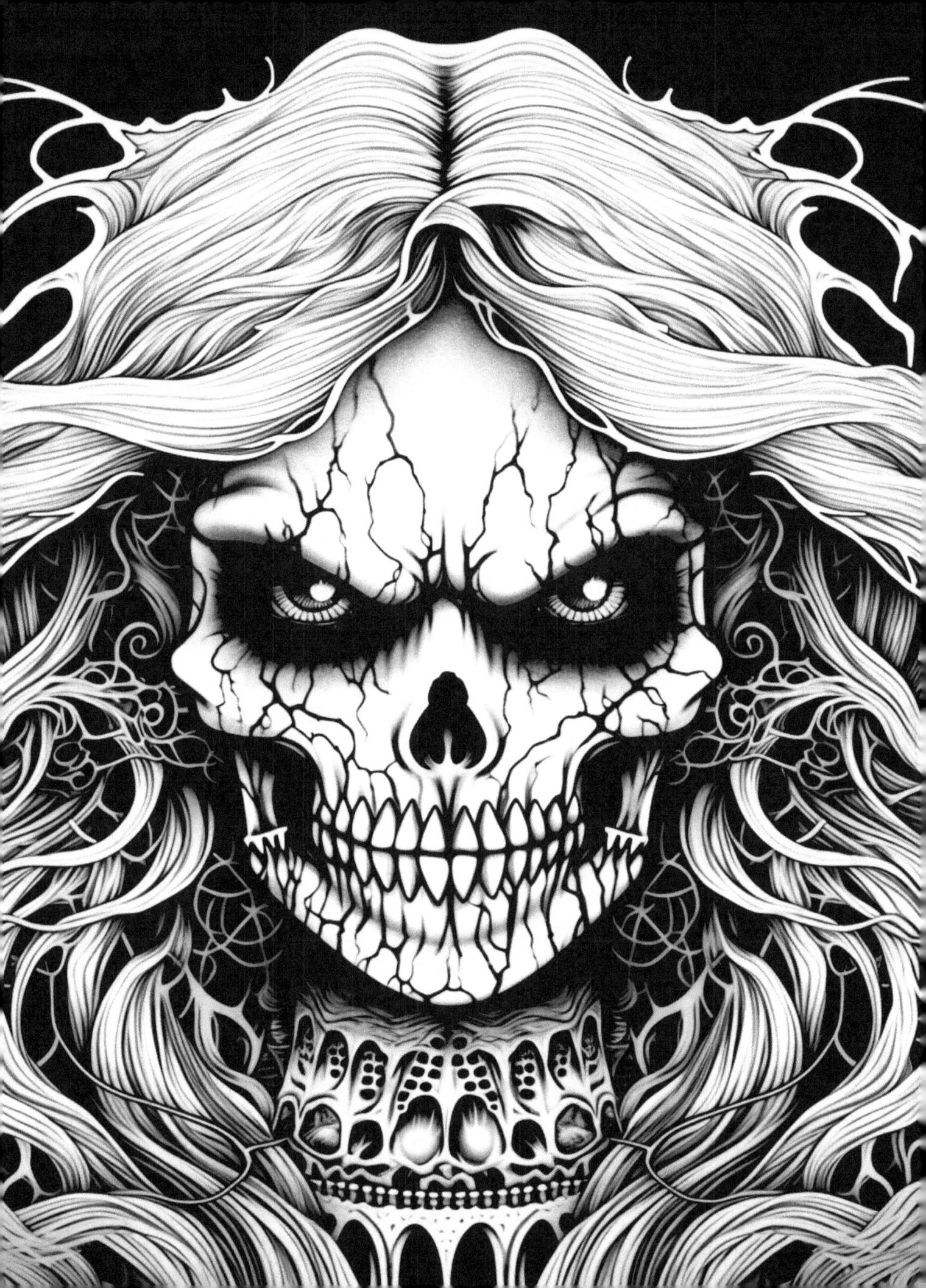

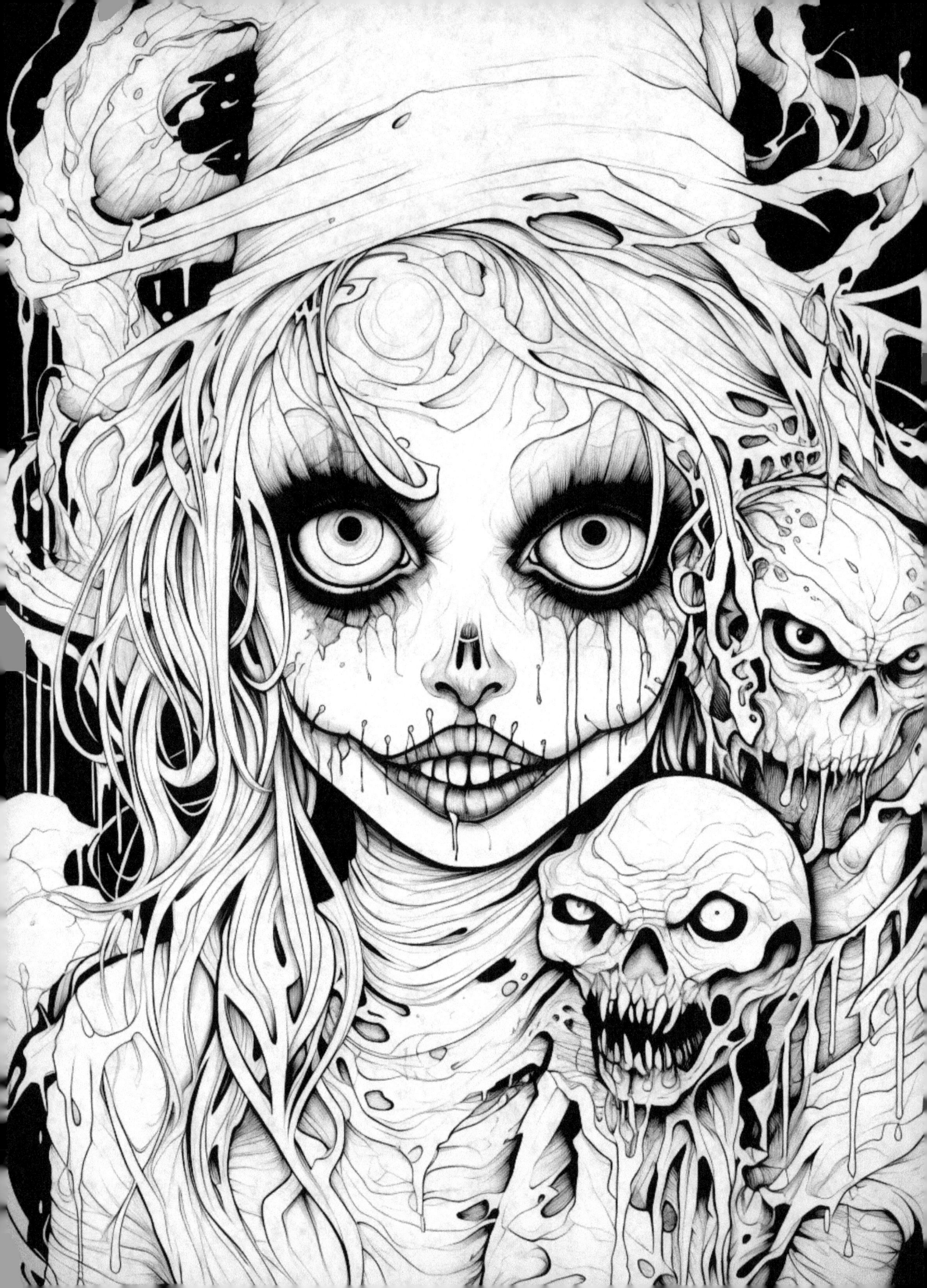

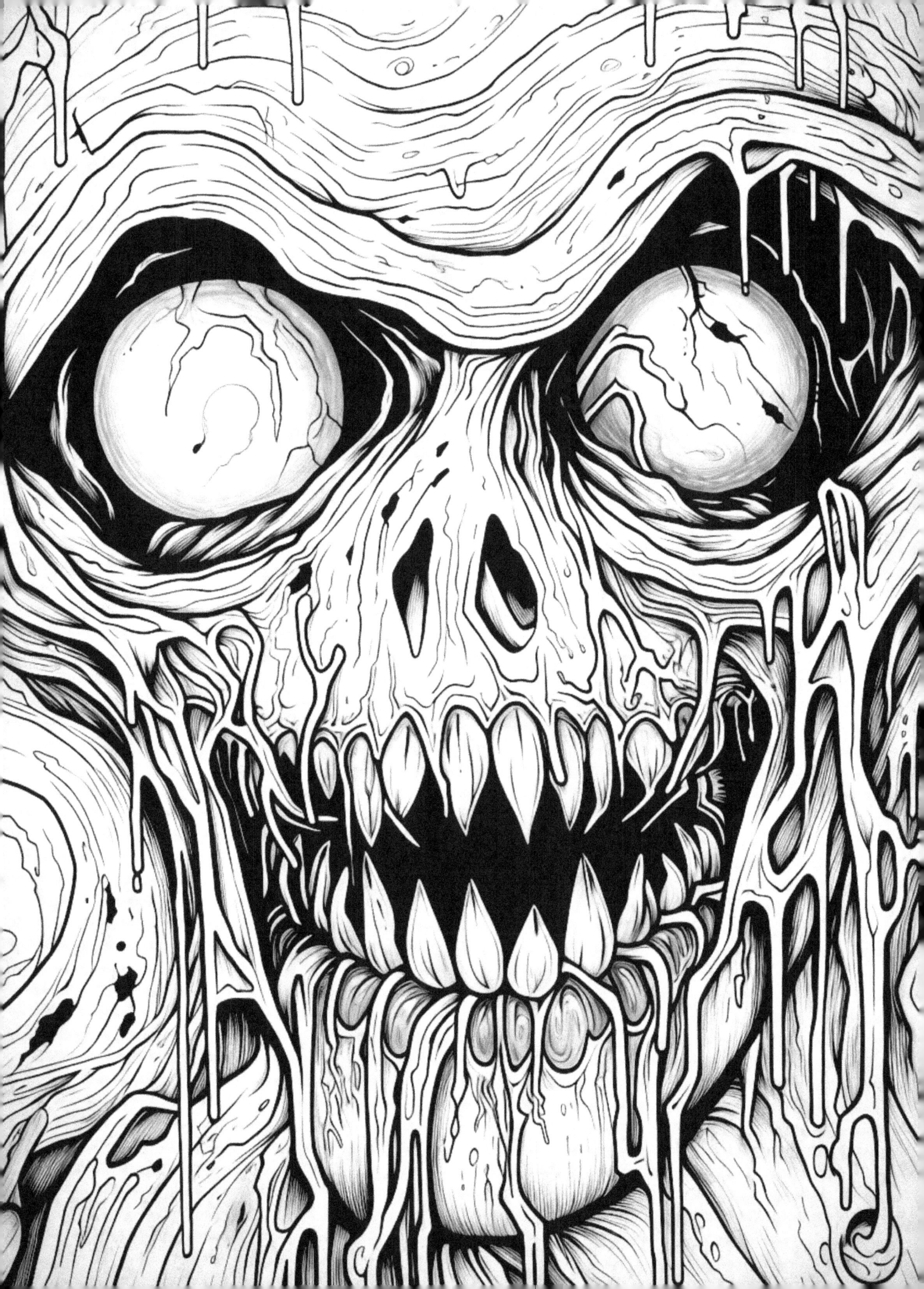

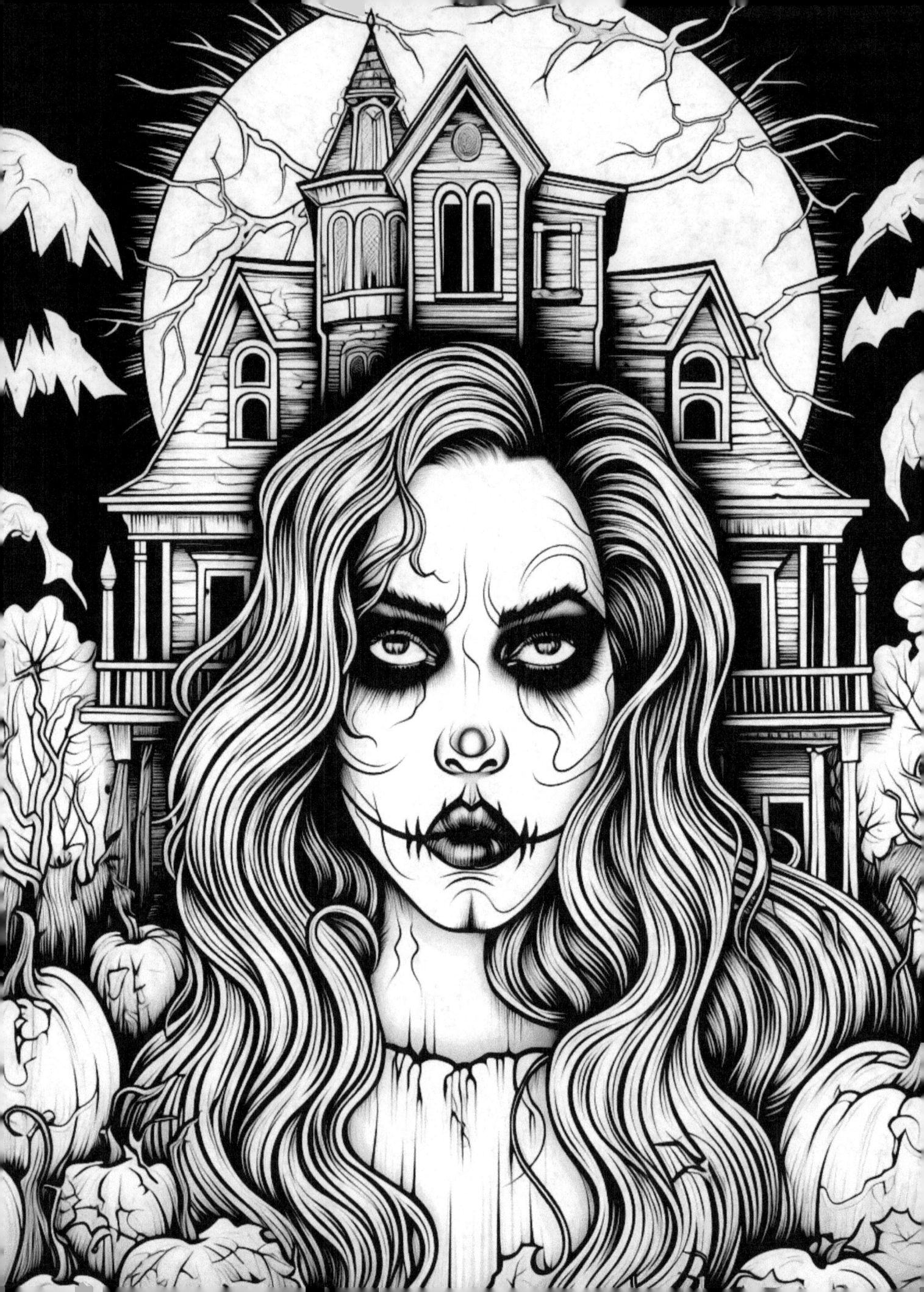

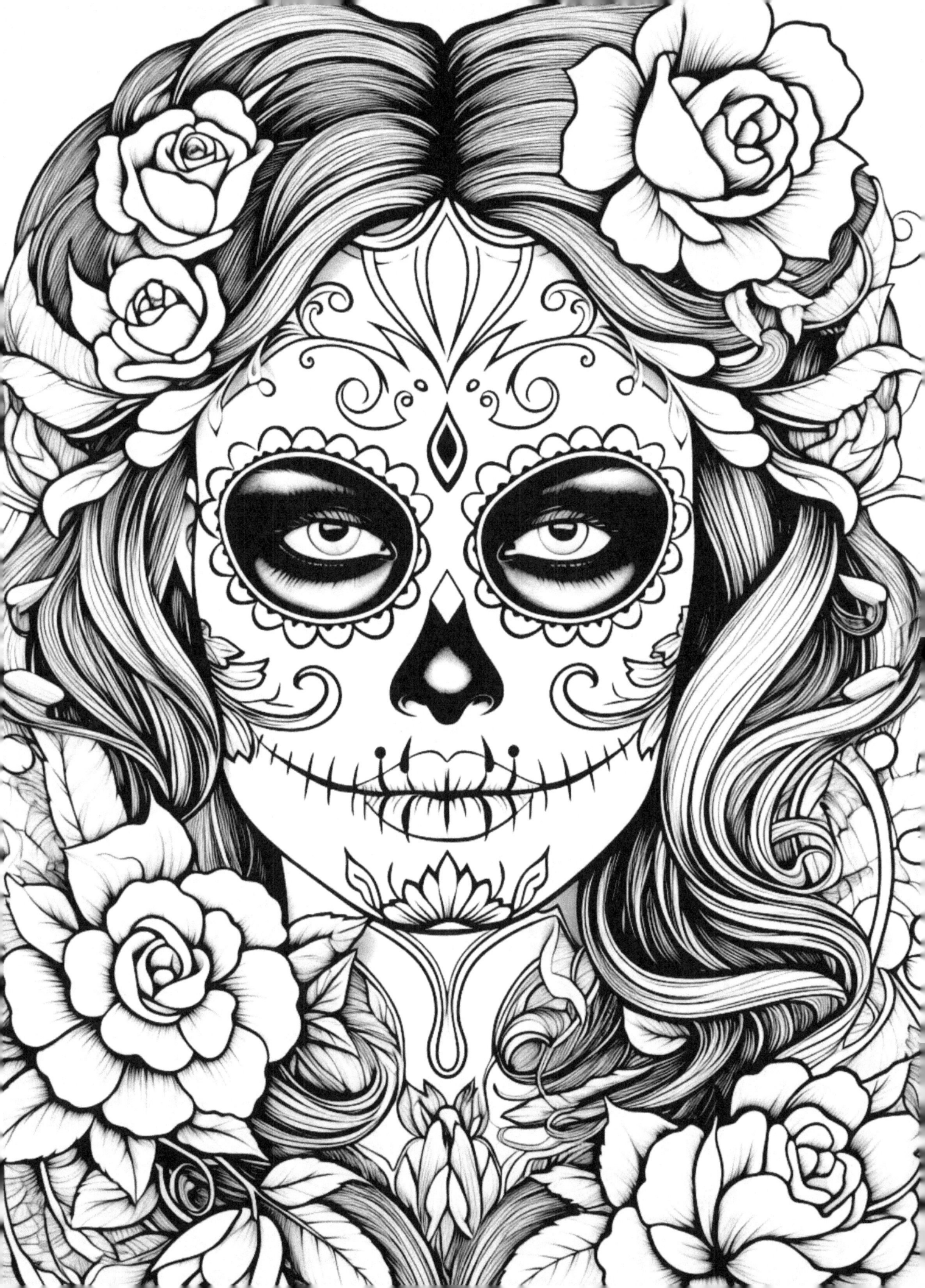

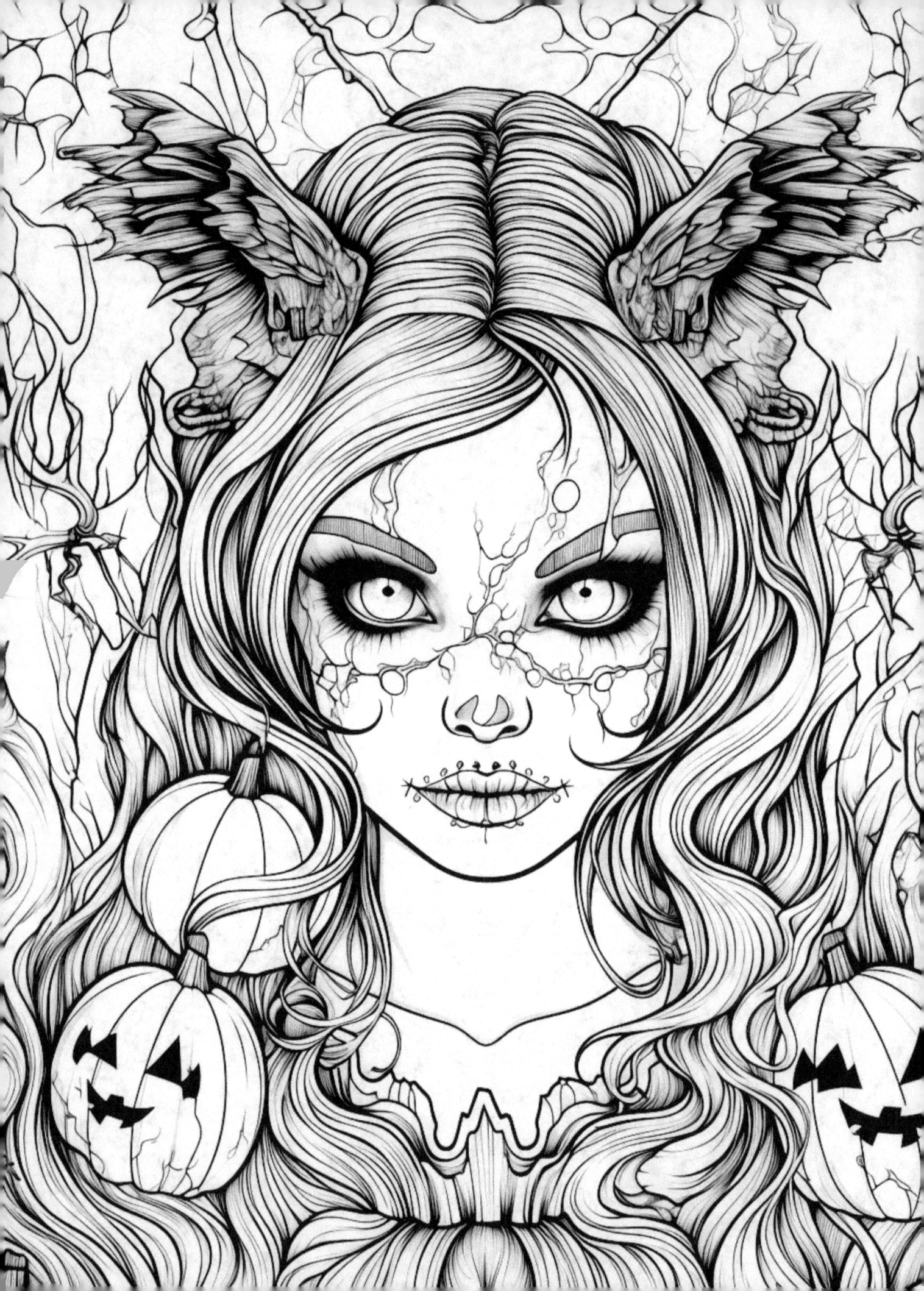

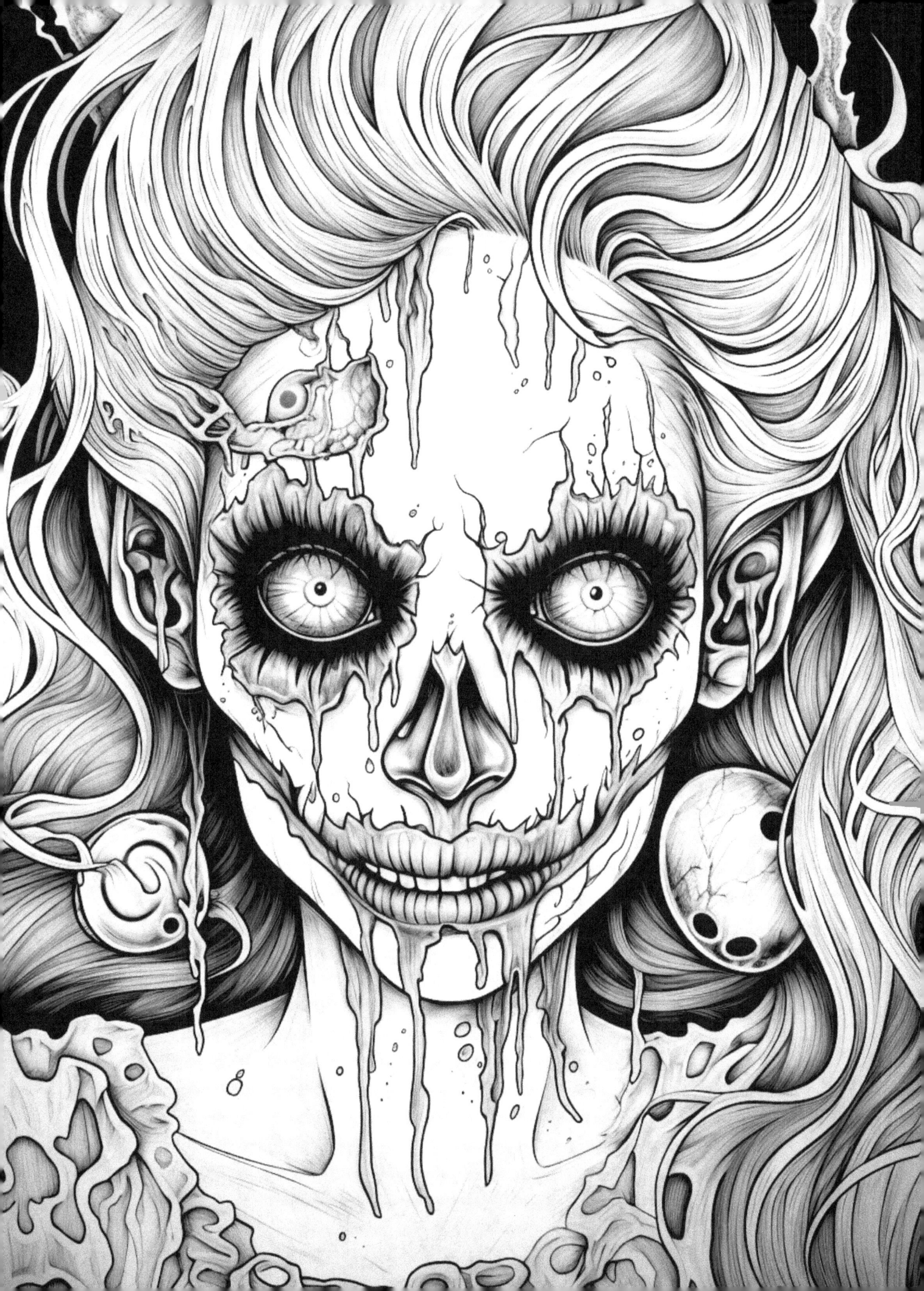

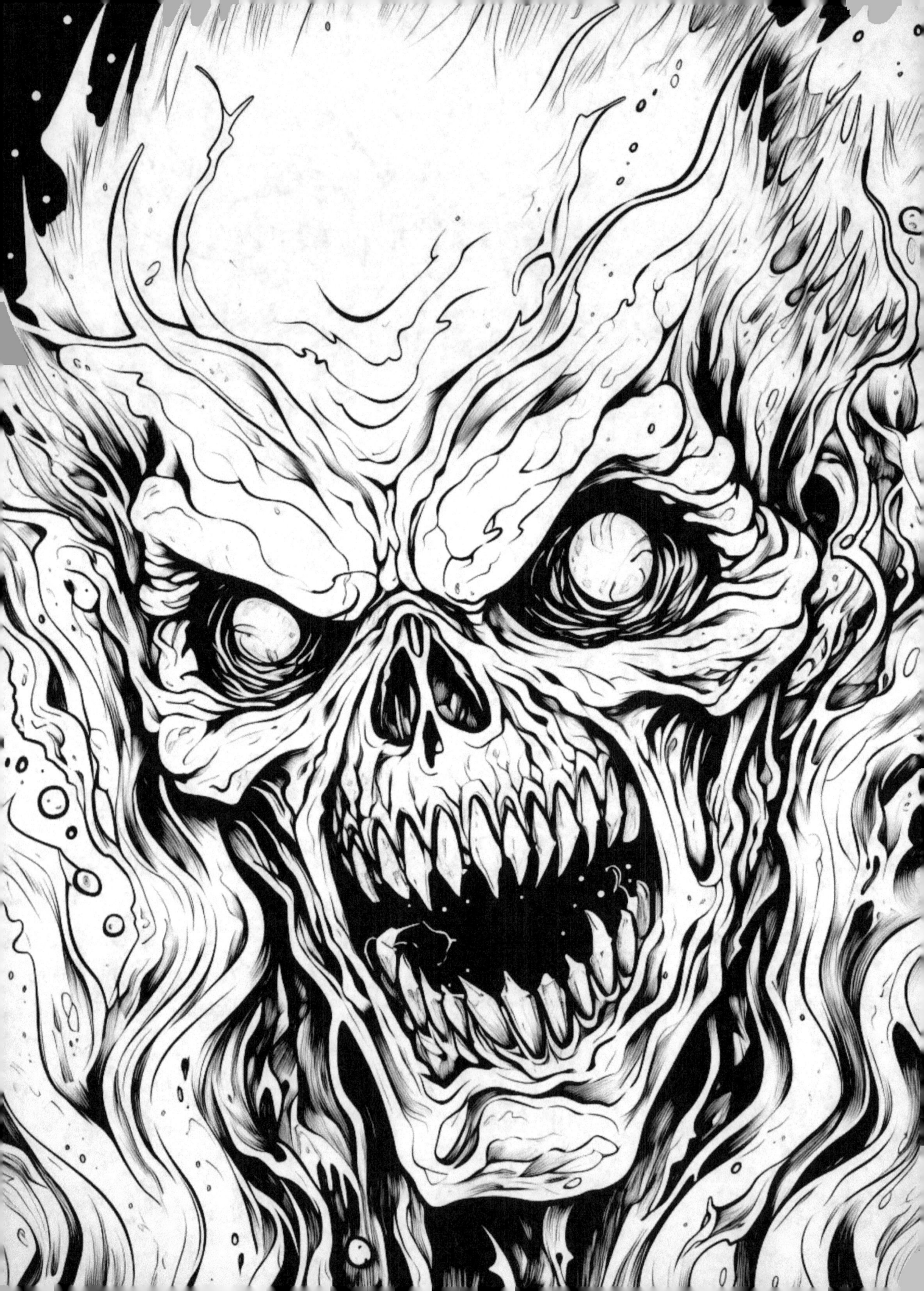

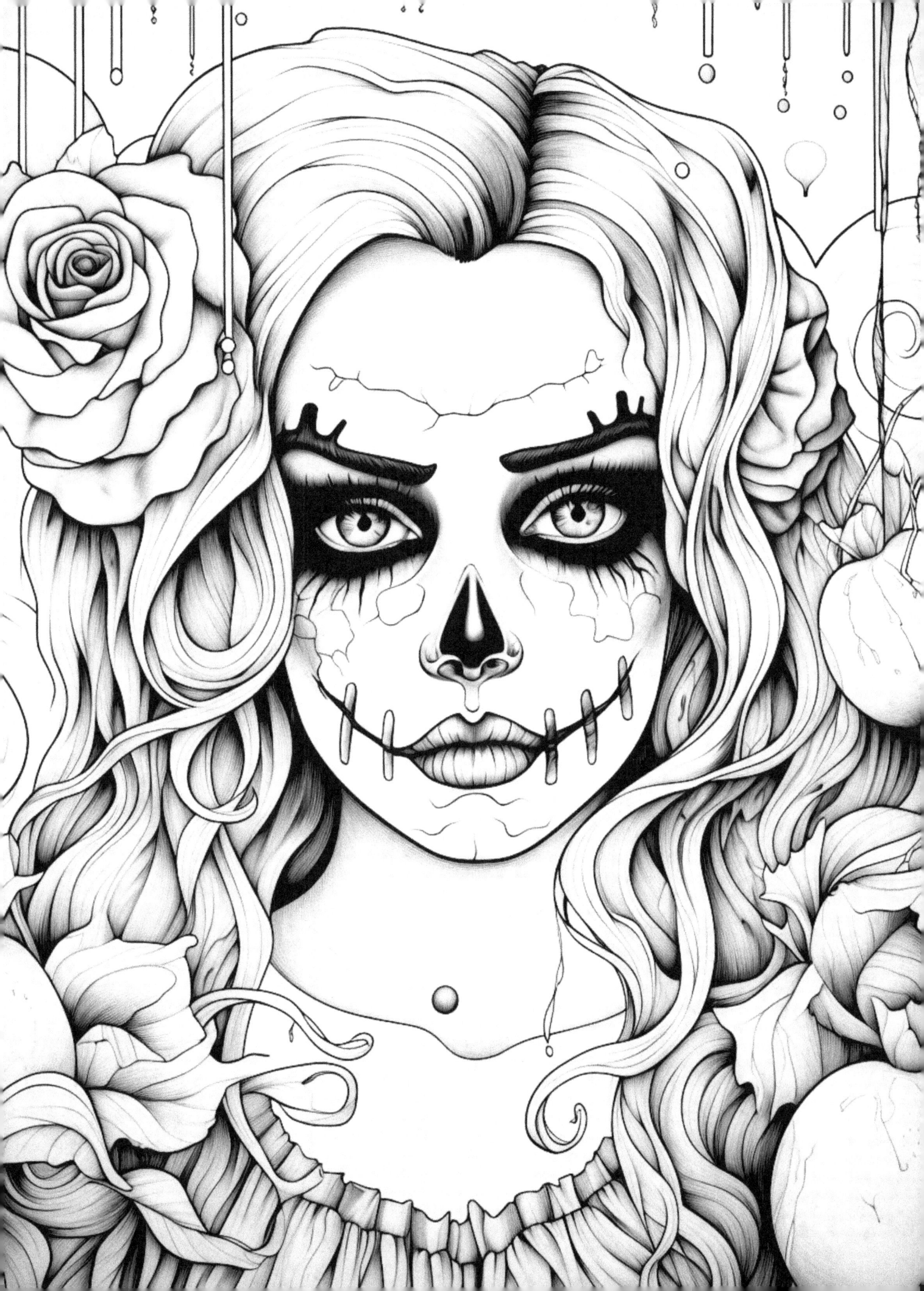

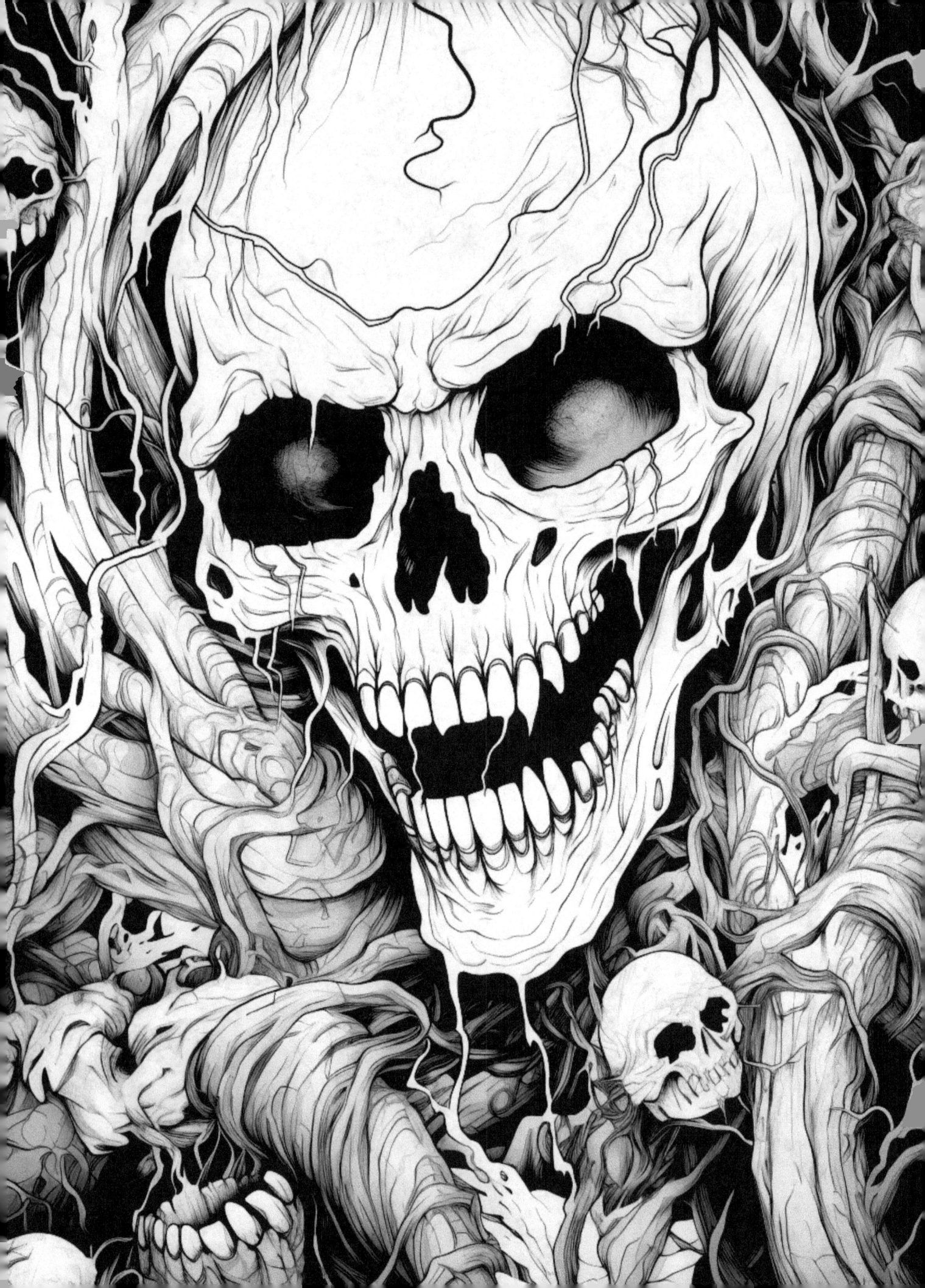

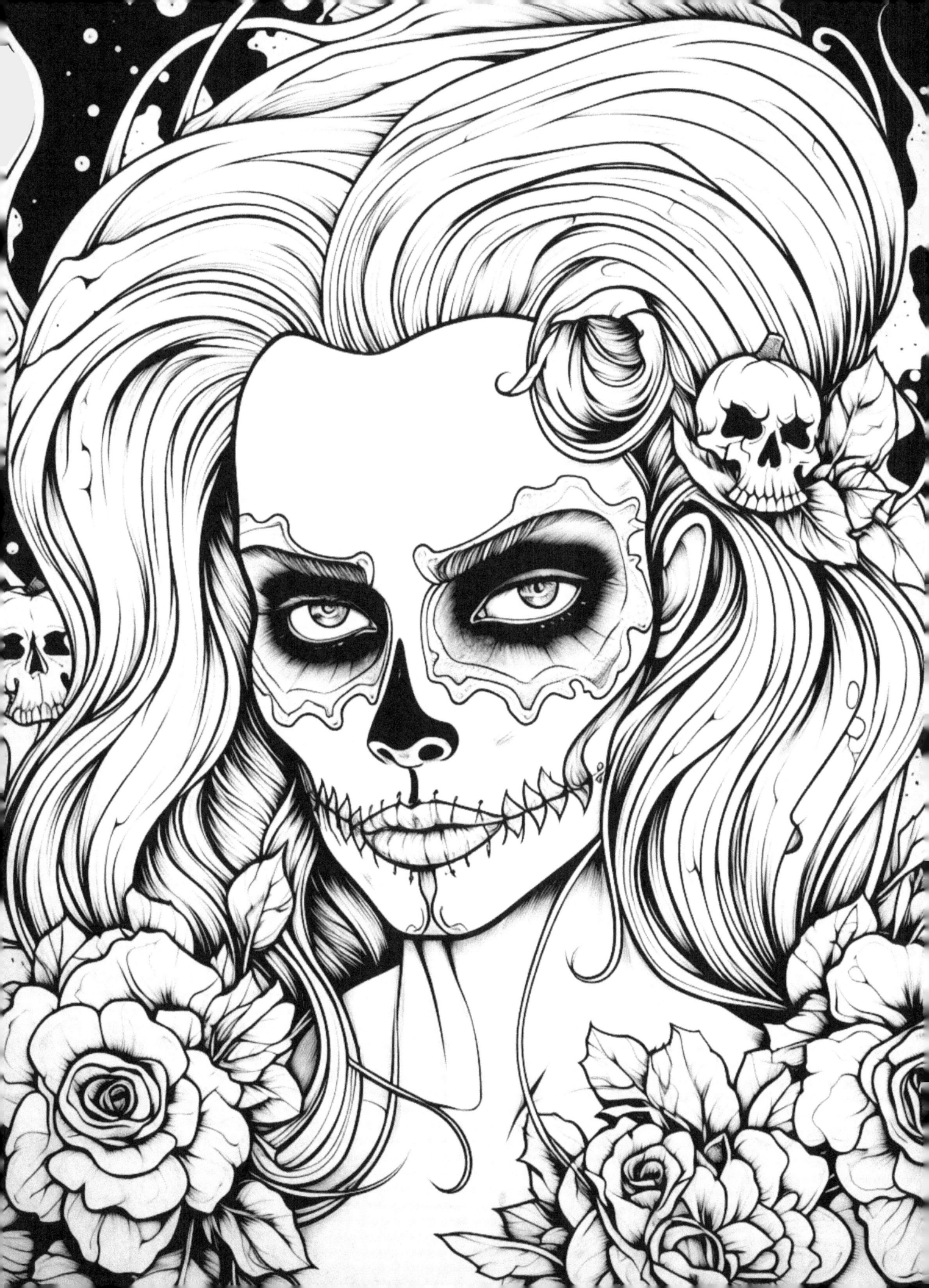

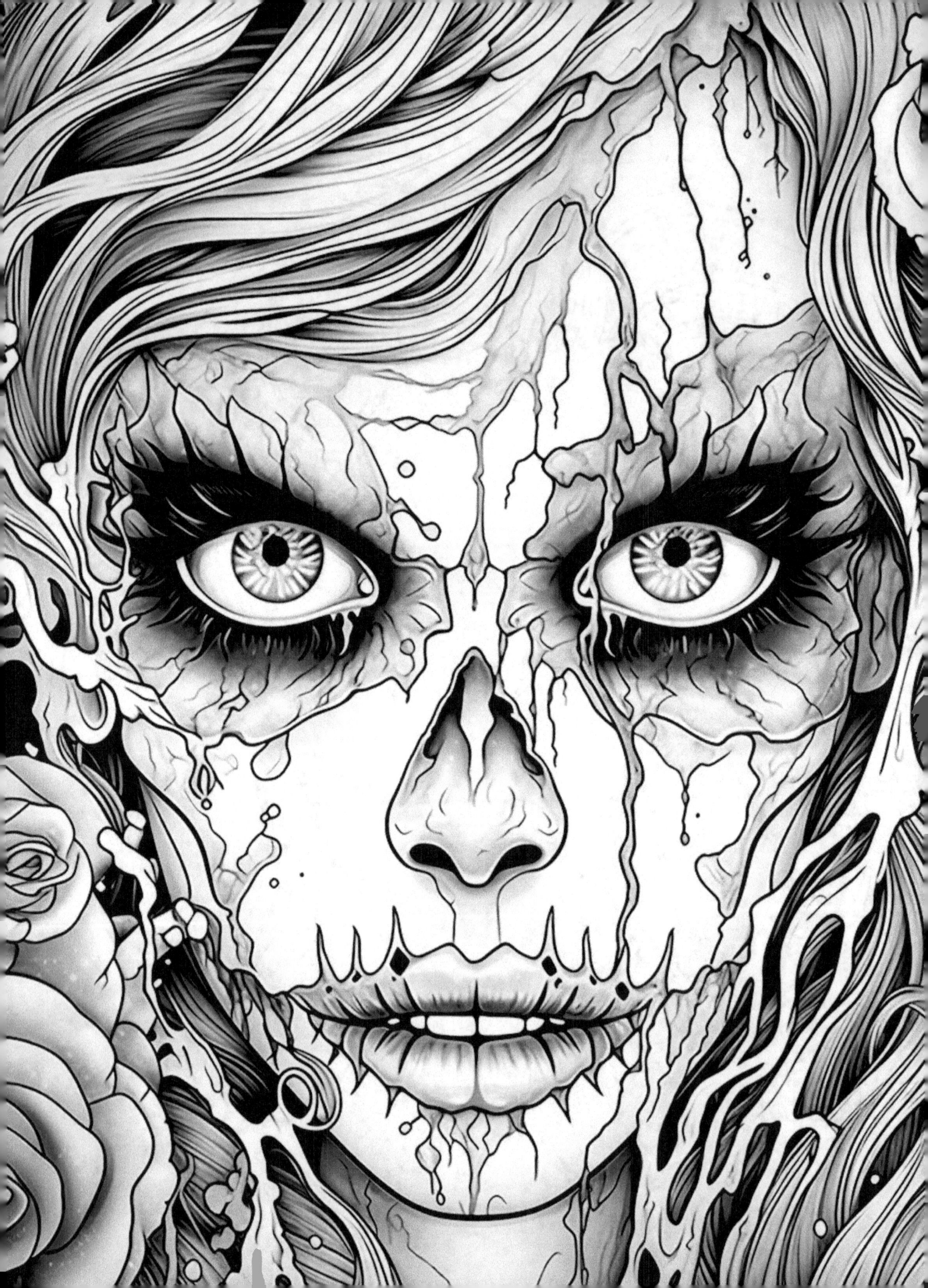

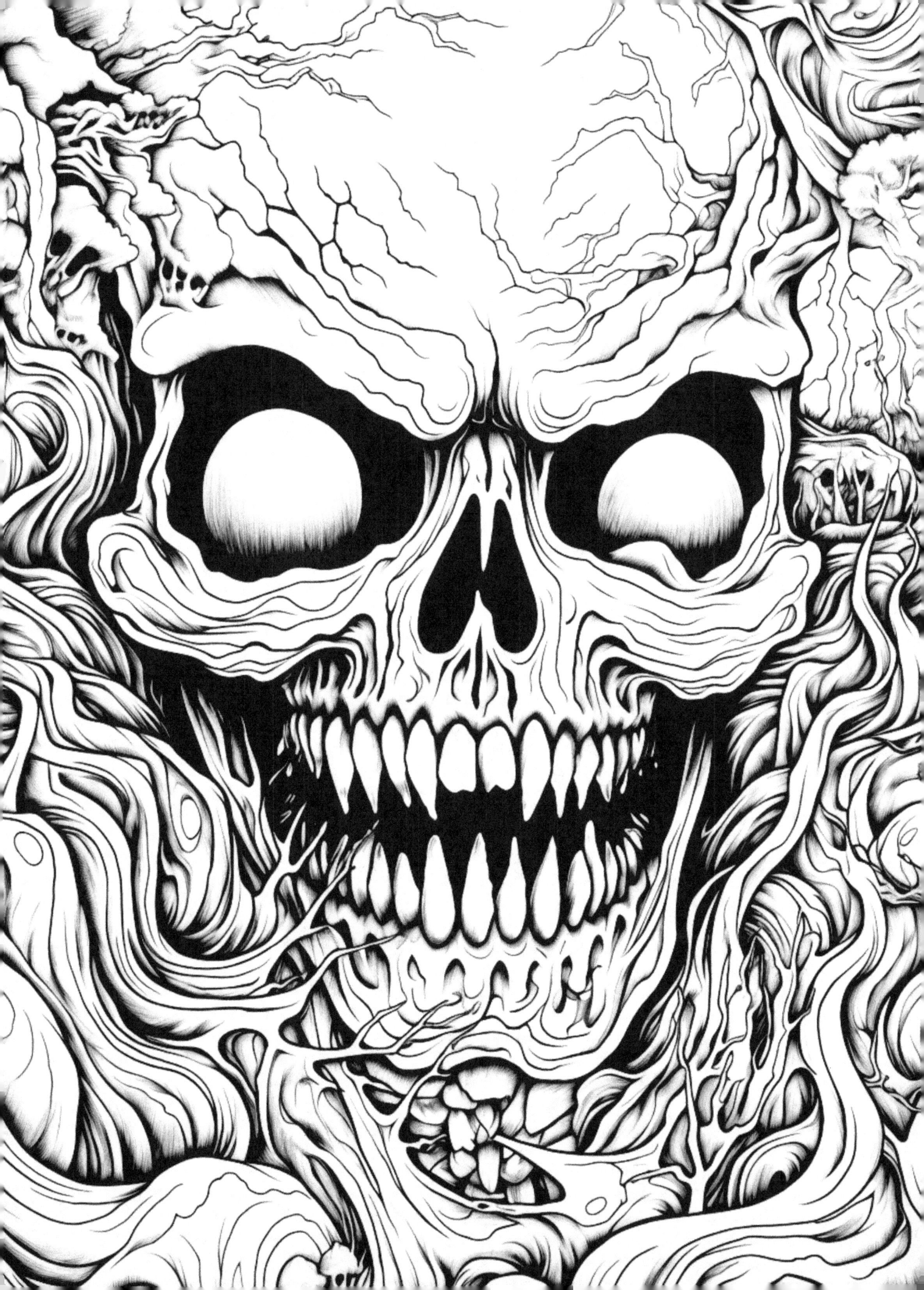

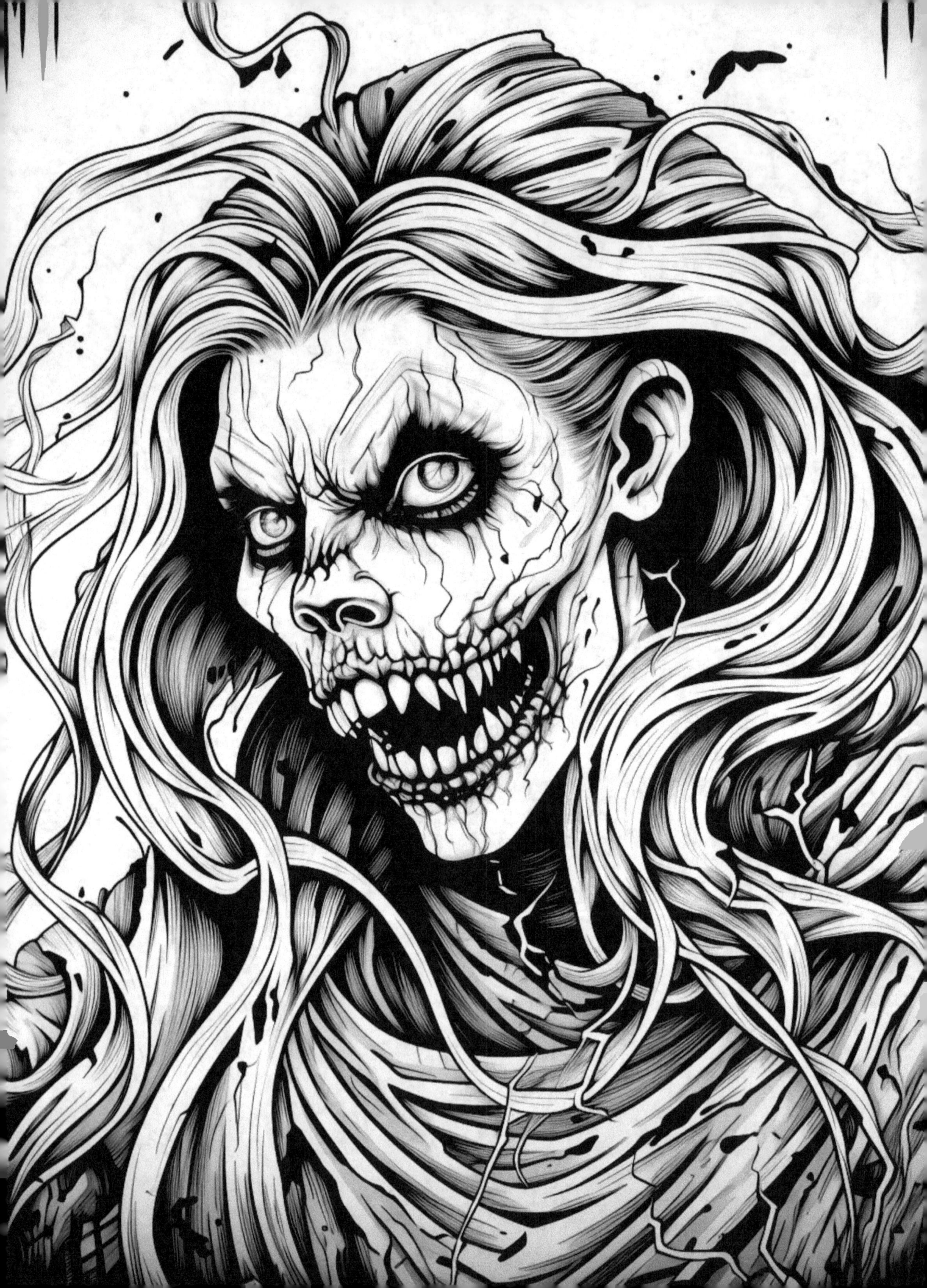

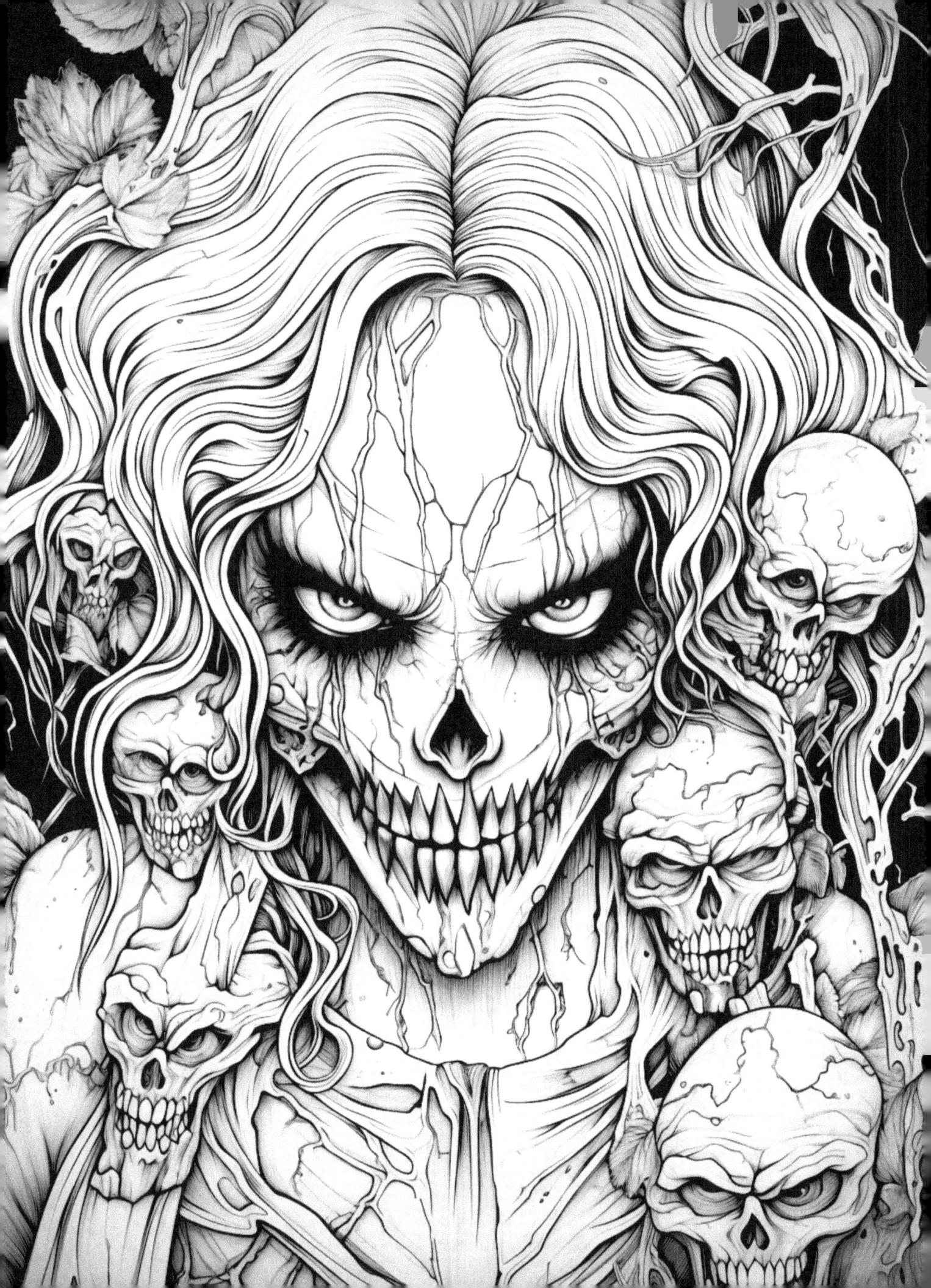

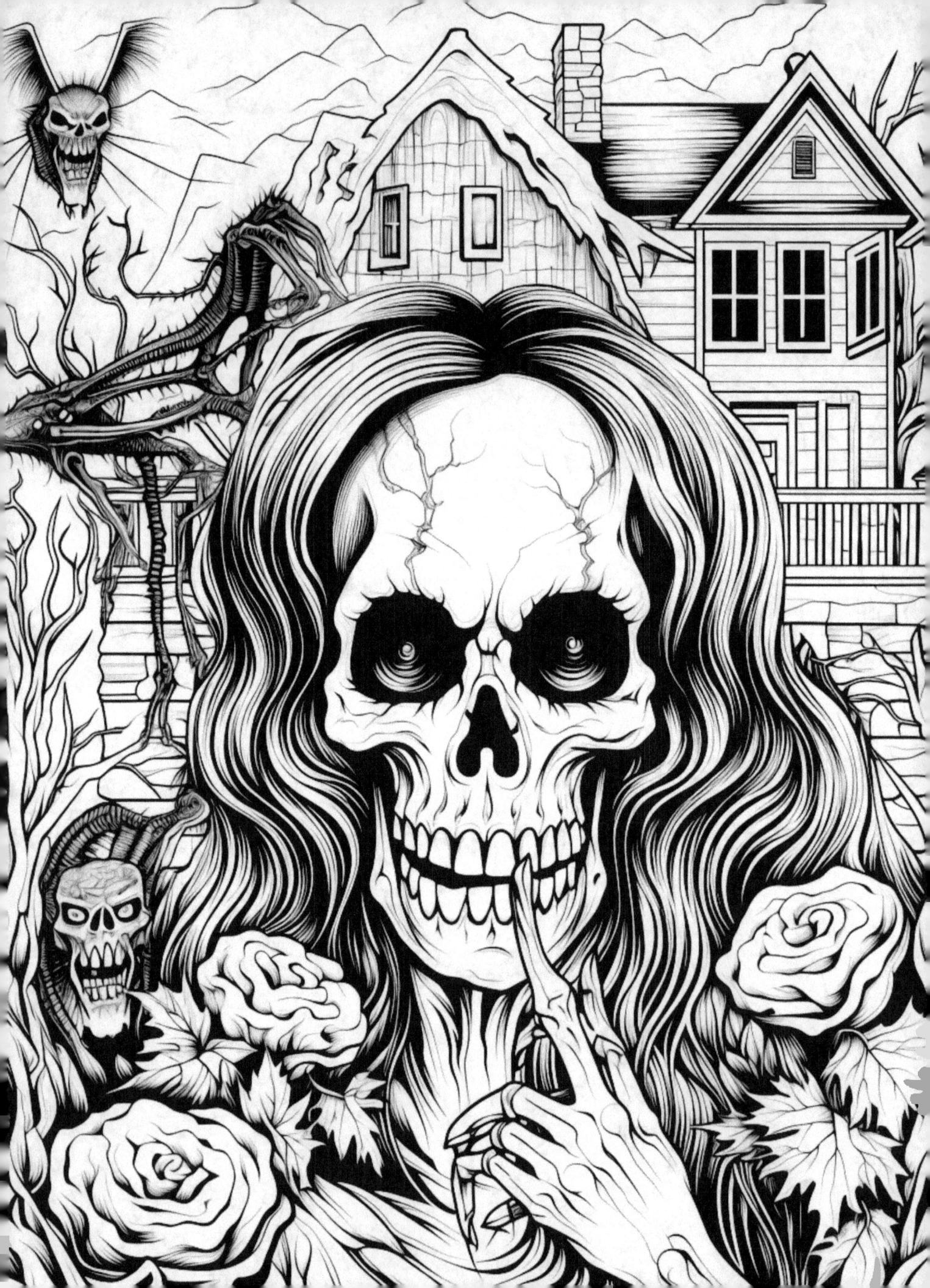

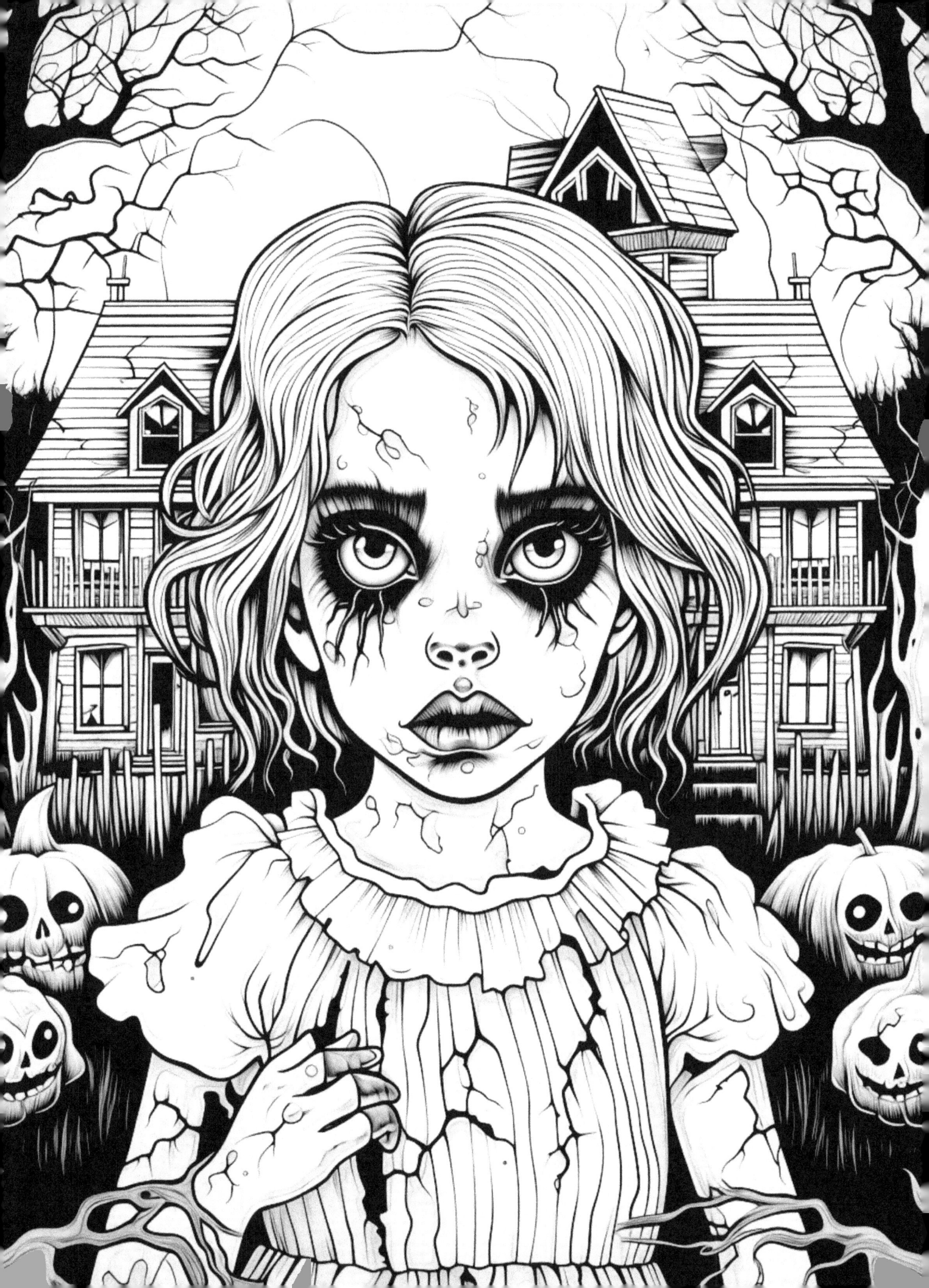

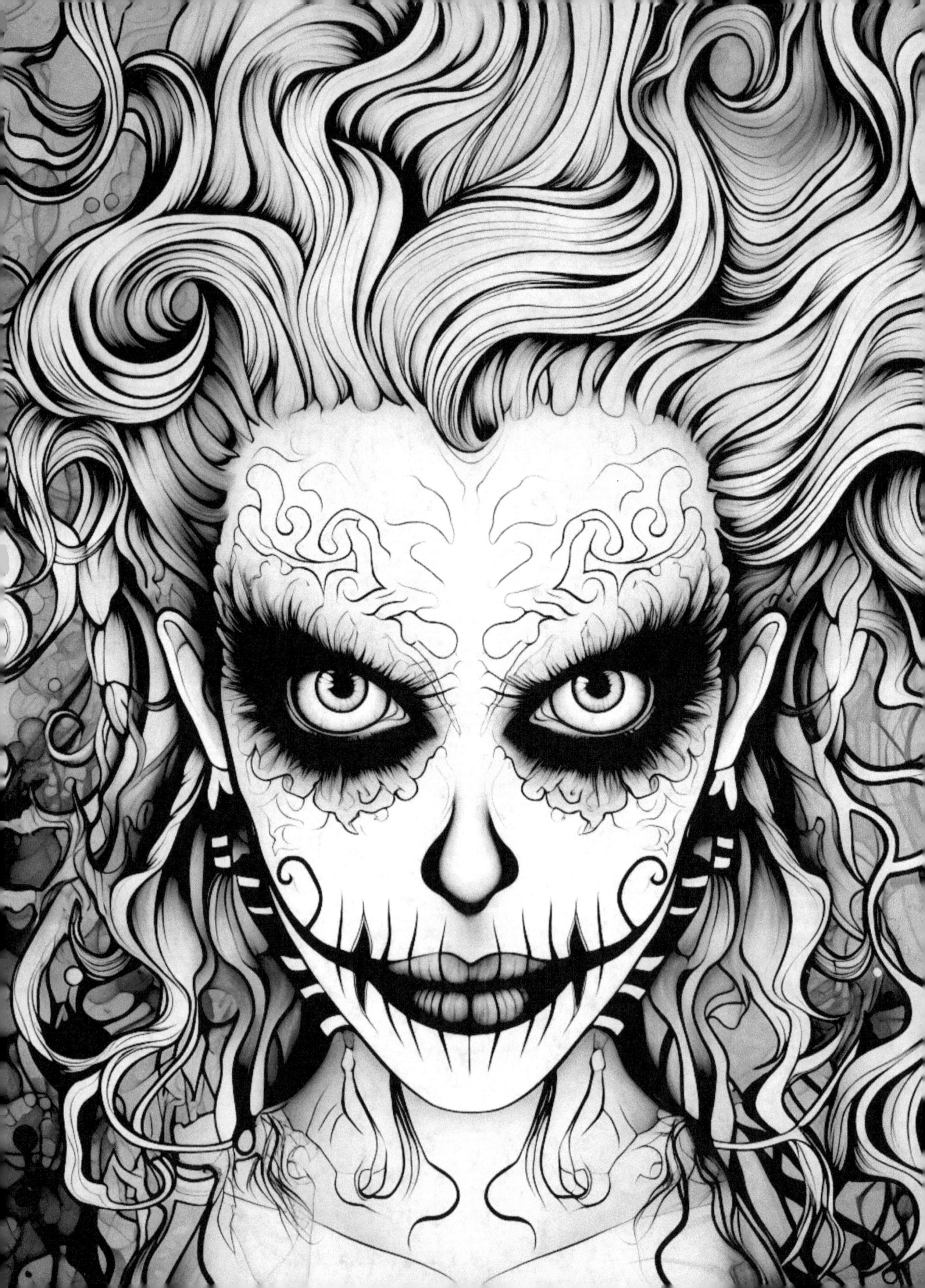

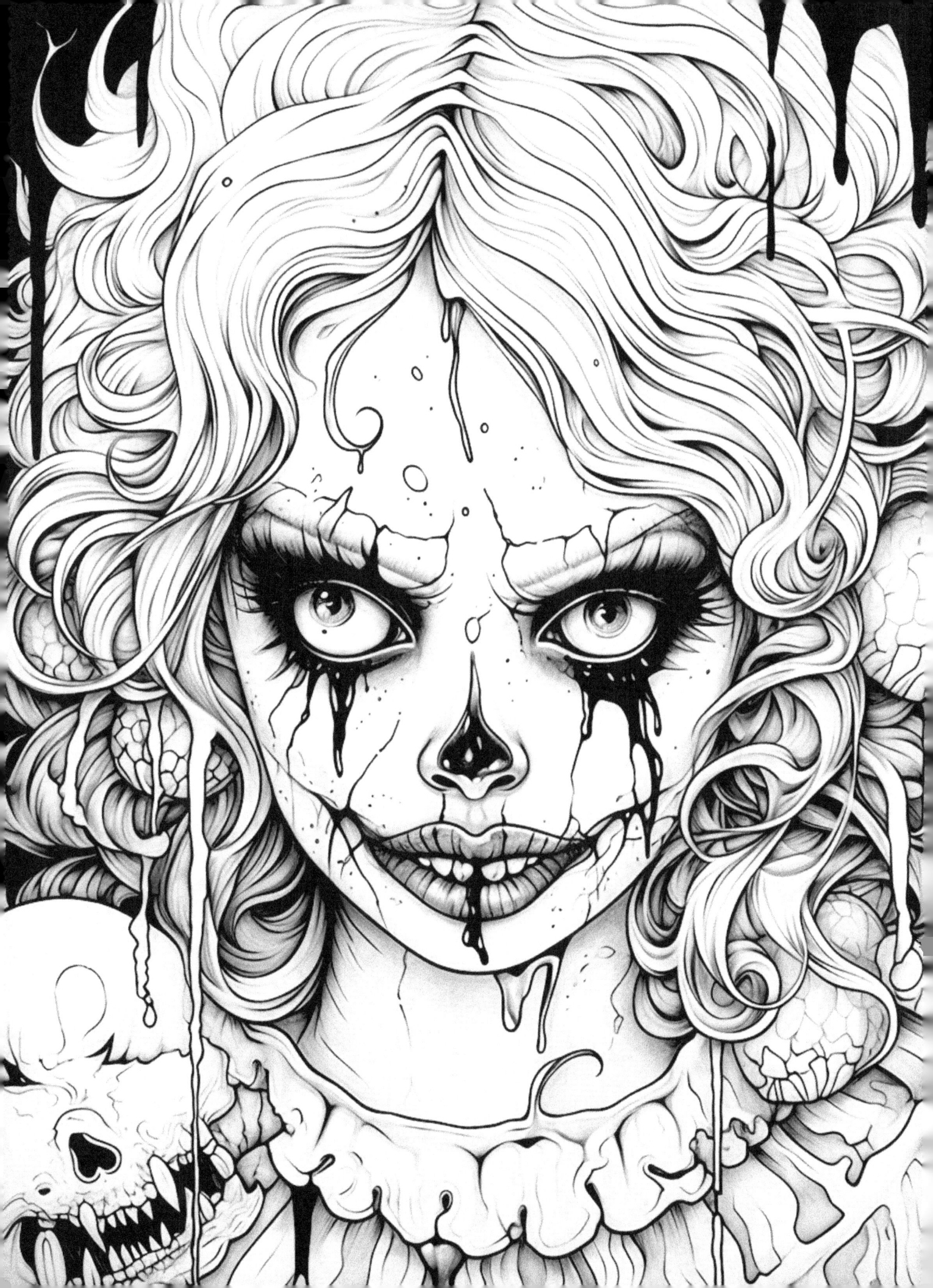

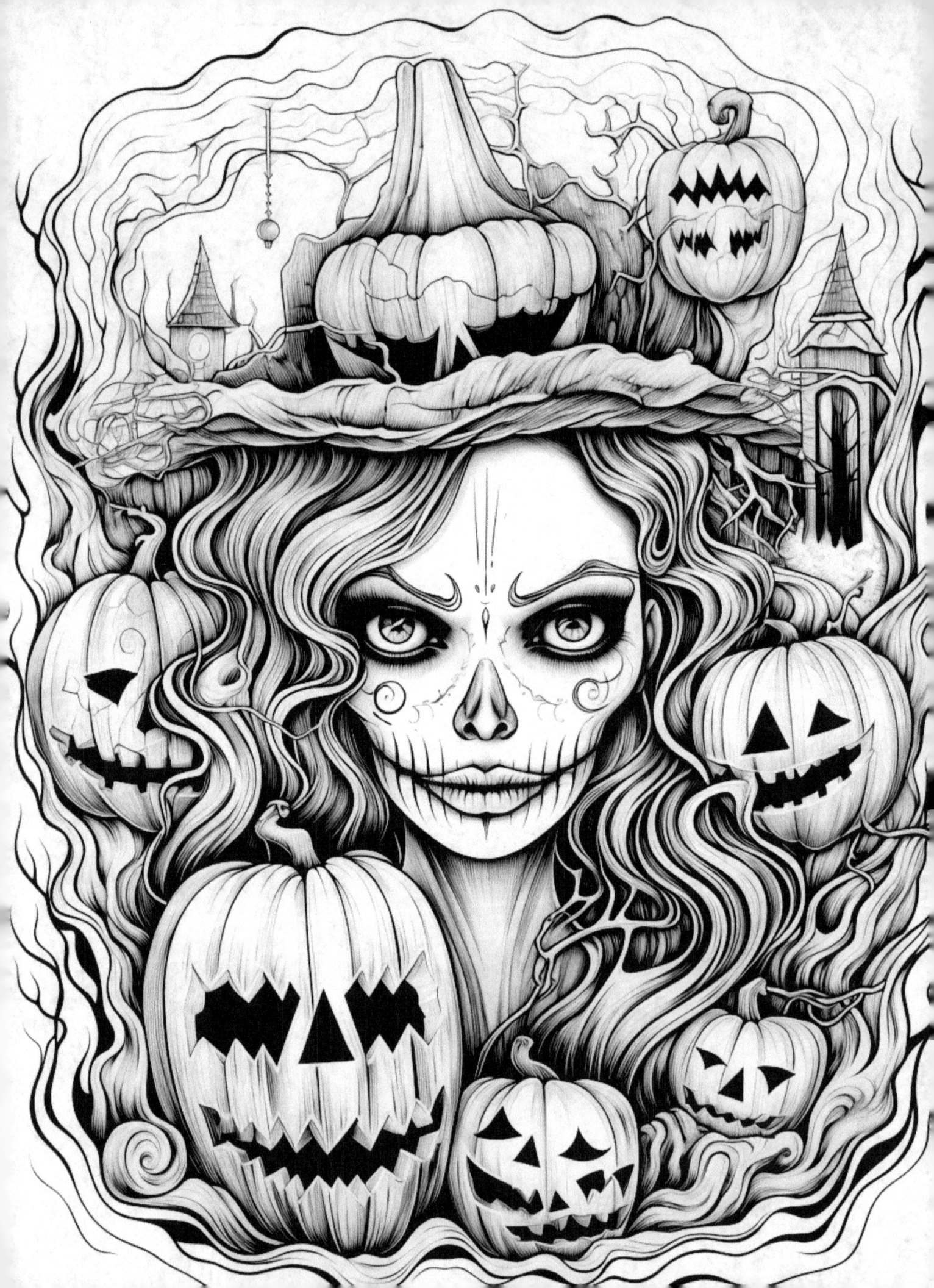

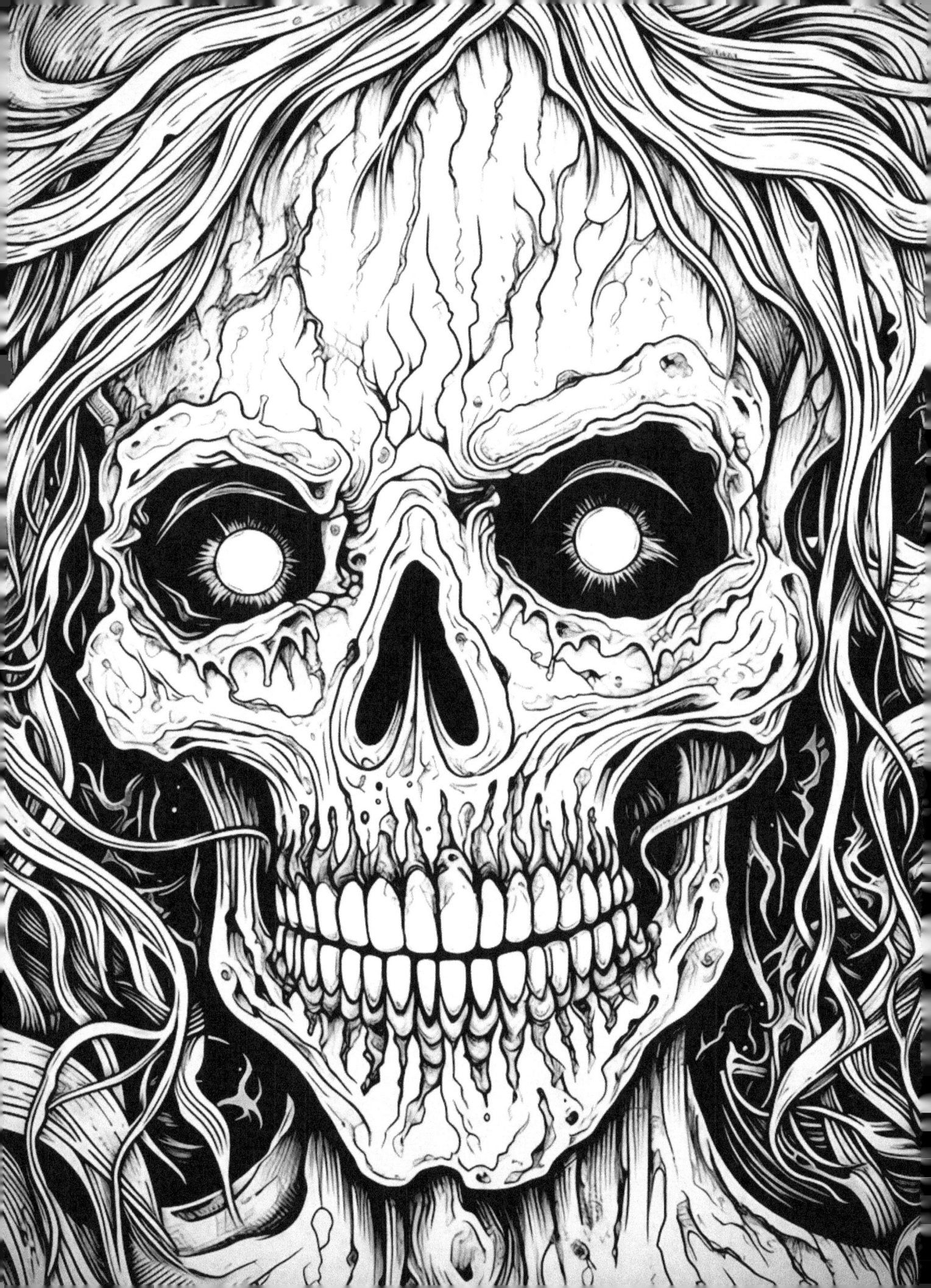

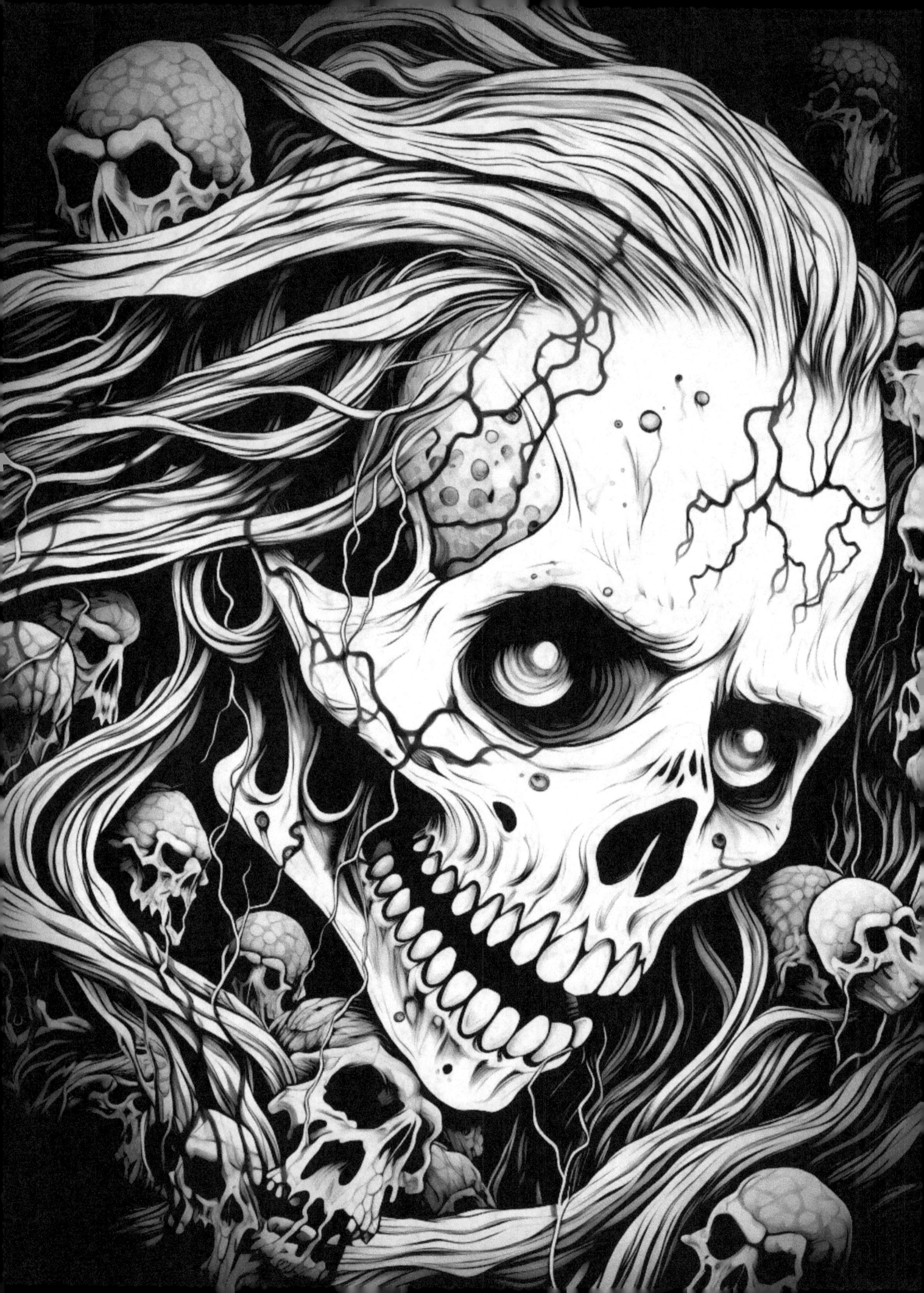

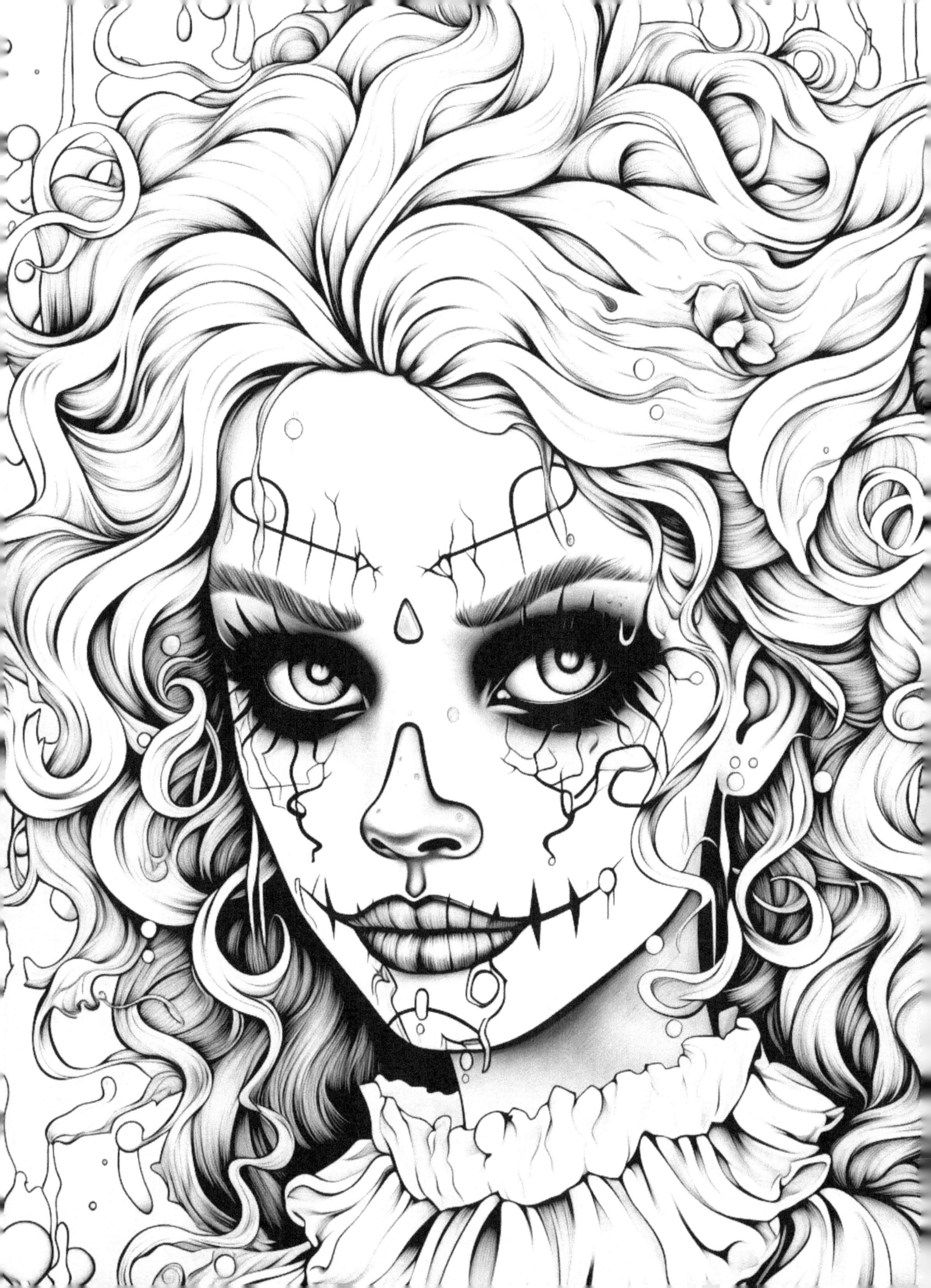

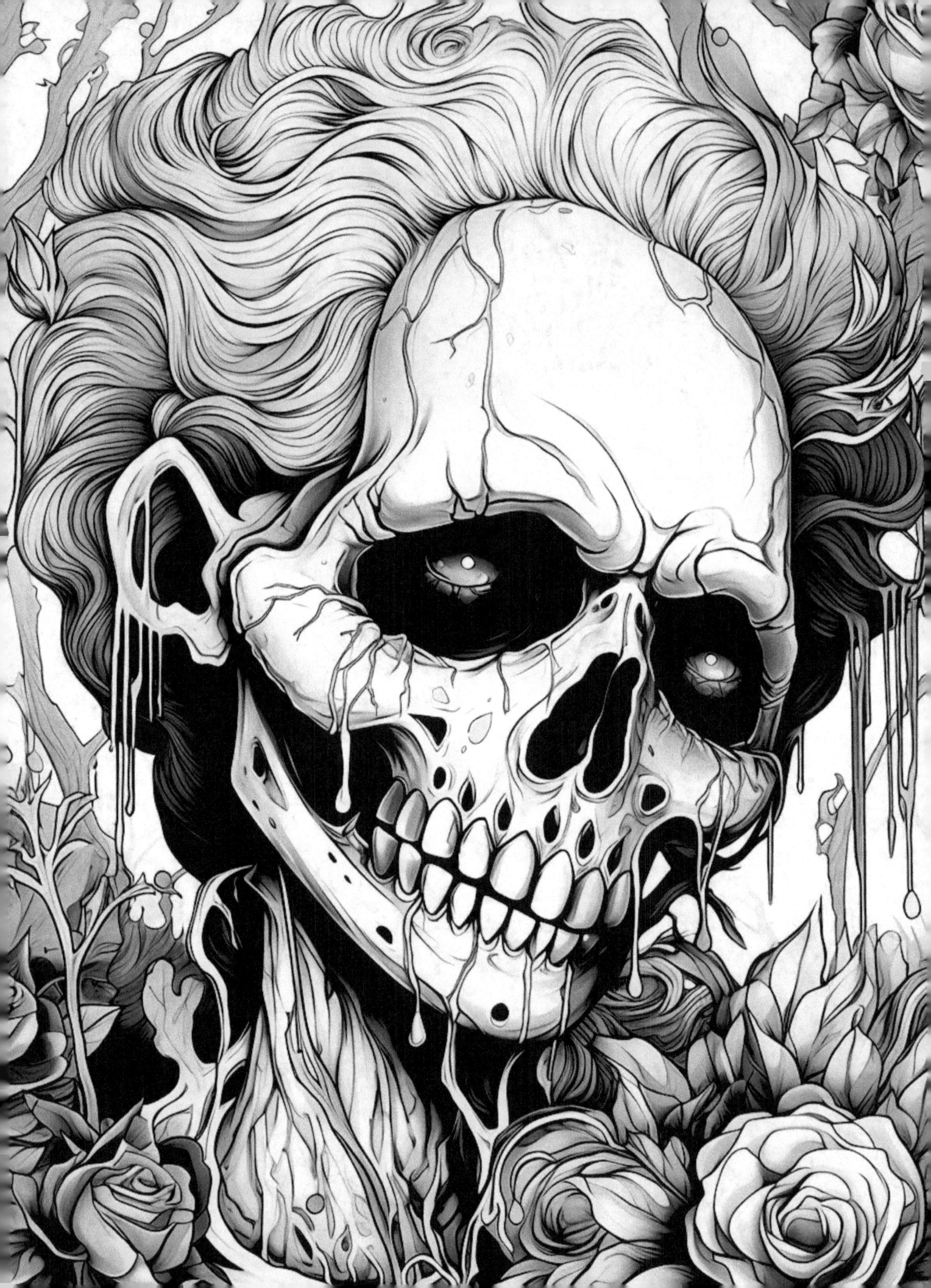

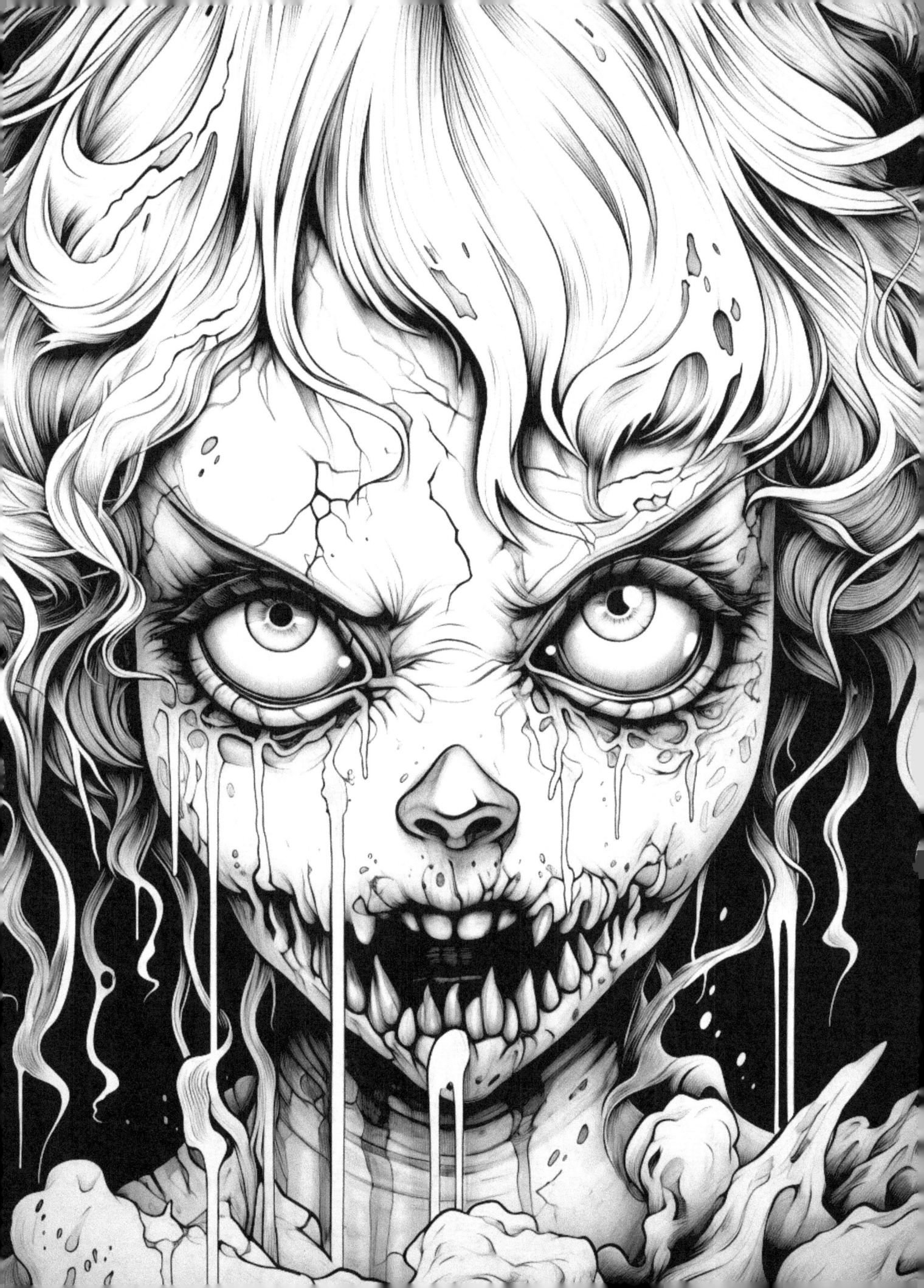

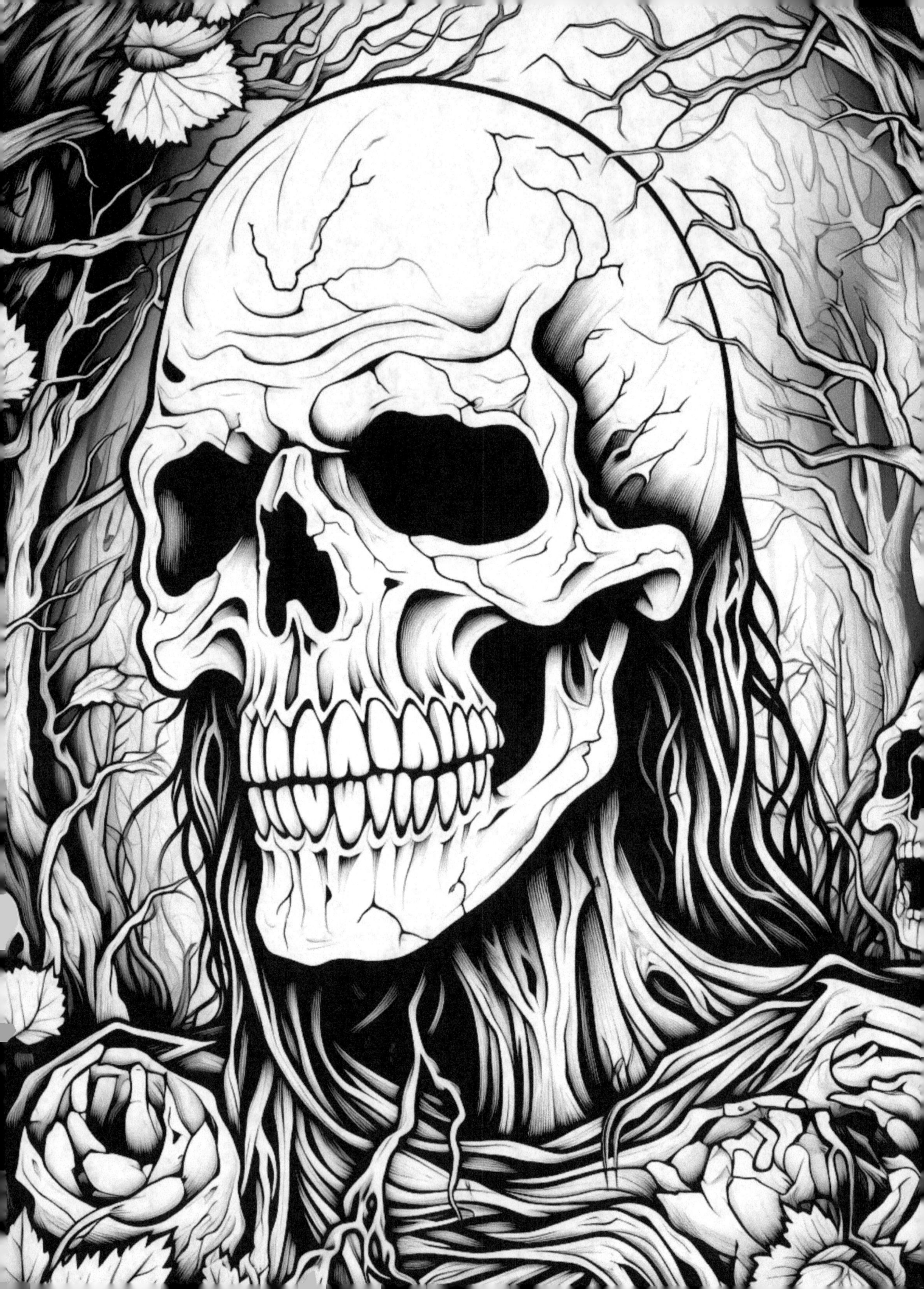

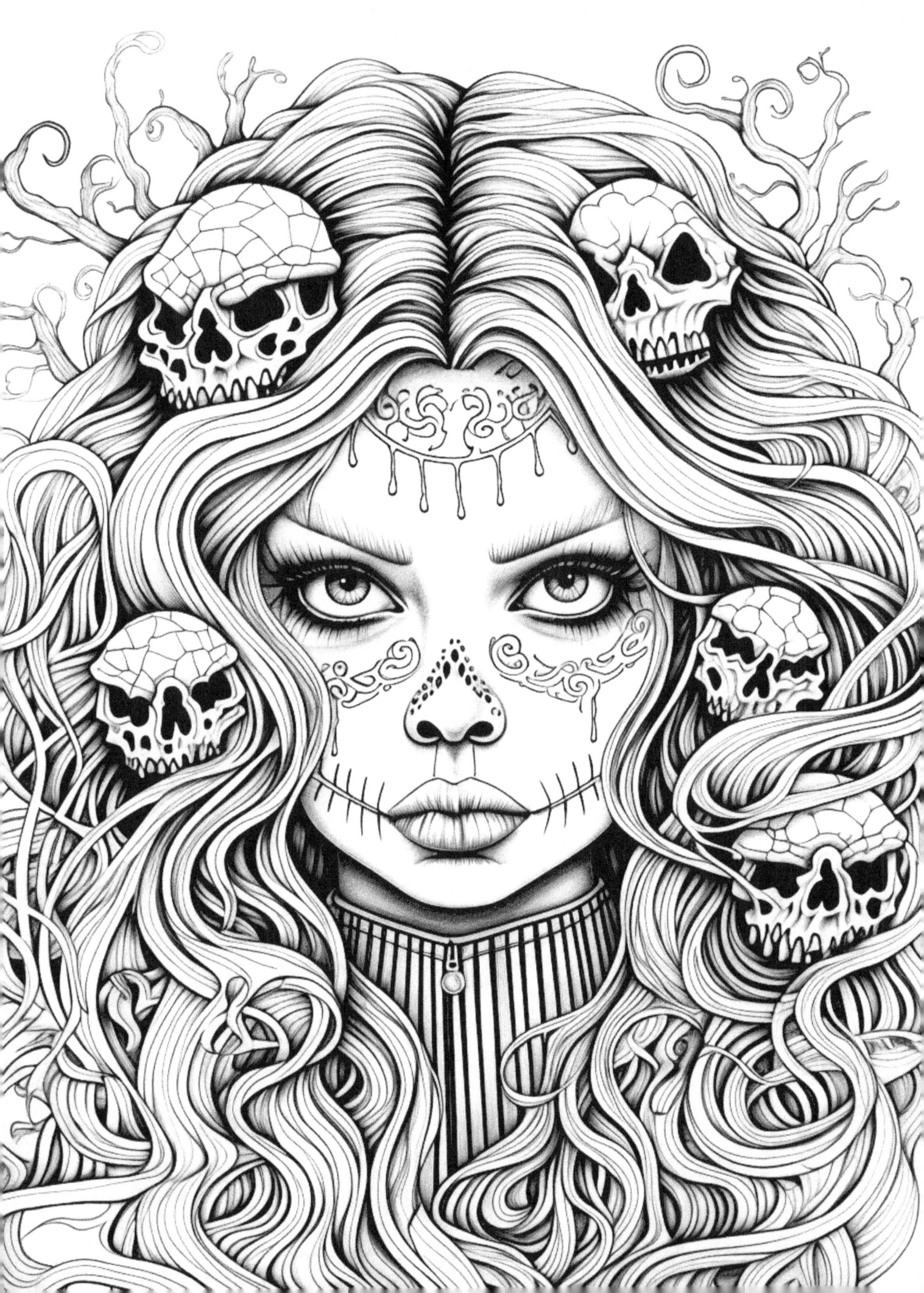

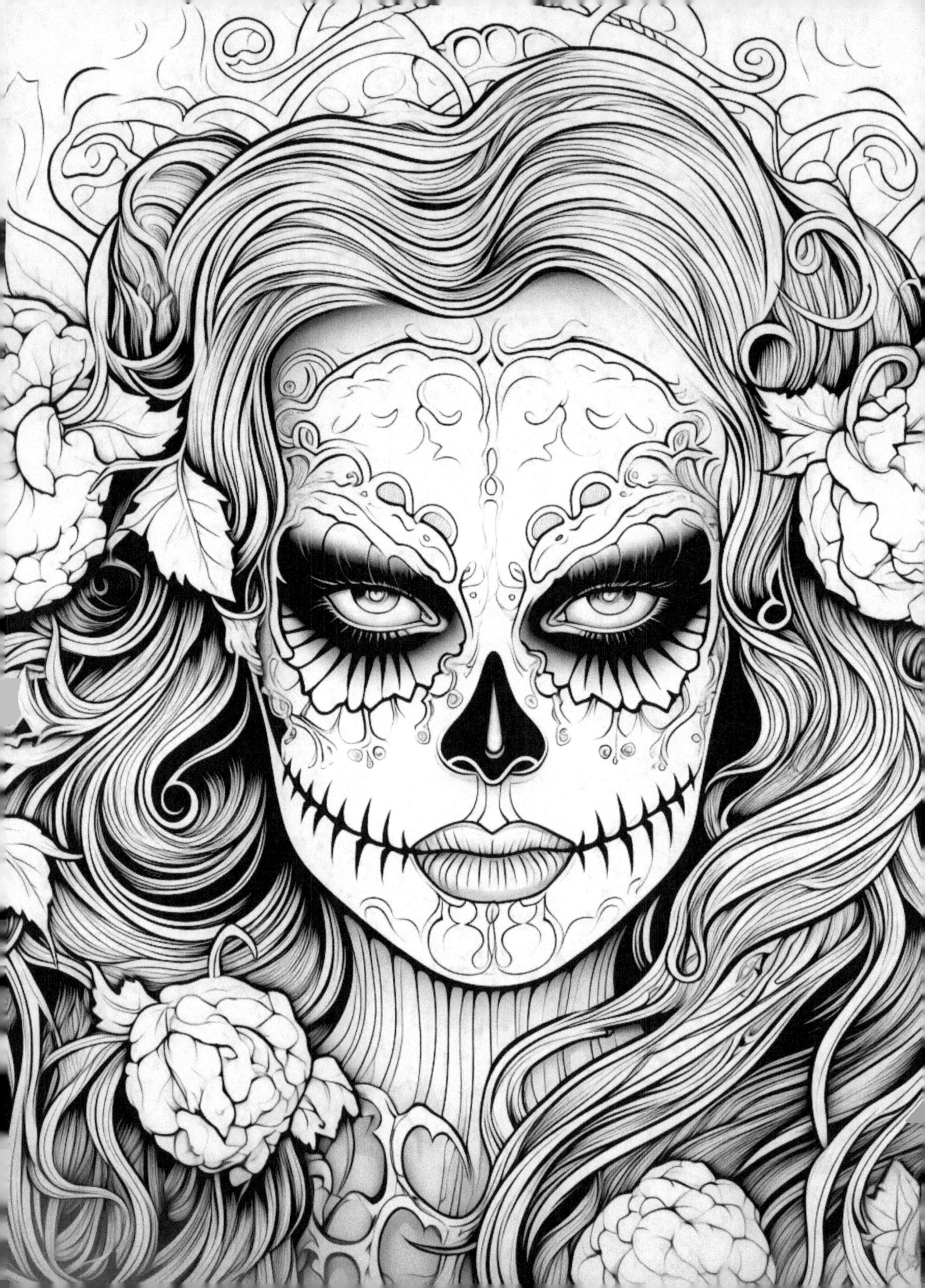

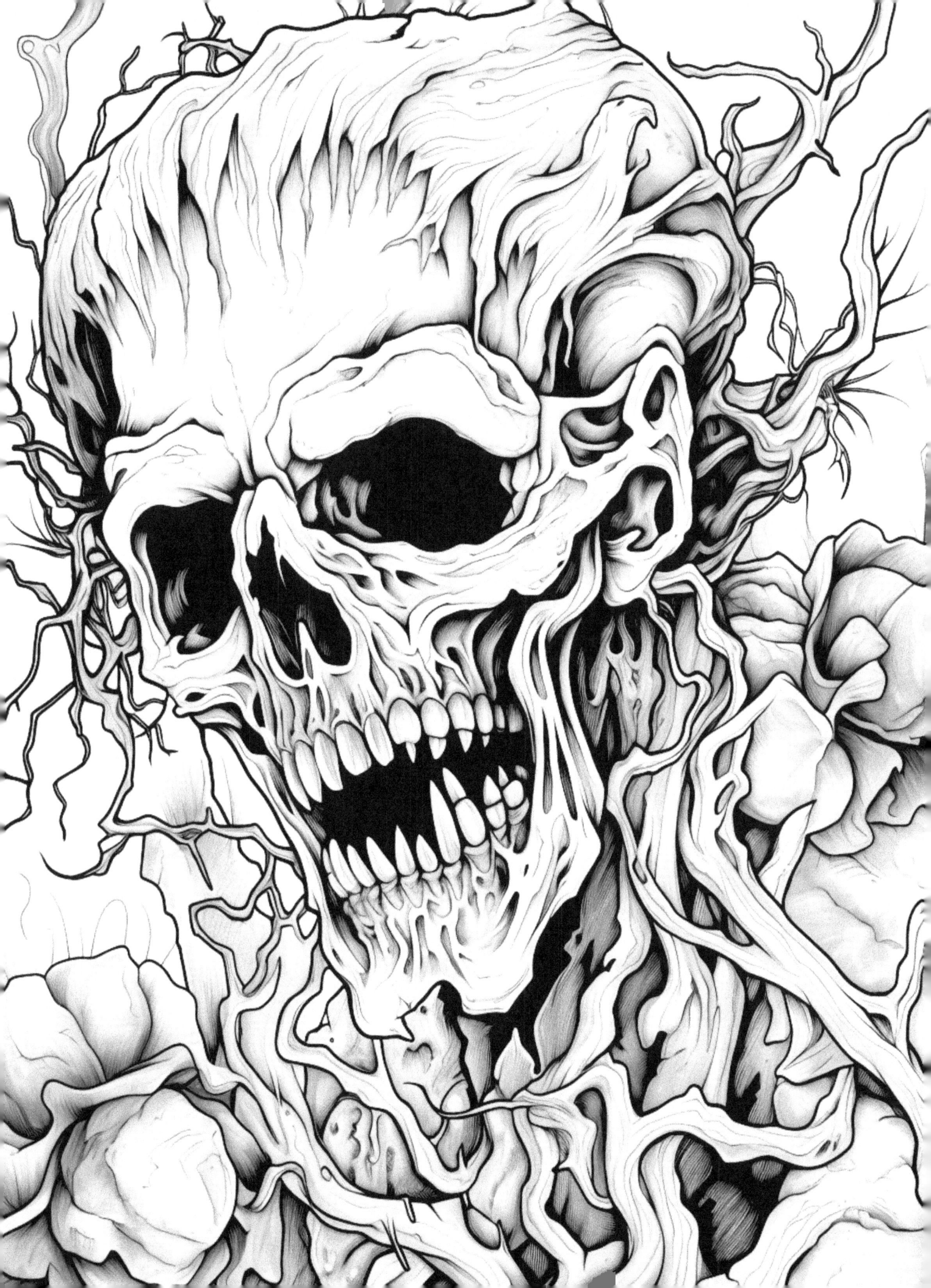